HUGH OF SAINT VICTOR

GREAT MEDIEVAL THINKERS

Series Editor
Brian Davies
Blackfriars, University of Oxford,
and Fordham University

DUNS SCOTUS
Richard Cross

BERNARD OF CLAIRVAUX
Gillian R. Evans

JOHN SCOTTUS ERIUGENA
Deirdre Carabine

ROBERT GROSSETESTE
James McEvoy

BOETHIUS
John Marenbon

PETER LOMBARD
Philipp W. Rosemann

ABELARD AND HELOISE
Constant J. Mews

BONAVENTURE
Christopher M. Cullen

AL-KINDĪ
Peter Adamson

JOHN BURIDAN
Gyula Klima

ANSELM
Sandra Visser and Thomas Williams

JOHN WYCLIFF
Stephen Lahey

HUGH OF SAINT VICTOR
Paul Rorem

HUGH OF SAINT VICTOR

Paul Rorem

OXFORD
UNIVERSITY PRESS

2009

OXFORD

UNIVERSITY PRESS

Oxford University Press, Inc., publishes works that further
Oxford University's objective of excellence
in research, scholarship, and education.

Oxford   New York
Auckland   Cape Town   Dar es Salaam   Hong Kong   Karachi
Kuala Lumpur   Madrid   Melbourne   Mexico City   Nairobi
New Delhi   Shanghai   Taipei   Toronto

With offices in
Argentina   Austria   Brazil   Chile   Czech Republic   France   Greece
Guatemala   Hungary   Italy   Japan   Poland   Portugal   Singapore
South Korea   Switzerland   Thailand   Turkey   Ukraine   Vietnam

Published by Oxford University Press, Inc.
198 Madison Avenue, New York, New York 10016
www.oup.com

Oxford is a registered trademark of Oxford University Press

Library of Congress Cataloging-in-Publication Data
Rorem, Paul.
Hugh of Saint Victor / by Paul Rorem.
p. cm.
Includes bibliographical references and index.
ISBN 978-0-19-538436-9; 978-0-19-538437-6 (pbk.)
1. Hugh, of Saint-Victor, 1096?–1141. 2. Theology—
History—Middle Ages, 600-1500. I. Title.
BX4705.H786R674 2009
230'.2092—dc22   2008047344

1 3 5 7 9 8 6 4 2
Printed in the United States of America
on acid-free paper

SERIES FOREWORD

Many people would be surprised to be told that there *were* any great medieval thinkers. If a *great* thinker is one from whom we can learn today, and if "medieval" serves as an adjective for describing anything that existed from (roughly) the years 600 to 1500 A.D., then, so it is often supposed, medieval thinkers cannot be called "great."

Why not? One answer often given appeals to ways in which medieval authors with a taste for argument and speculation tend to invoke "authorities," especially religious ones. Such invocation of authority is not the stuff of which great thought is made, or so it is often said today. It is also frequently said that greatness is not to be found in the thinking of those who lived before the rise of modern science, not to mention that of modern philosophy and theology. Students of science are nowadays hardly ever referred to literature from earlier than the seventeenth century. Students of philosophy in the twentieth century have often been taught nothing about the history of ideas between Aristotle (384–322 B.C.) and Descartes (1596–1650). Modern students of theology have often been encouraged to believe that significant theological thinking is a product of the nineteenth century.

Yet the origins of modern science lie in the conviction that the world is open to rational investigation and is orderly rather than chaotic—a conviction that came fully to birth, and was systematically explored and developed, during the Middle Ages. And it is in medieval thinking that we find some of the most sophisticated and rigorous discussions in the areas of philosophy and theology ever offered for human consumption—not surprisingly, perhaps, if we note that medieval philosophers and theologians, like their contemporary counterparts, were mostly university teachers who participated in an ongoing worldwide debate and were not (like many seventeenth-, eighteenth-, and even nineteenth-century philosophers and theologians) people working in relative isolation from a large community of teachers and students with whom they were regularly involved. As for the question of appeal to authority: it is certainly true that many medieval thinkers believed in authority (especially religious authority) as a serious court of appeal, and it is true that most people today would say that they cannot do this. But as many contemporary philosophers are increasingly reminding us, authority is as much an ingredient in our thinking today as it was for medieval thinkers (albeit that, because of differences between thinkers, one might reasonably say that there is no such thing as "medieval thought"). Most of what we take ourselves to know derives from the trust we have reposed in our various teachers, colleagues, friends, and general contacts. When it comes to reliance on authority, the main difference between us and medieval thinkers lies in the fact that their reliance on authority (insofar as they had it) was often more focused and explicitly acknowledged than is ours. It does not lie in the fact that it was uncritical and naive in a way that our reliance on authority is not.

In recent years, such truths have come to be increasingly recognized at what we might call the "academic" level. No longer disposed to think of the Middle Ages as "dark" (meaning "lacking in intellectual richness"), many university departments (and many publishers of books and journals) now devote a lot of their energy to the study of medieval thinking. And they do so not only on the assumption that it is historically significant but also in the light of the increasingly developing insight that it is full of things with which to dialogue and from which to learn. Following a long period in which medieval thinking was thought to be of only antiquarian interest, we are now witnessing its revival as a contemporary voice—one to converse with, one from which we might learn.

The Great Medieval Thinkers series reflects and is part of this exciting revival. Written by a distinguished team of experts, it aims to provide substantial introductions to a range of medieval authors. And it does so on the assumption that they are as worth reading today as they were when they wrote. Students of medieval "literature" (e.g., the writings of Chaucer) are currently well supplied (if not oversupplied) with secondary works to aid them in reading this literature. But those with an interest in medieval philosophy and theology are by no means so fortunate when it comes to reliable and accessible books to help them. The Great Medieval Thinkers series therefore aspires to remedy that deficiency by concentrating on medieval philosophers and theologians and by offering solid overviews of their lives and thought, coupled with contemporary reflection on what they had to say. Taken individually, books in the series provide valuable treatments of single thinkers, many of whom are not currently covered by any comparable books. Taken together, they constitute a rich and distinguished history and discussion of medieval philosophy and theology considered as a whole. With an eye on college and university students, and with an eye on the general reader, authors of books in the series strive to write in a clear and accessible manner so that each of the thinkers they write on can be learned about by those who have no previous knowledge about them. But each contributor to the series also intends to inform, engage, and generally entertain even those with specialist knowledge when it comes to medieval thinking. So, as well as surveying and introducing, books in the series seek to advance the state of medieval studies at both the historical and the speculative levels.

The subject of the present volume, Hugh of St. Victor, died in 1141. He wrote on a wide range of topics (including geometry, grammar, and history). Best known today for his *Didascalicon*, his *De sacramentis*, and his spiritual works on Noah's ark, he was extremely influential in the development of medieval theology. According to St. Bonaventure, "Anselm [of Canterbury] excels in reasoning; Bernard [of Clairvaux] in preaching; Richard [of St. Victor] in contemplating; but Hugh [of St. Victor] in all three."

Yet in spite of his encyclopedic output and historical significance, the overall contours of Hugh's thought still remain relatively unknown, at least among English-speaking readers. Hugh presents an impressive synthesis of biblical, doctrinal, and spiritual theology. But how does all of it hold together? What does Hugh's achievement look like when viewed as a whole?

In what follows, Paul Rorem seeks to answer these questions. He does so by presenting Hugh's teachings in accordance with the way in which the Victorines originally tried to do and in accordance with Hugh's own threefold understanding of biblical theology: the literal-historical meaning of scripture, the doctrinal (allegorical) meaning, and then the tropological-spiritual meaning. As Hugh used Gregory the Great's analogy of a building, so Rorem structures his presentation of Hugh's threefold synthesis in terms of the foundation, the framework, and the finale.

In documenting Hugh, Professor Rorem presents the big picture of his thought in all its complex structure and with judicious quotations and compact summaries. Nowhere else, in any language, will you find such an efficient and balanced presentation of Hugh's large and multifaceted corpus.

BRIAN DAVIES

PREFACE

Viewed from certain tables in the library of the School of Historical Studies at the Institute for Advanced Study in Princeton, a lovely pond and then the Institute Woods stretch out in peaceful beauty, symbolic of the institute's extensive and quiet support of creative scholarship. From start to finish, I wrote this book at such a table, inspired by that view and supported by the institute community, from autumn to winter to spring in 2006–2007. Thanks to Princeton Theological Seminary's generous sabbatical, I had the privilege of devoting every day to this form of teaching, writing an introduction to one theologian's comprehensive corpus. I thank Caroline Bynum of the institute's permanent faculty for encouraging me to attempt an overview of Hugh of St. Victor's major works, for the sake of students and general readers first of all but also for specialists who may know some aspects of Hugh's thought and would appreciate an attempt to present the larger panorama. The staff of the institute, especially in the library and dining hall, go out of their way to support the research and writing of the annual members and visitors. It was a privilege to be among them again.

The goal of this small book is simply to offer an introduction to Hugh of Saint Victor's major writings, with summaries of their contents amid an overview of the contours of his thought. The sheer breadth of this Victorine's output makes his integration of so many topics both impressive and challenging. On every point, there is much more to say: on the founding of the community at Saint Victor, on the context in early twelfth-century Paris, on each one of Hugh's works here merely glimpsed, and of course, on his legacy in later Victorines and other authors for generations and centuries to come. For these more specific items, there are other books, especially in French and German, and many yet to be written. I hope this introduction to Hugh will contribute to further Victorine studies, especially in English, so that our postmodern age can appreciate the breadth, depth, and synthesis of this one premodern theologian.

I am grateful to various friends and consultants for help on this project, but most of all to Grover Zinn: for his many insightful publications on Hugh, for his encouragement that I should offer a general introduction, and for his thorough comments on an initial draft. For helpful feedback on various sections, I thank Caroline Bynum, who has become a friend; Boyd Coolman, who was once my student; Karlfried Froehlich, who was and is my teacher; and Brian Davies, who graciously accepted into his series this work on Hugh as a Great Medieval Thinker. Finally, many thanks to our son, Joseph Albert Rorem, who regularly made room for Hugh in the family schedule, and to Judith Attride, who patiently converted into a presentable manuscript the longhand results of those months at the institute library.

CONTENTS

Part I

FOUNDATIONS

I

CONTEXT

1. The Early Twelfth Century and Paris

The explosion of cultural creativity in early twelfth-century Europe is well known, indeed a commonplace since Charles Haskins's *The Renaissance of the Twelfth Century*.[1] Latin literature flourished especially in Paris, as Haskins and many others have documented. The theological side of that story is not as well known, at least not in English, outside of the famous affair of Abelard and Heloise and perhaps the general career of Bernard of Clairvaux. Equally important, however, to the theological renaissance of the twelfth century is the work of Hugh of St. Victor and the school he represents. This brief book introduces Hugh's major works, voluminous and diverse, drawing on recent editions and studies, especially by French and German scholars. The challenge is not in narrating his life story, of which little is known, but rather in organizing a presentation of his rich corpus. "Learn everything,"[2] he said, and thus he taught not only all of theology in its broad sense (biblical, doctrinal, practical, philosophical) but also history and grammar, geometry and geography. The organization of such learning and teaching was his distinctive contribution to the development of medieval thought. How to hold so much together in one unified and holistic package of learning and life could also be his contribution to our own age of specializations to the point of fragmentation.

In the early twelfth century, Paris reflected the overall surge of creative energies in western Europe. With growing populations and booming economies, various communities shared in the flourishing of art, music, poetry, letters, and learning, but Paris above all. Western Europe seemed to be bulging at the seams, indeed, spilling out beyond old borders to reclaim from Islam parts of northern Spain and Sicily and then Jerusalem, in that spasm of military, economic, religious, and territorial expansion later known as the First Crusade. As the Franks spread outward in that geographical sense, so, too, their churchly ambitions took them upward in the new style of architecture, later called Gothic, at Saint Denis and Notre Dame of Paris and nearby Chartres in this same century. The crusades and Gothic architecture represented enormous expenditures of money, personnel, and initiative, equally indicative of the dynamic societal growth underway. On the larger scale, all of this, including the story of Hugh and his community at St. Victor, reflected "a dramatic growth of population, increased agricultural productivity, the cultivation of new land, the formation of new villages, the development of manufacture, and the growth of trade both within and beyond Europe."[3] Why all of this happened at that time is still debatable—perhaps the weather improved and thus the crops, the diet, and therefore also the health and output of western Europeans—but Hugh's Paris was certainly part of a much larger development.

More specifically, and of little interest to Haskins, the religious culture of the early twelfth century reflected a double reform movement of its own. On the one hand, local parish clergy were increasingly expected to live a disciplined life, often in community, as reflected in the Gregorian Reform of the eleventh century. The established monastic (Benedictine) pattern of life was also poised for its own reform movement of youthful energy and discipline at Citeaux, yielding Cistercian communities such as Bernard's Clairvaux. On the other hand, monks and priests were joined in great numbers by curious students who wanted to study theology, especially in Paris. New currents of philosophical and spiritual inquiry were stirring, and new schools flourished, both schools of thought and many new physical places of teaching. Peter Abelard represents this scholarly ambition to pursue learning at the highest level, also in Paris, and thus also represents the well-worn contrast with Bernard's monastic discipline. Let Haskins overdraw it: "Between a mystic like Bernard and a rationalist like Abaelard there was no common ground."[4] Labels aside (for Bernard was more than a mystic, and Abelard no rationalist in any modern sense), the juxtaposition of the scholarly pursuit by a "pre-scholastic" author with the religious community of daily prayer is instructive. That there was, in fact, some common ground between the two is the story of the Abbey of St. Victor, and it starts with William of Champeaux.

2. William of Champeaux, St. Victor, and Abbot Gilduin

Born around 1070 in Champeaux near Melun, not far from Paris, William wanted to study theology. He started in Paris under Manegold, an obscure figure who was nevertheless pivotal for his influence on Anselm of Laon. William also studied under Roscelin at Compiegne and eventually under Anselm himself at the great cathedral school of Laon. In the first decade of the twelfth century, William was the archdeacon of Paris, in full support of Bishop Galon's clerical reforms, and the head of the cathedral school there, where he taught dialectic and rhetoric.[5] Suddenly, his academic career changed. In Abelard's narration of William's move, he made himself the pivotal figure. Young Abelard had come to study with William, but when he challenged, refuted, and vanquished his teacher (so he says), the master yielded the field, retired from teaching altogether, and moved.[6] Indeed, William and a few students did leave the cathedral school precincts of Notre Dame in 1108 and set up quarters just outside the city walls on the left bank at a small (cemetery) chapel or hermitage apparently already dedicated to the martyr of Marseilles, St. Victor.[7] It was a religious decision, meaning that William wanted to live a disciplined life of daily prayer and contemplation. The whole Gregorian reform movement of "regular canons," clergy living together according to a rule, is the larger context here, and William's subsequent history suggests that this spiritual ideal was more important to his change of lifestyle than was losing a debate to a student. His daily devotion was no doubt genuine, and he maintained a life of spiritual discipline. Yet this new way of life did not exclude teaching. Other students had their say and indirectly prevented Abelard from having the last word.

William retired to St. Victor not alone but with companions, including some of his students; apparently they, too, adopted the communal life of daily prayer, and yet they wanted to keep studying. They asked William to resume his teaching, but now within the daily schedule of corporate prayer and life together. This fateful combination of scholarship and communal piety garnered decisive support in a letter William received from Hildebert of Lavardin, the reforming Bishop of Le Mans. Hildebert's exhortation, that William should offer his whole self to God, launches a distinctive Victorine synthesis of mind and heart, of learning and prayer.

> What use after all is hidden wisdom or buried treasure? . . . Is there any difference between common stones and jewels if they are not displayed to the light? It is the same with learning; when one shows it to others it bears increase.[8]

Hildebert here voiced not only a decisive integration of learning and piety, of mind and heart, of scholarship and prayer, but also expressed this evangelical ideal in terms of apostolic service, namely, teaching others. William of Champeaux, in fact, resumed his teaching, but now within the daily communal schedule of prayer as "canons regular." And the apostolic ideal that this ministry of teaching was for others spread to his students, who learned and then taught, by word and example,[9] on through a Victorine succession of teacher training for generations.

William of Champeaux, first master of St. Victor, thus found the common ground that Haskins thought impossible between the monastic Bernard and the scholastic Abelard. There was still a wide gulf, and William and his subsequent Victorines were not the only such bridge builders. As Beryl Smalley says, the whole movement of canons regular should be acknowledged: "A gulf had opened between monks and scholars. Contemporaries constantly stress their difference in function: the scholar learns and teaches; the monk prays and 'mourns.' The canons regular courageously refused to admit the dilemma."[10] This combination of comprehensive scholarship and disciplined prayer is all the more admirable over against recent centuries, when the gulf or "dilemma" became institutionalized. William of Champeaux's personal example and leadership in combining the daily life of communal prayer with advanced intellectual study set the course of St. Victor, both as a specific place and as a broader school of thought. His students were set on their Victorine way, and one of them in particular became the abbot who shaped the particulars for decades to come.

Among those who moved with Master William to form the new community at St. Victor was his student Gilduin. When William resumed teaching within the communal life of prayer, Gilduin and the others continued their study of the liberal arts, theology, and philosophy, yet now amid the biblical readings and psalmody of their new daily schedule. These first years of the Victorine community have left few details in the historical record, but at William's departure, Gilduin's leadership soon gave specific shape to the original ideal of study and prayer. After five years of initial leadership (1108–1113) in this rather spontaneous community, William was elected bishop of Châlons-sur-Marne. He went on to a substantial career as a church reformer, building on his foundations of study and spirituality, including a close tie to Bernard of Clairvaux. But before leaving St. Victor, he made one more decisive contribution there. William secured the approval of King Louis VI to charter St. Victor as a royal abbey including a school, indicating financial support; the king further entrusted the Victorines with the election of an abbot from within their ranks to be nominated to the bishop of Paris without needing separate royal approval. Thus, as he left, William secured the foundations of the community, now the "abbey" of St. Victor, just as he had originally embodied its spirit. Shortly afterward, on December 1 of 1114, Pope Paschal II confirmed these rights and privileges for the royal Abbey of St. Victor and ratified the election of Gilduin, further strengthening the reform movement of canons regular in Paris.

Upon William's departure, the community's first real election of an abbot fell to Gilduin, who led the community for forty years, from 1114 to 1155, namely, before, during, and after Hugh's career there. In quality and continuity, Gilduin's leadership was remarkable, yet we know very little directly about him. From the indirect evidence of the features of his community at this time—the library and various buildings, the sheer numbers of novices and students, the dozens of daughter houses, and above all, the writings contributed by Victorines, starting with Hugh and then a whole school—Gilduin must have been a remarkable leader. As with the earlier abbots of Cluny, and then the later Gertrude of Hackeborn (Abbess of Helfta), such administrative gifts and personal leadership should be honored and appreciated, especially in light of the famous authors who flourished precisely because of the community context. The Abbot Gilduin may be almost unknown, but his legacy is abundant, specifically in Hugh's career and indeed in the first major collection of Hugh's writings. Gilduin enjoyed the favor of Pope Innocent II and of King Louis VI, even becoming the king's confessor. Amid tumultuous times and conflicts, including the political murder of his prior Thomas in 1133,[11] Gilduin guided the community's steady growth. He applied royal funds to a building campaign and to creating a magnificent library, still evident in its extensive remains within the Bibliothèque Nationale in Paris.[12] He also developed the foundational document for St. Victor's communal life, namely, the *Liber ordinis*, or custumal for the community.

As with other communities not adopting all the specifics of Benedict's *Rule*, even if eventually following the general guidance of Augustine's brief and suggestive *Rule*, the particulars of such a custumal were largely local and thus heavily up to the discretion of the abbot at the time. There are general similarities with Cluny, the Premonstratensians, and indeed the Cistercians, such as the principles of poverty and contemplation and the apostolic life of service, but the specifics of the *Liber ordinis* were uniquely Victorine. Although some particulars may have been added later, the Victorine custumal reveals Gilduin's community in Hugh's time.[13] Daily life was spelled out, including the duties of various offices: abbot, prior, subprior, treasurer, librarian, and eventually the master or head of the school (Hugh's position). The daily rhythm of prayer and study was parallel to the canonical hours already standard among the Benedictines: the night office of matins and lauds, prime and daily Mass, work in the garden or library, common meals and chapter meetings, study and a free period for conversation, vespers with readings and Compline, and bed. The church year provided the familiar annual rhythm, but the Victorines had a distinctive weekly highlight: every Saturday evening featured the foot-washing service (*mandatum*) otherwise associated with Maundy Thursday,[14] thus dramatically reinforcing the lesson that all this prayer and study is for serving the neighbor. There is a definite emphasis on relating to others with kindness and humanity.[15] The periods of formal study, including lectures, could have been part of the morning chapter meetings, including guests, and again in the afternoon hour of open conversation. The resident community was of modest size (eighteen in 1134),[16] but students were numerous. As for a "school," the *Liber ordinis* mentions explicitly only the "school of novices," although it is clear that some external students who were not resident members of the community also came to hear William and later Hugh. One Lawrence, later Abbot of Westminster, went to Paris explicitly to study with the saintly scholar Hugh at St. Victor but did not live there; he wrote to a friend about how he was taking notes at lectures (an early *reportatio*) and about Master Hugh's interest in seeing and correcting them![17]

Thus under Abbot Gilduin's leadership, beginning in 1114, the community of St. Victor came to embody William's combination of advanced study and daily devotion within a disciplined community. With the further support of Stephen of Senlis, Bishop of Paris in the 1120s, St. Victor grew considerably in size, budget, and influence. Hugh came to St. Victor soon after Gilduin's leadership took hold, between 1115 and 1118, but where he came from was hotly debated for a long time.

3. The Life of Hugh

The disputes over Hugh's birthplace and early years started because the sources are few and ambiguous, raged on and off for centuries partially out of modern national and cultural loyalties, and in the end do not matter very much, at least regarding birthplace and thus ethnic or national identity. Whether French or German by birth, specifically Flemish or Saxon, Hugh came to represent St. Victor and Paris in a transnational way, both then and now.

His own writings are not much help regarding his origins or family, but there the inquiring begins. "From boyhood," he once wrote, "I have dwelt on foreign soil."[18] The classical allusions in this text make any further biographical conclusions murky, but at least some form of early dislocation is suggested. Elsewhere, Hugh writes so vividly of boyish observations on a manor befitting the nobility that it might reflect his own experience, although not a specific location.[19] Most concretely, he dedicated one of his most important essays to the Augustinian canons at the community of Saint Pancras (Pancratius) in Hamersleben (Saxony) with wording of personal familiarity and memory.[20] Hugh also mentions an uncle in a missive to one "Th," now taken to indicate Thietmar, the first prior of this Saxon community in the diocese of Halberstadt.[21]

With so little internal evidence to go on, a biographer naturally turns to the texts about Hugh, even if they came significantly later. The Victorines themselves early on embraced a thirteenth-century witness that Hugh was born in Saxony and first went to school among the Augustinians at Hamersleben. Then, with his uncle (an archdeacon, also named Hugh), he came to St. Victor. In 1675, Jean Mabillon interpreted some twelfth-century texts to say that Hugh was Flemish, from Ypres, and claimed that the entire Saxony story was a fiction. Mabillon's overall scholarship was persuasive, for a time. In 1745, Christian Gottfried Derling defended the Saxon claims against Mabillon, including new but controversial manuscript evidence about a noble German family, and he then seemed to prevail. In the twentieth century, the Flemish tradition was represented by E. Croydon, and the Saxon by Jerome Taylor.[22] Gradually, the old Victorine tradition of Hugh coming to St. Victor from Saxony with his uncle and namesake has come to dominate, albeit with occasional harmonizing of the Flemish claims. Roger Baron, for example, persisted by suggesting that Hugh was born in Ypres, then lived in Hamersleben, then came to Paris.[23] Yet the "uncle" language in Hugh's text, along with later sources identifying the archdeacon as from Halberstadt, makes a Flemish birth unlikely.[24]

All of these biographical arguments have recently been summarized by Dominique Poirel and supplemented with new twelfth-century evidence in favor of the Saxon tradition.[25] A Victorine calendar dating from near Hugh's lifetime carries special annotations identifying several Saxon names and death dates, including the uncle named Hugh and one Reinhard, bishop of Halberstadt. This Reinhard studied in Paris before becoming bishop in 1107, perhaps with William of Champeaux, and founded the Augustinian community of Saint Pancras at the same time that William moved to Saint Victor. More to the current point, he was also, according to the later texts, an uncle to our Hugh by his brother Conrad, Count of Blankenburg. Suddenly, Hugh of St. Victor has a solid Saxon pedigree and perhaps even a named father and a noble family, vindicating Derling and his sources. Saxon troubles with the emperor may have suggested to Bishop Reinhard that he send his young and talented nephew Hugh from the Hamersleben Augustinian community to the one in Paris, accompanied by his brother Hugh, the archdeacon and uncle. Together, by way of a traditional Marseilles pilgrimage to Saint Victor's tomb, they came to Paris and offered themselves (and relics of the patron saint) to Abbot Gilduin on June 17, perhaps in 1115. In all of this, the community of Augustinians at Hamersleben in Saxony is a key context for Hugh's life before Paris, wherever he was born.

The old arguments over Hugh's birthplace mean very little in the end, for two reasons. First, interpretations of Hugh's works have never turned on his origins. Whether Flemish or Saxon by birth, whether noble family or not, his life's work or at least his output starts at St. Victor. Granted, his evident grounding in St. Augustine's thought had an earlier basis among the Augustinians at Hamersleben, as did his identity as a canon. Second, such national concerns—especially the subtext in the older French and German literature—were largely irrelevant to early twelfth-century Europe, especially in the Parisian mixture of students and teachers from many different places, just as they are of minor importance to twenty-first century readers worldwide. However, Poirel does suggest that Hugh brought to Paris a formation influenced by German imperial factors, such as an interest in the quadrivium, beyond Parisian dialectic, as supported by the Carolingian and Saxon (imperial) authors and "renaissance," but only as a suggestion and not a definitive conclusion.[26]

Whatever his prehistory, Hugh's real career began in Paris, where he started writing and teaching within a few years of his arrival at St. Victor, surely before 1120, the de facto successor to William. By at least 1127, he is designated as a "master," and as head of the school by 1133. Hugh's teaching career includes his voluminous authorship, to be addressed shortly, but not much more can be said of his life. Perhaps he traveled a little, even to Italy sometime in the mid-1130s. His own spiritual life seems summarized in the "Confession" that concludes his *Soliloquy* and our overview of his works. Regarding his death day, however, on February 11, 1141, we have an eyewitness narrative and verbatim from Osbert, the abbey's infirmarian. The devout dialogue, the sacramental piety, the biblical and liturgical quotations, all served to support Osbert's final encomium:

> Then our venerable and most erudite teacher Hugh passed from this life in the confession of the supreme Trinity on [February 11] at 3: good, humble, sweet, and pious.[27]

By tradition, he was only forty-four at his death, putting the conjectured birth year at 1096. His writing career was not long, and the biographical details are sparse, except that he was a teacher above all; yet his works speak volumes and present multiple challenges to the reader: for example, where to start?

4. Approaching Hugh's Works

Hugh of St. Victor may be a familiar name for one or another of his major writings, quite apart from how they fit together as part of his overall work. The *Didascalicon* is famous for the pedagogical issues of the liberal arts, various branches of learning, and comments on the Bible. His *De sacramentis* (*On the Sacraments of the Christian Faith*) is a well-known early "summa" of all theology from creation to eschatology, including sacraments in the (later) narrow sense. Recent years have emphasized Hugh's works of spiritual contemplation or mystical theology, such as the major works on Noah's ark or smaller essays on love and the soul. Yet there are so many large works and hundreds altogether, on so many subjects, that any one choice can be partial and deceptive. Biblical books, chronology, grammar, geometry, the Dionysian *Celestial Hierarchy*, formation for the Victorine novices, sermons, and topics of all kinds interested Hugh, and he wrote about them all. How, then, do we approach his voluminous and diverse corpus? And how do we appreciate that he held together what many contemporaries and most moderns split up into disciplinary specializations?

Despite Hugh's obvious interest in history and chronological order, his own time line of authorship or career is not of decisive help here. His works can be put in chronological order of composition only roughly and very partially. One major effort to place them all in succession is helpful but too speculative.[28] Too many writings cannot be dated at all, and some of them underwent considerable revision and development over time. Furthermore, Hugh's career is not marked by successive external involvements or controversies that could help cluster his works. For all the events, exchanges, and meetings involving others, such as his contemporaries Bernard or Abelard or Peter the Venerable, Hugh barely hints at any external circumstances for his writings. Thus, neither internal nor external history provides a comprehensive order for introducing his works.

Theologians or philosophers may be tempted to launch a presentation of Hugh's work and thought according to a prominent concept or theme that has emerged in retrospect. The *Didascalicon* offers a pedagogical grid for classifying all knowledge; in the *De sacramentis* and elsewhere, Hugh speaks systematically of God's two works, the work of creation and the work of restoration; these and other hermeneutical writings insist that biblical interpretation starts with history, proceeds via allegory to doctrine, and ends with the moral/spiritual meaning; to the mystically minded, such spiritual restoration or ascent has seemed the goal or whole point of Hugh's corpus. These various possible themes testify to Hugh's multifaceted or comprehensive outlook, if only we could see it whole. Such has been the challenge from the beginning. Some Victorines, such as Andrew of St. Victor, continued his exegetical-hermeneutical line; others, like Richard of St. Victor, the spiritual-mystical side; still others, including Peter Lombard, who came to Paris to study with Hugh, the systematic-doctrinal impulse. Perhaps his scope was too wide for any one follower to continue, and thus they needed to specialize. A century later, a well-known sentiment attributed to Bonaventure,

himself both scholastic and spiritual, praised Hugh for this same comprehensive competence, relative to other prominent names:

> Hence all Sacred Scripture teaches these three truths: namely, the eter-
> nal generation and the Incarnation of Christ, the pattern of human life,
> and the union of the soul with God. The first regards *faith*; the second,
> *morals*; and the third, the *ultimate end of both*. The doctors should labor
> at the study of the first; the preachers, at the study of the second; the
> contemplatives, at the study of the third. The first is taught chiefly by
> Augustine; the second, by Gregory; the third, by Dionysius. Anselm fol-
> lows Augustine; Bernard follows Gregory; Richard (of Saint Victor) fol-
> lows Dionysius. For Anselm excels in reasoning; Bernard, in preaching;
> Richard, in contemplating; but Hugh (of Saint Victor) in all three.[29]

This quotation, with its famous names and triadic patterns, is a way to
glimpse Hugh's diverse legacy, but for the moment, the point is simply the
diversity itself, and also that Hugh, there praised the most for the breadth of
his comprehension, is now the least known. Choosing one of these themes
as an organizing principle for introducing Hugh's corpus is tempting, but
it could also distort the overall picture.

The challenge of finding an effective order for introducing Hugh's writings is itself a matter of pedagogy and could thus be turned back to the
Victorine emphasis on teaching and learning. Hugh was first and last a
teacher, and his own concern to present material to his students so that they
could effectively learn it (and teach it) marks many of his own works. The
famous *Didascalicon* concerns not only what and how to read but also in
what order. Hugh consistently organizes his presentations/treatises pedagogically, putting the topic in a teachable form. This concern for ordering
the subject matter will help us appreciate many of his writings, specifically
in letting their contents unfold in his chosen order, beginning to end. It
does not yet provide the overarching order or sequence for introducing
those works, but it does give the question a Victorine pedigree. There is,
I think, a properly Victorine way to enter Hugh's writings. It is neither
chronological nor thematic but rather pedagogical, putting us back into the
community of St. Victor, into the capable hands of Abbot Gilduin. After
Hugh died in 1141, and his literary legacy stood in need of organization,
the abbot who had first welcomed Hugh to St. Victor was still in charge.
Gilduin's remarkable career as abbot culminated in the decade after Hugh's

death with a collection of Hugh's known works arranged in four volumes. None of these volumes has survived, and they cannot be completely reconstructed; in any case, they do not provide the last word on all of Hugh's works. But Gilduin also drew up a list of these works, an invaluable aid to appreciating Hugh's corpus within that early context. Gilduin's "Index" (*Indiculum*) contains many specific details justly pursued by specialists,[30] but it also offers a way for general readers to start meeting Hugh's works. The venerable abbot of St. Victor presented certain of Hugh's works first, in a specific order at the beginning of volume 1, and there we, too, should start. Gilduin mostly listed the titles and/or opening words rather than explaining his pedagogical rationale for this order. Nevertheless, in assuming some wisdom in his editorial decisions, some reason for teaching Hugh to the reader in this order, we are at least being Victorine about it, joining the first readers of this corpus. Who better to set up a curriculum for introducing Hugh, at least at the outset, than Abbot Gilduin? Thus, in order we have the *Chronicles* or *De tribus maximis*, then *On the Scriptures* and the famous *Didascalicon*, followed by other works but still in Gilduin's order.[31] With these introductory works, Hugh's corpus and major themes will open up before us, as Gilduin apparently intended.

Furthermore, beyond trusting Gilduin regarding an initial sequence for introducing Hugh's works, the following chapters also trust Hugh when it comes to the order of exposition within each work. Instead of rearranging the material to fit some other definitions or topical headings, Hugh's works are each presented from beginning to end, according to the teacher's lesson plan, that is, Hugh's own orderly sequence of sections. Victorines like Gilduin and especially Hugh gave great thought to the order of learning; modern readers would do well to follow their lead.

PEDAGOGY

1. The *Chronicles*

Gilduin's edition of Hugh's works starts with his "Chronicles," and it is clear that both the author and the editor had a pedagogical starting point in mind. The work is for the true beginner, a "schoolbook of history,"[1] first advising the young novices on how to learn and where to start, and then supplying chronological tables and diagrams as aids to their foundational learning. Most manuscripts do not call it by Gilduin's title "Chronica" but rather "The Three Best . . ." or, precisely, *De tribus maximis circumstantiis gestorum, id est personis locis temporibus*, which could be loosely rendered, following Mary Carruthers, as "The Three Best Memory Aids for Learning History, Namely, Persons, Places, and Occasions."[2] The heart of it is in the prologue, not in the various detailed tables that follow, although they illustrate Hugh's pedagogical interests in supplying visual aids regarding ancient rulers, Jewish history, and emperors and popes up until 1130.[3]

Editor William Green aptly characterizes the opening lines and overall tone: "The prologue begins in the tone of a master giving his first instruction to a young student."[4]

Child, knowledge is a treasury and your heart is its strongbox. As you study all of knowledge, you store up for yourselves good treasures, immortal treasures, incorruptible treasures, which never decay nor lose the beauty of their brightness.[5]

Storing up such treasures means remembering them, by way of different compartments. "Evidently, at the beginning of their course Hugo's pupils were first taught how to study."[6] The memory is aided by visualizing a place, like a line or a numbered list, for example, or where an item was on the page of the book, or where you were when you learned it. Yes, it sounds childish, says Hugh, but it helps children learn.[7] Starting with the basics like memory means a solid foundation for all learning, as Hugh taps a long tradition of rhetorical training. His next paragraphs, the climax of the prologue, reveal that to Hugh the real foundation for all knowledge is the historical sense of biblical scripture.

> All exposition of divine Scripture is drawn forth according to three senses: history, allegory, and tropology or morality. History is the narrative of what was done, expressed in the first meaning of the letter. Allegory is when by means of this event in history, which is found in the literal meaning, another event is suggested whether past or present or future. Tropology is when in that event which we hear about we recognize what we should be doing.[8]

Here we meet a major theme in all of Hugh's corpus, that sacred scripture should be read according to its historical, allegorical, and tropological or moral sense. The Victorine will expand on these terse definitions often, starting with the next work in Gilduin's order. For the pedagogical moment, says Hugh, the point is to start with history as fundamental.

> But now we have in hand history, as it were the foundation of all teaching [doctrine], the first to be laid out together in memory. But because, as we said, the memory delights in brevity, yet the events of history are nearly infinite, it is necessary for us, from among all of that material, to gather together a kind of brief summary—as it were the foundation of a foundation, that is a first foundation—which the soul can most easily comprehend and the memory retain.[9]

Hugh then pays tribute to the traditional three categories for remembering history, namely, the persons, places, and occasions, as mentioned in the title and as laid out in the tables and diagrams to follow. But before the prologue ends and the tables begin, he provides a much simpler "brief summary" of history, with a built-in memory aid for the beginner who has much yet to learn. "The creation of nature was completed in six days and the renewal of man will be achieved in six stages."[10]

With deceptive ease, Hugh has linked creation and salvation (*conditio* and *reparatio*) by the simple and memorable number six, for both the biblical days of Genesis and the Augustinian ages of world history. The teacher then breaks down the six days, summarizing Genesis for his pupils. With the mention of the sixth day regarding Adam and Eve, the chronology begins, and the first age (from Adam to the flood) is diagrammed accordingly. With the simple symmetry of the six days of creation and the six ages of restoration (named *restauratio* in the diagram), Hugh has provided an overarching perspective for his pupils, one that will serve them and us well as the larger panorama comes into view. Many tables follow, with too many numbers to remember, but the pair of sixes, the days of creation and the ages of restoration, follow in several of Hugh's major works throughout his corpus. When his masterwork, *De sacramentis*, refers back to a first volume of history (and then goes on to develop doctrinal theology on the basis of God's paired works of creation and restoration), some think that Hugh meant this fundamental *Chronicles*,[11] although there is another and a better candidate, discussed in chapter 3.

Writing clearly for novices, indeed for boys, Hugh has here touched lightly on two enormous and complex themes: the triple understanding of scripture as history and allegory and tropology, and the pairing of God's works of creation and restoration. His students have much more to learn about these themes, including the way they fit together, but with the prologue to the *Chronicles*, Gilduin's edition of Hugh's works has gotten things started, pedagogically.

2. On the Scriptures

Next in Gilduin's edition (and first in Migne's *Patrologia* volumes of Hugh) is "On the Sacred Scriptures and Writers," along with specific exegetical materials. *De scripturis* bears a close and complex relationship to the next work in the abbot's order, the *Didascalicon*. The former is more explicitly and thoroughly concerned with biblical interpretation; the latter presents an overall curriculum of study. Many readers have taken the *Didascalicon*'s comments on scripture to represent Hugh's overall viewpoint, in part because some scholars have argued that *De scripturis* was an early work that was then incorporated or even subsumed into the later and better known work. However, others argue the reverse sequence: that the *Didascalicon* is earlier, "with *De scripturis* representing a much more developed set of ideas."[12] Without needing to argue or assume a chronology of composition, there are several reasons to give *De scripturis* our separate, and indeed prior, attention. First, it discusses certain crucial aspects of biblical interpretation more thoroughly than the *Didascalicon* does, and it includes a sharp distinction between sacred scripture and other worthy writings. Second (and perhaps for that first reason), Abbot Gilduin placed it here in Hugh's collected works, before the *Didascalicon*. Third, as Grover Zinn has shown through examination of various manuscripts, "the treatise on biblical interpretation that is most intimately associated with Hugh's actual exegetical works is not the *Didascalicon* but rather *De scripturis et scriptoribus sacris*."[13] Zinn's analysis is followed here, although his specific argument about the manuscripts and a prior literary model is more specialized than we need for this introduction. The point is that this treatise, along with something by Saint Jerome, of course, was the student's introduction to reading sacred scripture.

That scripture is sacred or even divine is first asserted by virtue of authorship (chapter 1). The poets may delight, and logic or mathematics or physics may teach certain truths, but not the truth unto salvation. The "divine" scriptures are those inspired by the Spirit of God, and the obvious difference from other writings is in the subject matter. Chapter 2 supplies the decisive difference of material and does so in terms that have been sampled already and will turn out to be supremely important for Hugh's overall career. The chapter is worth quoting in full.

> There are two works of God, in which all things which were made are consummated. The first is the work of creation, by which was made that which was not. The second is the work of restoration, by which was repaired that which was lost. The work of creation is the creating of the world with all its elements. The work of restoration is the incarnation of the Word with all his sacraments, whether those from the beginning that preceded the incarnation or those that followed afterwards until the end of the world. Therefore, the first works were made for servanthood, so that they might be subject to humanity, standing through justice. But the second [works] were made for salvation, so that they might raise up humanity, fallen through sin; for that reason these [latter] are the greater. Therefore those [works of creation] as something modest and a small

indication of the divine power, were completed in a brief time, namely, just six days. But these [works of restoration], as excellent in comparison with the prior and as having a greater effect in power, could not be consummated except in six ages.

Consider the subject matter of the divine scriptures in these [terms], therefore, so that you can distinguish them from other writings both in what they treat and also in the way they treat it. The subject matter of all other writings consists of the works of creation; the subject matter of the divine scriptures consists in the works of restoration. This therefore is the first distinction, concerning that which they treat. Further, even if other writings teach some truth, it is not without the contamination of error; even if they seem to commend some goodness, it is either mixed with evil such that it is not pure, or it is without the knowledge and love of God such that it is not perfect. Therefore, just as the soul of someone reading that which is supposed to be divine in those [writings] will fall to earth through related falsehood, so also [the soul of someone reading] that which seems earthly in the sacred scriptures will rise up through the true knowledge of the creator, which is commended in all these writings, to the divine and celestial things that should be thought and loved.[14]

This chapter propels the reader toward several subjects at once, starting with theology and categories of literature. As to theology, the pairing of creation and restoration aims at the systematic exposition in Hugh's later works, notably *De sacramentis*. Indeed, this very text is reused in that systematic summa, somewhat revised but still evident, as in the understanding of "sacraments" to encompass all of salvation history. (As we will see, Hugh often reappropriated portions of his own writings.) Further, categories of literature are here associated with creation and restoration, namely, the divine scriptures for the latter and all other literature for the former. This distinction can also be applied to Hugh's own writings, in that his scriptural expositions including *De sacramentis* pertain to God's saving work of restoration, whereas some other writings and forms of knowledge fall under works of creation. Besides beginning here to draw a sharp contrast between sacred scripture and other literature, a distinction not as clear in *Didascalicon*, this quotation hints at an interpretive principle for reading scripture itself, the subject of the whole *De scripturis*. Something may seem terrestrial even within a biblical passage, yet that is how the uplifting interpretive process starts, whereas attempting to start with the lofty may lead to a fall. Hugh is drawing his readers into a discussion of the different meanings or senses of scripture, and their relationship.

The triple understanding of scripture as history, allegory, and tropology is now expanded somewhat and deepened in chapter 3 of *De scripturis*, especially when compared with the terse presentation in the *Chronicles*.
The deep background to all this is Origen, Jerome, Augustine, and especially Gregory the Great. Hugh here mentions, with development later,
the Augustinian notion that it is not only the words that can signify things
in scripture but also that the things signified, the events being narrated,
can signify other things or events. "Alle"-gory means this "other" or alien
meaning.[15] The allegorical sense, for Hugh, is thus also framed historically
or typologically, as when one event signifies another, whether past or present or future. He here uncharacteristically subdivides the allegorical sense
into simple allegory and anagogy, "that is, upward leading," but never
makes anything of it.[16] The biblical Job, to introduce a Gregorian example,
can be triply understood: the words indicate a historical man, who signifies
Christ allegorically, and models the penitent soul for us. Not all biblical
texts have all three meanings, but many do, and it is all grounded in the
historical sense.[17]

At this point (chapter 5), Hugh simulates a lively debate with those who
would leap over the letter in their eagerness for the allegorical or spiritual
meaning. You cannot appreciate how Christ is like a lion, sleeping (humanity) with eyes open (divinity), unless you know something about real lions,
not just the word *lion*.[18] "Do not, therefore, wish to make a leap, lest you
fall into a ditch!"[19] The only way to the invisible is through the visible, as in
Christ himself. "Thus, do not wish to despise the humility in the Word of
God, for it is through the humility that you will be illumined to divinity."[20]
Did not Christ use the terrestrial mud under our feet to open the eyes of
the blind man? "Therefore, read scripture and first learn diligently what
it narrates corporally," according to the (historical) sequence of narration.[21]
As Grover Zinn has emphasized, regarding this text and many others, for
Hugh, history is the foundation.[22] It is on the historical foundation of scripture that he will build the (allegorical) framework of doctrinal theology and
then finish or decorate it with a spiritual way of life, as suggested already
but not yet developed.

For several chapters (6–12), Hugh's *De scripturis* next lists the books of
the Bible, their writers and translators, as taken in large part from Isidore
of Seville and also highlighted in book 4 of the *Didascalicon*. He then
returns to the double "fruit" of divine reading in chapter 13, namely, first
building up knowledge through history and (allegorical) doctrine, and then

adorning it all with the moral, or tropological, as also developed in book 5 of the *Didascalicon*. The seven liberal arts are applied: the trivium (grammar, dialectic, and rhetoric) to understanding the words, the quadrivium to understanding the things they signify. The ensuing Augustinian discussion of "words" and "things" parallels Hugh's other texts, yet Zinn's analysis highlights a distinctive emphasis at the end of this treatise, one that is not duplicated in the *Didascalicon* but is indicative of Hugh's career as a whole. With the concluding chapter 17, Hugh returns to the subject matter, the *materia* of divine scripture, namely, the salvation history of "the incarnate Word with all his sacraments whether preceding from the beginning of the world or future to the end of the age."[23] This fundamentally historical outlook on scripture has many varieties, all of them involving temporal succession: two states (old and new), three times (natural law, written law, and grace), the six ages (corresponding to the six stages of human growth), all developed elsewhere. Hugh's historical perspective has become evident and provides the distinctive mark to his view of scripture, over against his view of other (nonscriptural) literature. As Zinn concludes,

> Scripture is distinctive and superior to the writings of the philosophers precisely because it deals with deeds done in time, specifically with the deeds known as the works of restoration. Hugh has now discovered the theological key to his distinctive view of the cosmos, history, and salvation. God is revealed in the very material of existence and in the structures and events of history.[24]

Zinn rightly isolates the "theological key" to Hugh's work, namely, salvation history, more evident in this lesser known treatise than in the *Didascalicon*, with its overall discussion of all learning and teaching.

3. *The Didascalicon*

Third in our abbot's order for reading Hugh of St. Victor is the justly famous *Didascalicon de studio legendi*. Of the pedagogical foundations being laid in this presentation of Hugh's corpus, it is by far the largest, most detailed, and most influential. The reader's first and lasting impression is of the amazing breadth of learning involved, the diverse topics and sources, not only within Hugh's work but also prescribed therein for general study in the Victorine school. Every conceivable subject seems part of this curriculum, from the humanities to the sciences, from arts to crafts, with detailed pedagogical guidance on what to read, how, and why. Hugh's reputation for broad learning is rightly linked to this particular work, which today's readers can easily see for themselves, since translations and analyses abound.[25]

An introduction to the *Didascalicon* can only hint at the curricular details it presents but should suggest the educational and formational principles at work and can ask certain questions about the relationship of this book and these principles to Hugh's overall corpus and career. For example, following Abbot Gilduin's sequence, how does Hugh's historical perspective, specifically the schema of works of creation and works of restoration, relate to this curricular overview? Further, how does he develop his hermeneutical method of the threefold sense of scripture (history, allegory, and tropology) toward his other writings, the rest of his corpus, specifically in theology and spirituality? The *Chronicles* and *De scripturis* lead the reader to the *Didascalicon* with these and other questions, and still more come from Hugh's ambitious overview of reading and learning.

Hugh's own preface to the work supplies the tone and the outline. He wants to inspire students in the pursuit of knowledge and wisdom, specifically on what to read, in what order, and how. Meditation will come later. As he says,

> [This] book, moreover, instructs the reader as well of secular writing as of the Divine Writings. Therefore, it is divided into two parts, each of which contains three subdivisions. In the first part, it instructs the reader of the arts, in the second, the reader of the Sacred Scripture.[26]

Thus books 1 through 3 concern secular readings in "the arts," their origins and distinctions and authors, guiding the students in what to read, in sequence, and how (their "discipline of life"). Similarly, regarding books 4 through 6:

> In the second part it determines what writings ought to be called divine, and next, the number and order of the Divine Books, and their authors, and the interpretations of the names of these Books. It then treats certain characteristics of Divine Scripture which are very important. Then it shows how Sacred Scripture ought to be read by the man who seeks in it the correction of his morals and a form of living. Finally, it instructs the man who reads in it for love of knowledge, and thus the second part too comes to a close.[27]

As already indicated, some of this material duplicates what is in *De scripturis* and borrows extensively from sources such as Isidore of Seville. Yet it adds up to its own tour de force regarding an ambitious curriculum of secular and scriptural reading, all for the sake of personal (spiritual) formation in the Victorine sense.

Book 1 immediately shows the sophistication of Hugh's work, both in the concepts (a discussion of philosophy and Wisdom that turns out to be divine, the "living mind" of Christ) and also in sources (naming Apollo's epigram, Plato's *Timaeus,* Pythagoras, and Varro; quoting Chalcidius briefly and Boethius at length).[28] As the "love of wisdom," philosophy is defined as "the discipline which investigates comprehensively the ideas [*rationes*] of all things, human and divine,"[29] indicating the disciplinary breadth of what is to come, and aims especially at the Wisdom that "is the sole primordial Idea or Pattern of things," quoting Boethius regarding an overall theological, indeed Christological, goal.[30]

As chapter 5 turns to the promised discussion of the secular arts, their origins and categories ("Concerning the Rise of the Theoretical, the Practical, and the Mechanical," to be joined by the "logical"), Hugh first provides an overarching theological context regarding human nature: created good, suffering corruption, needing repair or restoration.

> Of all human acts or pursuits, then, governed as these are by Wisdom, the end and the intention ought to regard either the restoring of our nature's integrity, or the relieving of those weaknesses to which our present life lies subject.[31]

As Hugh goes on to explain, humanity is both good by nature and corrupted or lessened, thus needing repair. Evil as a deficiency needs to be tempered or removed. "This is our entire task—the restoration of our nature and the removal of our deficiency."[32] Theologically implicit in this framework is Hugh's familiar sequence of creation and restoration, now separated by the suggestion of the fall and thus a need for repair. Hugh does not here use his explicit language of "the work of creation" and "the work of restoration," but the conceptual framework is identical, and the language is similar. After digressing, he says, for a chapter on humanity's dual affiliations (necessary flux and eternal stability), Hugh returns to this overarching framework for everything human, including the explicit language of restoration.

> From this it can be inferred, as said above, that the intention of all human actions is resolved in a common objective: either to restore in us the likeness of the divine image or to take thought for the necessity of this life.[33]

In Hugh's basic bifurcation, "the necessity of this life" implies both the original creation and also our fall into corruption, whereas the repair of our nature is straightforwardly God's work of restoration, regarding truth and virtue. This framework yields the distinction between understanding and knowledge, and thus Hugh's first division of the arts.

When, moreover, we strive after the restoration of our nature, [we perform] a divine action, but when we provide the necessaries required by our infirm part, a human action. Every action, thus, is either human or divine. The former type, since it derives from above, we may not unfittingly call "understanding" (*intelligentia*); the latter, since it derives from below and requires, as it were, a certain practical counsel, "knowledge" (*scientia*).[34]

This basic distinction of understanding and knowledge, both stemming from (divine) Wisdom, is further classified into the basic categories familiar in the rest of the book.

Understanding, again, inasmuch as it works both for the investigation of truth and the delineation of morals, we divide into two kinds—into theoretical, that is to say speculative, and practical, that is to say active. The latter is also called ethical, or moral. Knowledge, however, since it pursues merely human works, is fitly called "mechanical," that is to say adulterate.[35]

With the addition shortly of the "logical," because it was the last to be discovered or invented, we have Hugh's fundamental four branches of knowledge or philosophy: the theoretical, the practical, the mechanical, and the logical, as further subdivided and defined in due course. The deep theological background fades away quickly, but it has launched the basic sequence. Creation/fall and the repair to truth and virtue pertain, respectively, to life's necessities and the restoration of the divine likeness, and thus to (lower) "knowledge" (the mechanical) and to (higher) "understanding." The higher realm of repair or divine restoration is twofold, namely, the contemplation of truth (the "theoretical" or speculative) and the practice of virtue (the "practical," or active, ethical or moral). Although mostly implicit, except for the clear language of restoration, Hugh's familiar theological framework of the work of creation and the work of restoration is also foundational for his classification of knowledge in the *Didascalicon*.

Thinking about such things requires logic, and thus, as Boethius had argued, the "logical" is last to develop. "Linguistic logic" contains grammar, dialectic, and rhetoric, and the fourfold division of knowledge (theoretical, practical, mechanical, and logical) is set up for further elaboration in book 2. A comprehensive and ambitious curriculum has come into view, and the theological foundation is assumed. Philosophy as the "love of wisdom," including the divine Wisdom or "living Mind" (requoting Boethius), is again the overarching category for Hugh's further specification and classification of the arts in the *Didascalicon*, book 2. The larger context of creation and restoration is glimpsed only briefly. "This, then, is what the arts are concerned with, this is what they intend, namely to restore within us the divine likeness."[36] The theological language of restoration or repair then disappears as Hugh divides and subdivides philosophy into the various arts or branches of knowledge, but it remains the doctrinal context for all the details of the *Didascalicon*. In that sense, the liberal arts concern not only creation but also the beginnings of restoration. Philosophy, repeats Hugh, is the study of all things, human and divine, as seen in his fourfold scheme.

> Philosophy is divided into theoretical, practical, mechanical, and logical. These four contain all knowledge. The theoretical may also be called speculative; the practical may be called active, likewise ethical, that is, moral, from the fact that morals consist in good action; the mechanical may be called adulterate because it is concerned with the works of human labor; the logical may be called linguistic from its concern with words. The theoretical is divided into theology, mathematics, and physics.[37]

Now begins an itemizing and further subdividing of these various classifications, beginning with theology in the specific (Boethian) sense of the contemplation of God, even though the entire discussion of philosophy has also been framed theologically from the beginning, and the second part of this entire work concerns theological scripture.

The theoretical divides into theology, mathematics, and physics, and then mathematics is further identified, again in Boethian terms, as the quadrivium: "Mathematics, therefore, is divided into arithmetic, music, geometry, astronomy."[38] Each of these terms is discussed, and that field of knowledge sometimes subdivided further, as in the varieties of music or geometry. (Hugh's separate treatise *On Geometry*, discussed shortly, illustrates some of his pedagogical patterns.) Physics is also discussed, albeit briefly, and these various categories are compared and contrasted.

Hugh's second major subdivision, the practical, is tersely subdivided into three: the solitary (ethical or moral), the private (economic or managerial), and the public (political or civil), meaning, respectively: individuals, families, and governments.[39] Again quoting Boethius, Hugh adds little of his own. Turning quickly to the third of his four major branches of knowledge, the mechanical, Hugh has already admitted that most previous classifications of philosophy had no such category.[40] Perhaps in conscious compensation, Hugh here innovates with a comprehensive array of examples in chapters 20 through 27. The seven basic subdivisions (grouped as three and four, like the trivium and quadrivium) are fabric making of all kinds, armaments including all construction and crafts, commerce, agriculture, hunting including everything to do with food and drink, medicine, and theatrics. On display here is Hugh's breadth of mind and generosity of judgment. The broad definition of *hunting* to include food and drink generates a dazzling list of breads and meats and beverages. "Hunting, therefore, includes all the duties of bakers, butchers, cooks, and tavern keepers."[41] The Victorine teacher also shows a generous or positive judgment about commerce (*navigatio*) and theatrics (entertainment generally), although both topics were sometimes subject to ecclesial censure. "The pursuit of commerce reconciles nations, calms wars, strengthens peace, and commutes the private good of individuals into the common benefit of all."[42] Overall, these lists of specific subdivisions and lively examples of the mechanical read like a comprehensive affirmation of daily life in the world at large, the world of blankets, saws, trade, meadows, beer, surgery, and amphitheaters. Here and elsewhere, Hugh does not disparage the physical created world but affirms it, as seen more directly in his discussion of creation.

The fourth part of philosophy is the logical, meaning grammar (with all its subdivisions, treated in another work) and argument, including dialectic and rhetoric. "Grammar is the knowledge of how to speak without error; dialectic is clear-sighted argument which separates the true from the false; rhetoric is the discipline of persuading to every suitable thing."[43]

Hugh himself sums up all of this.

> Philosophy is divided into the theoretical, the practical, the mechanical, and the logical. The *theoretical* is divided into theology, physics, and mathematics; mathematics is divided into arithmetic, music, geometry, and astronomy. The *practical* is divided into solitary, private, and public. The *mechanical* is divided into fabric making, armament, commerce, agriculture, hunting, medicine, and theatrics. Logic is divided into

grammar and argument: argument is divided into demonstration, probable argument, and sophistic: probable argument is divided into dialectic and rhetoric.[44]

This scheme, at the opening of book 3 about the various authors of all these topics, can also be laid out as an outline.

Philosophy (love of Wisdom)
encompassing all the arts,
aiming at the repair of the divine image in us.

Theoretical
   theology
   physics
   mathematics
      arithmetic
      music
      geometry
      astronomy
Practical
   solitary
   private
   public
Mechanical
   fabric making
   armament
   commerce
   agriculture
   hunting
   medicine
   theatrics
Logical
   grammar
   dialectic
   rhetoric

With twenty-some headings, the Victorine curriculum of secular writings was comprehensive and ambitious indeed. Hugh's list of selected authors is equally formidable, such as Varro, John the Scot (Eriugena), Pliny, Pythagoras, Boethius of course, Plato and Aristotle, Cicero and Vergil.[45]

Hugh's real concern is not merely to list works or authors but to shape or form the student-readers in the way of wisdom. Even the words "tri*vium*" and "quadri*vium*" concern the ways (*viae*) "into the secret places of wisdom."[46] "We find many who study but few who are wise."[47] Hugh's advice here encompasses not only students (who should privilege the "arts" as named, not the "appendages" such as poetry) but also teachers, because some other lecturers tend to blur the arts or topics together. Hugh seems particularly critical of some other teachers, albeit anonymously: "It is not the teaching of others that they accomplish in this way, but the showing off of their own knowledge."[48] His concern for effective teaching is explicit here, as well as implicit throughout his teaching and writing career, for he embodies this advice.

> When, therefore, we treat of any art—and especially in teaching it, when everything must be reduced to outline (*compendium*) and presented for easy understanding—we should be content to set forth the matter in hand as briefly and as clearly as possible, lest by excessively piling up extraneous considerations we distract the student more than we instruct (*aedificemus*) him.[49]

Hugh's concern is consistently pedagogical, in his own writings elsewhere in practice, and for the rest of this work in theory.

How the student learns depends not only on natural ability and practice but also on an effective order or sequence of readings, as set forth by good teaching. This entire concern, explicitly applicable both to secular writings and to the divine scripture considered later in the *Didascalicon*, is a pedagogical expression of Hugh's overall interest in temporal succession, in a sequential order of events, in historical narration. Whether the macro of cosmic salvation history or the micro of a curricular order, Hugh was consistently historical. Specifically, the order of exposition is clear, for divine scripture as well: "first the letter [*littera*; the words themselves]; then the sense [*sensus*; the plain meaning of the words], and finally the inner meaning [*sententia*; the deeper understanding]."[50] Hugh's own commentaries, whether on scripture or on Dionysius, follow this pattern, especially in the patient analysis of the text as it stands (the "letter," meaning a close look at each word) before moving on to the "sense." Such reading, the subject of this whole work, thus includes exposition by analysis and leads to meditation that ranges more freely without such rules. As the goal of disciplined reading, such meditation (chapter 10) reminds the student of the larger spiritual goods, for meditating upon the creation can lead one to the Creator. The world of secular reading is God's world after all, as appreciated in "continual meditation upon the wonders of God."[51]

Many pedagogical virtues and capacities are then extolled, including memory of a summa (with the familiar imagery of a treasure chest),[52] discipline, and especially humility. The fervor and specificity of Hugh's praise for humility, the beginning of discipline, and especially his diatribe against those who lack it (swollen namedroppers and peddlers of trifle who wrinkle their noses at lecturers in divinity) have led some to see Peter Abelard between the lines.[53] The positive side of Hugh's advice on humble and patient learning also applies to learning about him and his work: "The man who proceeds stage by stage moves along best. Certain fellows, wishing to make a great leap of progress, sprawl headlong. Do not hurry too much, therefore."[54] Humble willingness to learn everything, but in a good and productive order or succession, marks Hugh's own works of pedagogical foundation and also allows these particular works to lay the foundations for our own encounter with Hugh's life and work. Among the final virtues or conditions for effective learning is the situation of exile invoked earlier for its hints of Hugh's own background. Here, finally, in its original pedagogical context, is the teacher's poetic touch of autobiography.

> The man who finds his homeland sweet is still a tender beginner; he to whom every soil is as his native one is already strong; but he is perfect to whom the entire world is as a foreign land. The tender soul has fixed his love on one spot in the world; the strong man has extended his love to all places; the perfect man has extinguished his. From boyhood I have dwelt on foreign soil, and I know with what grief sometimes the mind takes leave of the narrow hearth of a peasant's hut, and I know, too, how frankly it afterwards disdains marble firesides and paneled halls.[55]

In moving to the second half of the *Didascalicon*, and thus completing one entry into Hugh's world, his life, and his pedagogical foundations, our author works with a symmetry that is both obvious and also implicit. Obviously, as in the preface, the two parts present what to read, in what order, and how, with respect first to the secular writings (books 1 through 3) and then to the divine writings (books 4 through 6). Many aspects of reading and learning apply equally well to both kinds of literature. In moving from the secular to the sacred, the *Didascalicon*'s fourth book does not make much of a theological contrast, just that the philosophers may look attractive while containing falsehood, whereas the sacred scriptures look simple but contain pure truth and carry the authority of the church. Implicit, or perhaps not yet developed, is the overarching doctrinal framework seen in *De scripturis* regarding creation and salvation.

> The subject matter of all other writings consists of the works of creation; the subject matter of the divine scriptures consists in the works of restoration.[56]

Hugh's views of scriptural interpretation consistently cohere with this correlation of philosophy and the arts with creation and the sacred scriptures with salvation, but he does not make much of it in the *Didascalicon*.

Hugh's introduction of the biblical writings invokes another pattern of explicit symmetry, indeed, like the work as a whole, two symmetrical triads.

> The whole of Sacred Scripture is contained in two Testaments, namely, in the Old and in the New. The books in each Testament are divided into three groups. The Old Testament contains the Law, the Prophets, and the Hagiographers; the New contains the Gospel, the Apostles and the Fathers.[57]

The list of biblical books and the meanings of their names then draws on Jerome and especially (verbatim) Isidore's *Etymologies*, as does the whole of book 4, but the inclusion of "the Fathers" to complete the triadic symmetry is Hugh's own creative addition. How the New Testament can include these patristic authors outside the canon is never fully explained.[58]

In listing the biblical books and their writers, the translators, and apocryphal books, the canons and synods of the church, Hugh is quoting large passages of Isidore, as also seen in *De scripturis*. When he itemizes the Fathers, he also quotes from the pseudo-Gelasian decretals for most of the names (adding to Isidore's trio of Origen, Jerome, and Augustine a longer list starting with Athanasius, Hilary, and Basil), but on his own he adds Cassiodorus regarding the Psalms and this: "Dionysius the Areopagite, ordained bishop of the Corinthians, has left many volumes as testimony of his mental ability."[59] Hugh will return to Dionysius, at length, in another work, as covered in my appendix. Book 4 closes without further discussion of how the Fathers could be included within the New Testament, merely quoting more Isidorean etymologies on terms like *codex* and *homily* and *gloss*.

With books 5 and 6 of the *Didascalicon*, Hugh comes to the pedagogical foundation of biblical interpretation. Although still at times quoting Isidore at length and sometimes overlapping verbatim with his own *De scripturis*, Hugh's distinctive method is clear. "First of all, it ought to be known that Sacred Scripture has three ways of conveying meaning—namely, history, allegory, and tropology."[60] Not that every biblical text will necessarily contain all three. "Often, however, in one and the same literal context, all may be found together, as when a truth of history both hints at some mystical meaning by way of allegory, and equally shows by way of tropology how we ought to behave."[61] What Hugh means by "history" or "allegory" or "tropology" is not so immediately plain, and the relationships of these three ways to each other and to Hugh's overall method and, indeed, his entire corpus can be clarified only gradually. "History," for starters, can mean both the events and the narrations thereof, "allegory" relates directly to doctrine, and "tropology" covers much more than ethics or morality in the modern sense. To follow Hugh's own uses of these terms, and thus his hermeneutical method, leads to many other texts beyond the *Didascalicon*, indeed, in due time to an overall perspective on his works as a whole. For now, however, Hugh gives glimpses not only of his goals for all of this but also of his sources. From Augustine, especially *On Christian Doctrine*, comes the familiar claim that not only scriptural words but also scriptural events ("things") signify further meanings.[62] From Tyconius by way of Augustine and Isidore come the "seven rules," although Hugh never develops any of them any further.[63]

For students to progress in reading scripture in the right order and in the right way, they must keep its goals in mind, and here history, allegory, and tropology apply.

> Twofold is the fruit of sacred reading, because it either instructs the mind with knowledge or it equips it with morals. It teaches what it delights us to know and what it behooves us to imitate. Of these, the first, namely knowledge, has more to do with history and allegory, the other, namely instruction in morals, has more to do with tropology. The whole of sacred Scriptures is directed to this end.[64]

Of these two categories, the knowledge or doctrine that comes in the move from history to allegory (the interpretation of history as the work of restoration, namely, as salvation history) receives no further explanation until book 6, and of course, the entire *De sacramentis*. But the realm of tropology, the way of life, is immediately expanded by way of the saints' lives and explicit reference to Gregory the Great, apparently his *Dialogues*. In this context, *morality* does not mean ethics in the narrow modern sense of social justice, but rather the entire spiritual life of meditation, prayer, and contemplation. Hugh explicitly itemizes the steps of such a life as study, meditation, prayer, performance, and contemplation.[65] Such is the way of life, the mores of tropology, meaning that much of the meditative or contemplative patterns we might call spirituality are implied in this culminating sense of scripture. In particular, contemplation will remain an important category in Hugh's works, correlated to tropology, just as his doctrinal works correlate to allegory. Students should want to gain scriptural knowledge, says Hugh's conclusion, not for its own sake and certainly not for wealth or fame, but rather to teach others and to grow in love, two distinctive Victorine emphases.[66]

The concluding book of Hugh's magisterial *Didascalicon* contains some of his most important methodological and therefore theological statements, yet they must also be considered in light of his overall career and corpus. Even here, he is explicitly teaching and addressing himself "to you, my student,"[67] as to pedagogical foundations, that is, how to study. There is clear curricular order, namely, history, then allegory, then tropology, as discussed here in theory but as carried out elsewhere (in other works) in practice and in detail. Hugh invokes, and later quotes, Gregory the Great's instructive image of constructing a building: first the foundation (history), then the structure (allegory/doctrine), then the decorative finish (the way of life).[68]

First is history, a necessary foundation, even if some want to skip ahead. (Hugh testifies to his own patient learning of basic facts, although his examples are from nature or language rather than history.) As with secular learning, Hugh's advice here is humility, indeed in the same terms of patient steps instead of a precipitate leap.[69] It is in this context of patience with scriptural history that we find Hugh's famous words: "Learn everything; you will see afterwards that nothing is superfluous. A skimpy knowledge is not a pleasing thing."[70] The historical books most suited for this foundational study are Genesis, Exodus, Joshua, Judges, Kings, and Chronicles, and then the four Gospels and Acts. "The foundation and principle of sacred learning is history."[71]

Before summarizing this history, from creation to the sending of apostles, Hugh reviews the threefold sense of scripture, first by quoting Gregory's analogy of a building, then in his own words.

> You have in history the means through which to admire God's deeds, in allegory the means through which to believe his mysteries [sacraments], in morality the means through which to imitate his perfection.[72]

Biblical history thus leads to the doctrinal structure of belief, including the *sacramenta* or mysteries, eventually elaborated in *De sacramentis*. Elaborating on the construction metaphor, Hugh itemizes ("Pay attention now!") the layers of doctrinal stones or mysteries (*sacramenta*) laid upon the historical foundation. The sequence here is indeed the same one later taken up in *De sacramentis*: the triune God, creation, fall; restoration under the natural law, under the (written) Law, the incarnation, the New Testament's mysteries/sacraments, and the resurrection.[73] This, says Hugh, is the whole of divinity: first the foundations of history, then the superstructure of the faith, as guided by other specific biblical books pertinent to this doctrinal study and developed more fully in *De sacramentis*. Thus Hugh's later and mature doctrinal outline was already in place in his early pedagogical work. The next step, he says (namely, the tropological sense), has already been discussed sufficiently for now.

The *Didascalicon* concludes with a characteristic concern for order, for several specific sequences, but only one of them is historical in the usual sense. There is one order for reading the books of sacred scripture in terms of history but another for the "alien" or other (allegorical) sense that involves doctrine. "History follows the order of time; to allegory belongs more the order of knowledge,"[74] namely, that clear teachings like the New Testament should precede the shrouded figures of the Old Testament. Thus the later New Testament events regarding Christ will help the student understand the earlier Old Testament prophecies.

The order of exposition of such texts is the same as already presented regarding the exposition of secular texts: first is the letter (or literal sense, involving immediate grammar and syntax), then the sense (*sensus*) as when an idiom or symbolic way of speaking needs to be understood, and then the divine deeper meanings (*sententia*), which are "always harmonious, always true"[75] but not fully explained here, as Hugh merely quotes St. Augustine on the general idea. As earlier regarding worldly writings, Hugh closes this sixth book (and the whole treatise) with reference to the method of expounding a text, namely, through analysis or distinguishing the parts, and with mention of the further topic beyond reading, namely, meditation. As Hugh said in the preface, this entire work concerns reading, whether worldly or sacred scripture, but reading is followed by meditation, "the remaining part of learning," another subject altogether: "so great a matter requires a separate treatise."[76] Hugh has already indicated this sequence ("the start of learning, thus, lies in reading, but its consummation lies in meditation"[77]), and indeed he will lead the student to rich works of meditation in due time.

Although chapter 13 of book 6 thus seems to have been the original conclusion ("those things pertaining to reading have been explained as lucidly and briefly as we know how"[78]) Hugh himself added two more chapters, 14 and 15 in Buttimer's edition and appendices A and B in Taylor's translation. They sum up, respectively, the "Division of the Contents of Philosophy" and an overview of false knowledge ("Magic and Its Parts"), such as sorcery, necromancy, and horoscopes. Since Abbot Gilduin explicitly supplied the last words of his edition,[79] we know that it included this material.

This fuller conclusion, especially the penultimate chapter, shows Hugh's pedagogical principles at work, in two ways. First, he again sketches the larger context for "every art and every discipline." The theoretical, the practical, and the mechanical pertain respectively to wisdom, virtue, and need, which are themselves three "remedies against three evils to which human life is subject: wisdom against ignorance, virtue against vice, and need against life's weaknesses."[80] Here Hugh echoes his initial presentation (book 1) that all human pursuits "ought to regard either the restoring of our nature's integrity, or the relieving of those weaknesses to which our present life lies subject."[81] In other words, in his conclusion, Hugh has restated the theological context for all this "philosophy" or reading in general, namely, the creation-fall-restoration sequence of salvation history. These culminating categories (evils and remedies) were earlier presented in terms of "the restoration of our nature and the removal of our deficiency,"[82] and thus the larger theological framework (the "work of restoration") is here glimpsed again as the *Didascalicon* concludes.

The second pedagogical benefit of this concluding summary is that he helpfully provides the reader with another overview listing of the various parts of philosophy, also as a curriculum of learning: logic first, starting with grammar, ethics or "the practical" next (solitary, private, and public), the theoretical arts next (theology, physics, and mathematics, including geometry), and the mechanical arts fourth and last.[83] Indeed, the abbot's corpus next moves quickly to *On Grammar* and *Practical Geometry*, and so shall we. Although this summary mostly repeats what was presented earlier—for example, at the beginning of book 3—it is helpful here for the reader to have a concluding overview, as the teacher no doubt intended.

4. Summary

The *Didascalicon* is Hugh's most important work of pedagogical foundation, yet it is best appreciated in the context of the several works that Abbot Gilduin placed at the start of his edition of Hugonian works. For a simple example, Gilduin's next work, the early and brief *Epitoma Dindimi in philosophiam* on these same themes, seems appended here as in the shadow of the larger work. The *Didascalicon* covers the same ground and usually in much more detail. Presented in a charming dialogue, the *Epitoma* has the same breakdown of philosophy, its definition, origin, and divisions, as summarized at the beginning of Roger Baron's part 4 and the table sometimes appended.[84] It also mentions, albeit briefly, the theological context of three evils[85] and frames the whole work in terms of the creator: "The goal of all philosophy is knowledge of the highest good, which is situated in the sole maker of all things."[86]

From here, Gilduin's corpus continues with Hugh's pedagogical treatises on specific topics, namely, *On Grammar* and *On Practical Geometry*, as we shall see shortly, but the initial works covered so far are of larger methodological importance regarding pedagogical foundations generally. They have introduced several principles or deep structures in Hugh's thought that can help organize further presentation of his many works.

The Chronicles, *On the Scriptures*, and the *Didascalicon* all show Hugh, first of all, as pedagogue. These and other texts are "teaching tools,"[87] as Grover Zinn calls them, and indicate Hugh's concern throughout for effective teaching. His entire corpus testifies to this concern for pedagogy, specifically for organizing the material into a teachable, learnable order.[88] He explicitly advises his students at length about how to read and to learn. For his part, how to teach seems to mean especially how to order the material in an effective sequence, which is itself a matter of temporal order and often explicitly a historical order. Hugh's ordering of history does not always mean chronological details, although that is the basis. Glimpsed in his early guidance to the boys in his care and placed first by Gilduin, and then developed further in many other works, Hugh's overarching historical order is creation and restoration, God's work of creation in six days and God's work of restoration in six ages. According to *De scripturis*, the work of creation is the subject of all worldly literature, whereas sacred scripture is devoted to the works of restoration. Hugh's own work can also be allocated accordingly, but unevenly so, for he is mostly concerned for the scriptural story of restoration.

Specifically, sacred scripture should be read according to a triple meaning. The historical comes first, meaning the events narrated by the text itself; then comes the doctrinal interpretation of scripture that he calls the allegory; and then the personal or spiritual appropriation called tropology. The biblical texts themselves, the letter, yield the sense of a basic story. For Hugh, the world's story or history should be interpreted doctrinally or theologically as God's work of restoration. This biblical interpretation he calls allegory, the "other" meaning, but that word for him means doctrine or theology in the modern sense, as we will see when we come to his culminating exposition of it in the *De sacramentis*. Similarly, the tropological or moral sense of scripture that comes next is not a narrow (later) matter of ethics but the whole of life, especially the spiritual life including prayer and contemplation, as in many of Hugh's later works.[89]

Thus building on the foundations of history, in this pedagogical construct, is the framework of doctrine and then the final adornment of spirituality. All of this is within the heading of the divine work of restoration. Many although not all of Hugh's other works and concerns can fall into these two categories of (allegorical) doctrine and (tropological) spirituality and will be taken up in due course. Other works can fall into the prior category of the works of creation, such as the treatise on geometry. Still other writings parallel this initial overarching concern for pedagogy and formation, such as Hugh's guidance for Victorine novices.

Thus, in summary, Hugh's pedagogical foundations can indicate an order for encountering his other works and his overall corpus, but only gradually. After all, three times already he has warned that those who wish to make a great leap will fall into a big ditch![90] Under works of creation come Hugh's introductions to grammar and geometry, the next works in Gilduin's order. Under works of restoration, the realm of sacred scripture, come many of Hugh's writings, here triply divided according to his own hermeneutical method. First, the letter or foundational text of scripture is the starting point for many of Hugh's biblical commentaries, especially the historical sense of the Pentateuch. Of course, there are sermons too numerous to itemize. Second, Hugh's doctrinal (allegorical) interpretations of the biblical story are summed up in his magisterial *De sacramentis*, along with other theological works in this specific sense. Last, and at length, the (tropological) results of all of this for life, for the personal lives of the faithful especially in prayer and contemplation, are the subject of many of Hugh's works, great and small, whether the full treatise on Noah's ark or the small essays on love and a very personal *Soliloquy*. Thus, a strategic grouping of Hugh's remaining works, mostly according to his own conceptual framework:

Works of creation/worldly literature

> *On Grammar, Practical Geometry* (chapter 3, A)

Works of restoration/sacred scripture

> the literal/historical: commentaries (chapter 3, B)
>
> the allegorical/doctrinal: *De sacramentis* (and others) (part II: chapters 4 through 6)
>
> the tropological/spiritual: the ark treatises and meditations, ending with Hugh's most personal spiritual essay (part III: chapters 7 through 9).

Even such a comprehensive framework cannot do justice to the multifaceted nature of Hugh's writings or contain all of his different types of writings. Many of his works cannot be so simply classified, and a few fall outside this schema altogether, such as his extensive commentary on the Dionysian *Celestial Hierarchy*, presented in an appendix. Nevertheless, creation-restoration and historical-allegorical-tropological are Hugh's own pedagogical foundations for his work, especially according to Abbot Gilduin's initial ordering of the Victorine corpus, and thus suggest themselves as the ordering principles of a sequence for gradually encountering Hugh's many other writings.

CREATION AND HISTORY

A. The Works of Creation

1. Introduction

In Hugh's basic framework of God's works of creation in six days and works of restoration in six ages, "worldly" writings pertain to creation, and sacred scripture pertains mostly to restoration. The novice reader begins with the former, starting with human language itself, including grammar, and then moves to the Divine Writings, as indicated in the *Didascalicon*. The latter correlation of the scriptural story with the history of salvation from the fall to the final restoration can serve to frame Hugh's own numerous explicitly theological writings, but the prior pairing of creation with secular writings is somewhat ambiguous as an organizing principle for presenting Hugh's own works, for two reasons.

First, when he says that "secular writings" pertain to the creation, he is not referring to his own writings but to the world's literature, the "books of the gentiles,"[1] appreciating the way this world is, its human culture such as language, and its physical makeup, whether mathematics or physics. In that light, much of the *Didascalicon*'s overview of secular readings for the student concerns this realm of creation and gives a positive place for "pagan" literature in a Christian curriculum. Arithmetic or music, for example, concerns the world as it is, apart from God's work of restoration. In (theological) principle, the theoretical, practical, and mechanical arts may be needed as remedies against the evils implied in the fall (respectively, "wisdom against ignorance, virtue against vice, and needs against life's weaknesses," as the *Didascalicon* concludes[2]), but in fact they are presented in terms of creation by itself rather than as part of the process of restoration. For example, Hugh lists the particulars of the seven mechanical sciences without the theological overlay of this "fallen" world but with a delightful array of details about the created realm of fabrics, construction, commerce, farming, hunting, medicine, and theatrics. For him, not as an author but as reader and teacher, the "works of creation" include all of this, and more, in a comprehensive appreciation of this world and its components. As noted already regarding the *Didascalicon*'s itemization of mechanical knowledge, Hugh shows a robust pleasure in the rich variety of our created world, the world of weaving and saddles, swords and trowels, commerce and orchards, fishing and porridge and mead.[3] The teaching task, broadly understood, embraced all these subjects, and the Victorine novices in particular would have started with such basic learning.

Hugh's affirmation of this world as God's good creation can also be seen in other treatises not explicitly devoted to the works of creation but appreciating the created realm along the way. The visible creation leads us to the invisible Creator, as Hugh's *De tribus diebus* expounds on Romans 1.20 with explicit appreciation for marvelous creatures in the "book of nature" such as crocodiles and salamanders, sunsets and starlight.[4] While discussing the different kinds of contemplation in his spiritual treatise on Noah's ark later in the Victorine curriculum, Hugh includes a vivid appreciation of creation as the gift of God. The created world even tells us so, if we have ears to hear.

> The sky says, "I offer you light by day so that you may awake, darkness by night that you may rest. I change the seasons for your delight: the spring warmth, summer's heat, autumn's bounty, and the cold of winter. I vary the lengths of days and nights in an ordered way, that the variety might relieve monotony and the order might offer interest." The air says, "I offer you breath for life, and send you birds of all kinds just for your pleasure." Water says, "I offer you drink, I wash away dirt, I moisten the dry spots, and supply your meals with all kinds of fish." The earth says, "I carry you and feed you. I nourish you with bread and

delight you with wine. I treat you with fruit of every kind and fill up your table with meat."[5]

Of course, because of sin, the created world is not only an original gift but also now a debt to be repaid, or even a threat, as Hugh goes on to specify. For any Augustinian, disordered love for the perishable creation is, of course, a distraction from love for the Creator. But that all comes later, under "restoration."

Second, the pairing of creation with the worldly writings rather than with scripture is ambiguous because the sacred writings themselves start with creation, at least briefly, before moving on to restoration. Genesis 1 and 2 receive Hugh's attention as a biblical interpreter, on the subject of creation, both in exegesis according to the literal-historical sense and also in doctrinal summary, as we shall see, especially regarding *De sacramentis*. There Hugh explicitly says in the prologue that although the proper subject of scripture and thus of *De sacramentis* is restoration, nevertheless, this subject matter entails the background of sin and the fall and thus first of all the original condition or creation before the fall. Therefore, Hugh's summary of Christian doctrine begins with the six days of creation building on an exegesis of Genesis 1 and 2, as presented more fully later. In that respect, Hugh's writings on the works of restoration begin with a theological understanding of the original creation rather than leaving the works of creation entirely to secular writings.

Nevertheless, Hugh's own writings also include items that fall on the creation side of the creation-restoration schema. Abbot Gilduin's sequence of Hugh's works continues to show the way. After the *Didascalicon*, itself half devoted to secular writings and thus to this realm of creation, the *Epitoma Dindimi in philosophiam* next reprises much of the same overview of all the arts and ends in some manuscripts with a chart of them all. Baron's edition supplies a look at a major manuscript of Hugh's work (BMaz 717) with this table of the arts, starting, as Hugh said, with the logical and thus with *grammatica* first of all.[6] Indeed, next in Gilduin's order and starting on the very same page of this manuscript is Hugh's treatise *De grammatica*. He does not have extant essays on all the other logical arts, but this one, *On Grammar*, as well as his sole literary foray into mathematics, *On Practical Geometry*, comes next. Creation as it is, apart from its restoration, includes human speech and grammar, as well as the physical and mathematical phenomenon of geometry. Both subjects, and thus both treatises, fall under the works of creation.

2. On Grammar

Hugh's primer *On Grammar* employs the same dialogical format as the preceding *Epitoma Dindimi*, indeed the same dialogue partners, Sosthenes and Dindimus. Much of the work is a didactic listing of forms of speech and the like, with explanations, but their dialogue gets things started pedagogically. "Sosthenes: What is grammar? Dindimus: Grammar is the knowledge of speaking rightly. . . . Sosthenes: Whence is it called 'grammar'? Dindimus: Grammar takes its name from letters. . . ."[7] The treatise goes into considerable detail, certainly in contrast to the sketchy treatment of grammar in the *Didascalicon* (II, 29). There, Hugh mentions several different ways to divide the subject (letter, syllable, phrase, and clause; written letters and spoken sounds; Isidore's list of nouns, verbs, etc.), but he explicitly says he needs to be brief about it, and the interested reader should consult Donatus or Isidore, among others. In the *Didascalicon*, he did not mention his own work on grammar, suggesting (but not proving) that it was not written yet but comes afterward, as in Gilduin's order of Hugh's works.

Hugh adapts Isidore and the others to his own outline, using the category of "letters" to give a brief historical overview of Hebrew, Greek, and Latin letters, such as aleph, alpha, and A. Under "syllable," Hugh discusses long, short, and diphthong varieties, with many subcategories and examples. All of this is for the student who has already learned some Latin but needs an organized presentation of grammatical theory. Next come the parts of speech, with extensive subdivisions and examples for each group: nouns, pronouns, verbs, participles, adverbs, conjunctions, and interjections. The preceding *Epitoma Dindimi* is explicitly mentioned, with grammatical rules for subject-verb agreement, proper use of cases with specific verbs, and so forth. The detail is impressive. Sosthenes and Dindimus go on to "discuss" orthography (spelling), analogy (comparisons), etymology, glosses, differences, punctuation (including accents, pointing, and special marks like an asterisk), abbreviations, metric feet, meter, and more, including tropes such as onomatopoeia and periphrasis.[8] The sheer accumulation of specialized terms must have been daunting for the students, yet it was probably useful to have collected together as a reference work. R. Baron lists all these headings in his introduction and uses them to break up the work itself into its parts. His edition can be consulted for the (many) details, and his introduction can provide us with one major methodological point. When Baron discusses how Hugh adapted prior literary traditions regarding grammar, such as Isidore of Seville, he concludes that Hugh's modifications show his overall interest in a logical and methodological order, in other words, a "pedagogical concern."[9] Hugh, as a teacher first and foremost, has reorganized some basic grammatical material for the sake of pedagogical method, so that his student-readers could profitably learn, in order, the basic points of grammar. Although the logical arts arose last, says Hugh elsewhere, they need to be learned first, beginning with grammar, so that the novice student can read the other writings. The right order is the key, both within the subject (in this case, grammar) and among the arts, here placing grammar first. Hugh may not have written treatises on all the arts or divisions of knowledge pertaining to the works of creation, but he started the sequence off with his own work, *De grammatica*.

3. *Practical Geometry*

Next in Gilduin's edition of Hugh, but far down the list or table of the arts, is *Practical Geometry*. Whether our Victorine master may have also written (lost) works on rhetoric or dialectic and why he did not write on arithmetic or music but did write on geometry are open questions. The curricular gap between grammar and geometry, between Hugh's pedagogical essays *On Grammar* and *Practical Geometry*, permits some speculation, such as textbooks and/or lectures on intervening subjects by other authorities or perhaps Hugh's special interests in geometry, as we shall see, but the gap itself remains. Only the *Didascalicon* supplies Hugh's explicit perspective on certain intervening subjects, such as dialectic or arithmetic. "Ethics," too, is not given a separate treatise, although Hugh's guidance for the behavior of the Victorine novices covers some related material, as covered in the next section.

Geometry itself is mentioned only briefly in *Didascalicon*, with no hint that it, unlike the neighboring paragraphs on arithmetic or music or astronomy, has received or will receive expanded treatment at Hugh's hands. (As often noted, the chronological sequence of Hugh's works is impossible to reconstruct with complete certainty. We are here following the pedagogical sequence suggested by Abbot Gilduin.) The name itself, says the *Didascalicon*, means earth measure ("geo-metry"), and there are three parts: planimetry, measuring any (flat) plane; altimetry, measuring height or depth; and cosmimetry, measuring any sphere from a ball or egg to the spherical universe itself.[10]

Calling his treatise "practical" geometry indicates immediately that Hugh will discuss specific instruments like the astrolabe and various methods for making specific types of measurements. That a treatise with such concerns, and in such technical detail, is authentically by our Hugh, although it also circulated anonymously, is proven by Gilduin's glimpse at the opening and closing words of the work, edited in full by R. Baron and translated into English by Frederick A. Homann.[11]

Hugh's first words indicate his intention and his debt to prior works. "My goal is to teach practical geometry to our students, not as something new, but rather as a collation of older, scattered material."[12] Although he here honors the labors of predecessors and later credits some of them, such as Eratosthenes, he is also critical of Macrobius and never acknowledges his debt to Gerbert of Aurillac (later Pope Sylvester II) or the pseudo-Gerbert materials.

As in the *Didascalicon*, geometry is divided into three: altimetry, planimetry, and cosmimetry, although here the micro examples of a ball or egg drop out in favor of the macro of the celestial spheres. Points, lines, planes, and solids are about to be explored in considerable detail. "Weighty topics, indeed, and remarkable ideas, well worth study,"[13] says the teacher.

A simple right-angled triangle, understood in conjunction with surveyor's instruments like the quadrant and astrolabe, can lead to concrete mathematical measurements of all kinds, from local architecture to the earth's sphere to the solar orbit. One needs to know the overall history of geometry to appreciate the specific place of Hugh's treatise, as introduced by Homann. The range of topics and technical detail can also best be glimpsed in Homann's topical outline.

Preface: Purpose and tribute to predecessors. Praenotenda (#1–6): Definitions; division of geometry into theoretical and practical; specific goals; geometry of similar right triangles; models of the celestial sphere and its great circles.

I. Altimetry (#7–35): Triangles and circles in measurement problems, and their geometry. The astrolabe and its quadrant face. Isoplane height problems for objects on the horizon and for nearby objects. Four ways to measure height when the triangle base is known; three ways when the base is not known. Two-station methods. Other instruments and their use: triangles, rods, and mirrors. Heteroplane techniques. Depth measurement: visual techniques, mechanical devices.

II. Planimetry (#36–38): Three astrolabe techniques to measure level lengths.

III. Cosmimetry (#39–57): Introduction: Earth as a center point in the cosmos. Ancient received values for the diameter and circumference of the earth. Altitude of the sun computed in Egypt and elsewhere; the diameter of the solar orbit. The diameter of the sun and the length of the earth's shadow. Lemmas for geometric optics, horizon and vision problems.[14]

As suggested by the breadth and depth of terms and topics in this synopsis, Hugh goes into remarkable scientific detail, as also illustrated by Homann's numerous diagrams. Among the many specific questions raised by this material, many of them pursued by Homann or others, the overarching impression and query is simply Why? Why was Hugh so interested in geometric details and surveyor's methods? Why would Victorine novices and other students need to know so much about using an astrolabe and other such instruments?

In terms of pedagogical theory, Hugh's breadth of learning is well known, and here he embodies his own advice to learn everything. This treatise is the most striking testament to his expansive view of the Victorine curriculum. The fact that geometry, with hypotenuse and astrolabe and all, should be taught at St. Victor in such detail is itself remarkable, perhaps stemming from Hugh's earlier education,[15] and anticipates the comprehensive scientific agenda of an Albert the Great. R. Baron calls it typical of Hugh's "immense curiosity."[16] There may be no more specific explanation than this general curiosity and breadth of interests for Hugh's remarkable foray into geometric details as if writing a handbook for medieval surveyors. It is God's world, after all, the divine work of creation. Still, there is also the specific application of such spatial dimensions and measurements to the spiritual appreciation of Noah's ark, so thoroughly presented elsewhere in the Ark treatises, which in fact come next in Gilduin's edition. While developing his spiritual interpretation of the ark, Hugh there invokes "the great discipline" of geometry to mention some measurements, perpendiculars, and the hypotenuse.[17] He then forgoes further detail in the Ark treatise itself, but his interest is plain, and so is one application of practical geometry. (Whether his contemporary Suger of St. Denis took such a detailed interest in measurements and instruments, or even whether such Victorine theory and training overlapped with the actual construction projects on the famous Abbey church, must also be left to other contexts.[18])

In the end, aside from direct application to Noah's ark, Hugh's geometrical pursuits may simply illustrate the breadth of his interests in creation, in all branches of knowledge, including, rather eloquently, the "high seas and the depth of heaven."[19] He had a confidence in learning ("reason illuminates nature, and everything is open to understanding"[20]) and could apply it globally. Along the way, Hugh's pedagogical patterns are also on display, at least to those historians of science who can compare his "text book" with others before or since. Baron remarks on Hugh's "qualities of order and of clarity," citing prior conclusions about Hugh's distinctive abilities to structure or to order this subject pedagogically.[21] Homann concurs and provides a conclusion to this glimpse of Hugh the orderly teacher, in this case of geometry:

> The disciplined exposition in the three distinct but related parts of practical geometry is a refreshing development after the randomly arranged material in the Gerbertian texts.... [*Practical Geometry's*] projects are taken in order, each developed from clearly marked starting points.[22]

4. On the Formation of Novices

With the Abbot Gilduin's sequence as our guide, we have glimpsed the pedagogical foundations put down for Victorine student novices by Hugh's early works. The *Chronicle* introduced the works of creation and works of restoration, which were then correlated in *De scripturis* with worldly writings and sacred scripture, respectively. The *Didascalicon* explored all such reading, there further grouped into "philosophy's" many arts and scripture's several meanings: the literal-historical, the allegorical-doctrinal, and the moral-spiritual. The "Epitoma of Dindimus" summarized this classification of knowledge, and the very first "art" follows immediately, in Hugh's essay *On Grammar.* Next in Gilduin's edition, but further down the table of subjects, came *Practical Geometry* and then the Ark treatises. Although there is a slim geometric connection to the ark itself, as mentioned previously, at this point Gilduin's order of treatises completes the pedagogical or foundational task of introducing Hugh's work generally and his early treatises in particular. The Ark treatises are explicitly not for beginners and come later in our overview. Yet Gilduin's order does offer one more item in this sequence for our summary of foundational formation at St. Victor, namely, Hugh's *De institutione nouitiorum*, or *On the Formation of Novices.*[23]

As noted already, and often observed about St. Victor, daily life there was a distinctive combination of the hours of prayer, as in the traditional monastic communities, and sophisticated sessions of study, as in the developing schools of that creative period. The holistic formation of the novices meant more than the curriculum of subjects covered in class and also more than the liturgical order of the canonical hours and the church year. Knowledge and prayer were prominent, of course, but full-scale Christian formation, at St. Victor and elsewhere, extended to the behavior of daily life, to gestures and postures and overall attitude, as explicitly explained by Hugh's *On the Formation of Novices*.

Hugh's *De institutione novitiorum* has attracted considerable attention in modern scholarship, especially for what it reveals about Hugh's perspective on daily life and formation at St. Victor.[24] From early in Hugh's career, although it presupposes some teaching seniority, this essay on the novices' formation is clearly central, perhaps foundational, to the master's pedagogical purposes and writings. The spiritual goal is clear, with biblical warrant providing the outline: "the way to God is knowledge, discipline and goodness," citing Psalm 119.66; "through knowledge one comes to discipline, through discipline one comes to goodness, and through goodness to beatitude."[25] This triad indicates the structure of the essay, although unevenly. "Knowledge" here (chapters 1–9) is not a reprise of all the disciplines or arts of philosophy as covered in the *Didascalicon* but rather knowledge of how to behave. "Discipline" (chapters 10–21) is not a matter of the curricular disciplines but rather, and the real point of the work, proper behavior regarding clothing, gestures, speech, and table manners. "Goodness," given equal billing in the prologue, is merely tacked on at the end, almost casually. "So, brothers, we have told you these things about knowledge and discipline. As for goodness, however, pray that God may grant it to you. Amen."[26]

Hugh's work had few precedents (although some sources are noted besides the obvious biblical ones) but a wide distribution later, not only among Victorines but also for other religious communities and Christian formation generally.[27] His theme of humility and harmony found many appreciative readers.

Knowledge of how to behave *"recte et honeste"* (chapter 1) comes from several sources: from reason (chapters 2–5) or common sense (are you in the chapel or the refectory? is it a festival day or ordinary time? are you speaking with the abbot or each other?); from teaching (chapter 6), meaning humble biblical listening and not proud worldly disputations as others do;[28] from receiving the examples of the saints (chapter 7) as a soft surface receives the imprint of a seal; and, of course, from scripture (chapter 8):

> You, brothers, who have entered the school of discipline, you ought to seek first in the *lectio divina* that which instructs your morals to virtue, rather than that which sharpens your sense toward subtlety, more to be informed by the precepts of Scripture rather than impeded by Questions. . . . Read this way, Scripture confers saving knowledge.[29]

Turning to "disciplina," Hugh moves the definition away from its etymology about learning to a broad view of behavior.

> Discipline is good and proper behavior; to attain it one must not only avoid evil but also strive to appear above reproach in all things that one does well. Discipline is also the governed [ordered] movement of all members of the body and a seemly disposition in every state and action.[30]

This concept of discipline is the heart of Hugh's treatise, with many examples, and coheres with his overall interests in pedagogical/ethical formation. He covers four arenas of disciplined behavior where inner virtue matches outward appearance: clothing (chapter 11), especially gestures (12), speech and silence (13–17), and table manners (18–21). As with grammar or geometry, Hugh goes into considerable detail on various points: fancy robes, raised eyebrows, struts and swaggers, thoughtful words and strategic silences, and even what and how to eat and drink. Hugh's chapter on gestures was particularly thorough and widely influential, as documented by J.-C. Schmitt.[31] Stephen Jaeger calls Hugh's essay "a school for gentlemen" and discusses some of the particulars relative to other literature of this kind.[32]

Overall, *On the Formation of Novices* strikes several distinctive Hugonian notes, now becoming Victorine generally. Humility especially is emphasized, not only before God but also before one's neighbors.[33] As in the *Didascalicon* and throughout Hugh's works, humility leads to formation, for it is by bowing low that we are built up (edified). Throughout the essay, Hugh emphasizes the ideal of harmony or equilibrium, a peaceful order balancing the interior and exterior, spirit and body, inner being and outward appearing.[34] Often the goal is explicitly serving others, specifically by teaching them effectively. Chapter 16 advises when to speak and when not to speak, teaching by words and by the example of silence. "To teach by word and example" as Caroline Bynum isolates it,[35] captures a distinctive

Victorine interest, implied throughout the treatise. If these novices are to become effective teachers in their own right, by word and example, then solid learning and honorable overall behavior is part of their calling. After all, first William of Champeaux and then Hugh himself were known at the time for both. Hugh's student Lawrence of Westminster supplies the personal look at his teacher and our author: "The moral excellence of his life decorates his learning, and the saintliness of this teacher illuminates his polished doctrine with beauty of manners."[36]

On the foundations of basic learning together with honorable behavior, the learned and saintly teacher leads his pupils and readers from the works of creation through the works of restoration, from secular writings to sacred scriptures with their ascending triple meanings, and thus to God. The unified Victorine curriculum called for no less, and Hugh was its master.

B. The Foundation of (Biblical) History

1. The Biblical "Works of Restoration"

In moving from "works of creation" to "works of restoration," we have already seen how Hugh gives a prominent and complex place to sacred scripture in the architecture of his work. He adapts and applies Gregory the Great's dynamic image of building, namely, starting with the foundation of the literal-historical interpretation of the biblical texts, then moving to the doctrinal framework that is erected when the same texts are understood in another way (the allegorical sense), and then finally to the finishing touch or the personal application regarding a (spiritual) way of life, the so-called moral sense.

In fact, the *Didascalicon* quoted Gregory on this key point, without acknowledgment.

> As you are about to build, therefore, "lay first the foundation of history;
> next, by pursuing the 'typical' meaning, build up a structure in your mind
> to be a fortress of faith. Last of all, however, through the loveliness of
> morality, paint the structure over as with the most beautiful of colors."[37]

This image of construction recurs throughout Hugh's works, especially regarding the restorative process of scriptural interpretation. As foundation, framework, and finish, it will help organize the remaining presentations of Hugh's works, all regarding God's works of restoration. The hermeneutical sequence is the restoration itself: from the foundation of history in the letter, to the framework of doctrine, to the spiritual finish or finale. The subject matter of sacred scripture is God's works of restoration in general, and the process of reading and contemplating scripture in this way (from history to doctrine to personal application) is *itself* the process of that same restoration for each individual.

There are very few compact examples in Hugh's works of a single biblical text interpreted according to all three senses and explicitly identified. Noah's ark is treated at length later. The book of Job in its entirety is a triplex example offered by Hugh in *On the Scriptures*, as also well known from Gregory the Great. The literal-historical sense is obvious, as we move from the letters/words to the things/events: the words tell the story of a man who descended from wealth into misery, even to sitting on a dung heap. This historical narrative is then the foundation for more, much more.

> Now we come to allegory, so that through the things signified by words we might consider other things to be signified, and through the thing done, [we might consider] another thing done. Now Job, which means "lamenting," signifies Christ, who had been co-equal with his Father in the wealth of glory but condescended to our misery and sat humbly on the dung heap of this world, sharing all our defects except sin.[38]

Thus, the "other" meaning of Job, the "alle"gory yielding doctrinal truth, is Christ's own kenosis (and his final exaltation, also like Job). The allegorical sense is the doctrinal.

Last is the moral of the story, the tropological sense that applies this history and doctrine to ourselves, what moderns might call the spiritual meaning. What has been done, in Job and in Christ, indicates what should be done, by the reader/believer.

> For Job can signify any just or penitent soul who assembles in his memory the dung heap of all the sins he has committed, sitting on it and meditating on it not for an hour but continually, and does not stop lamenting.[39]

The tropological or moral sense here, as Hugh discusses explicitly elsewhere,[40] pertains not to morality in the modern sense of ethics but to the personal appropriation by the readers regarding their own lives, specifically in contemplation and meditation, as retained in the expression "the moral of the story." Thus the tropological or moral sense of scripture could also be called the spiritual or devotional sense, although tradition has called all the senses beyond the literal-historical sense the "spiritual senses," often subdivided into the allegorical, tropological, and anagogical.

Although Hugh's actual exegesis and homilies do not supply all three senses for many other scriptural texts (applying hermeneutical theory flexibly to exegetical practice), this pedagogical example of Job provides a template. What Hugh sometimes calls the literal, allegorical, and tropological turns out to mean the historical, doctrinal, and spiritual. (The "literal" sense of scripture, however, becomes more complicated when the texts are not narrative or historical, as seen in many other authors and studies.[41])

This triplex sense of scripture also provides a way to classify some of Hugh's works, especially his correlation of allegory with doctrine (as in the *De sacramentis*) and his understanding of the tropological sense of scripture to include the spiritual way of life, as in contemplation and meditation, namely, the large category of spiritual writings such as the Ark treatises and many brief essays. This dynamic view of scriptural senses (and Hugh's corpus) also entails moving or progressing from one to the next, from the historical to the theological/doctrinal, and thence to the spiritual.

All of this biblical interpretation is also correlated by Hugh to the "works of restoration" from the fall to final consummation, as also previewed previously. This correlation of scriptural understanding to God's restoration of humanity is complex, for at least two reasons. First, it means that the dynamic process of interpreting the scripture rightly and fully through the three senses is itself part of the progression of restoration of the divine image in the human; thus hermeneutical progress is salvific and even has implications for ontology, since what is being restored is the human being itself as originally created. The house being constructed is really the soul being rebuilt. This interrelation of hermeneutics and salvation, of inner individual history and outer corporate history,[42] will need to be explored along the way. Second, Hugh immediately qualifies his correlation of sacred scripture with restoration by noting that the Bible itself starts with creation, and therefore his biblical interpretation must start there, too.

> Now although the principal subject matter of Divine Scripture is the works of restoration, yet, in order to approach the treatment of these more competently, it first, at the very commencement of its narrative, recounts briefly and truthfully the beginning and constitution of the works of foundation. For it could not fittingly have shown how man was restored, unless it first explained how he had fallen; nor, indeed, could it fittingly have shown his fall unless it first explained in what condition

he was constituted by God. But to show the first condition of man, it was necessary to describe the foundation and creation of the whole world, because the world was made for the sake of man.[43]

In this chain of explaining the necessary background for the repair or restoration of the human, the fall itself must be explicated but only when the original created human condition is presented, and that presentation must be in the context of creation overall. Thus does the Bible start with creation in general, then the human creature, and then the fall, all by way of prologue to the principal subject matter of scripture from the fall through salvation history to final consummation. The *De sacramentis*, accordingly, devotes its initial attention to the "Work of Foundation" as a theological interpretation of the scriptural text of Genesis. Yet Hugh also says that this entire work, his summa, is the doctrinal sense of scripture, the allegorical reading that comes second, after the first literal-historical sense. Here enters a puzzle, and a puzzling lack of extant texts. The *De sacramentis* begins its prologue with this reference back to a prior reading of scripture as if to prior works by Hugh.

> Since, therefore, I previously composed a compendium [literally, "dictated a compendious volume"] on the initial instruction in Holy Scripture, which consists in their historical reading, I have prepared the present work for those who are to be introduced to the second stage of instruction, which is in allegory.[44]

On the face of it, we should expect to find elsewhere Hugh's literal-historical reading of Holy Scripture as a preparatory counterpart to his doctrinal interpretation of scripture, the allegorical sense. Indeed, if history is the foundation, as he says, we should expect to find plenty of historical exegesis. Yet no works by Hugh fully fit this description. The *Chronicon* presented before has been proposed, for it certainly pertains to history. Yet it is not the historical reading *of scripture* in this exegetical sense. Indeed, as summarized previously, it barely mentions scripture, and when it does, all three senses are noted with equal brevity. We know that Hugh did lecture or "dictate" on scripture, according to the literal-historical sense, apparently only on certain books. He recommended a course of reading the biblical books according to the historical sense in the *Didascalicon*, and his extant works of that sort are largely confined to the *Pentateuch*. His *Notulae* on Genesis, for example, seem to be lecture notes by students that can give us further insight into his teaching on creation, specifically the literal-historical meaning as a first foundation for the doctrinal interpretation added in the *De sacramentis*.

2. The Historical Sense of Genesis on Creation (*Notulae*)

Jan W. M. van Zwieten has argued that when Hugh refers to a previous "compendium" of historical reading of Holy Scripture, he cannot mean the *Chronicon* (*De tribus maximis*), as many have supposed.[45] That work is rather a primer on learning, as introduced previously and it only tersely mentions scripture without ever interpreting any actual scriptural passages. For a more likely candidate, he points to Hugh's *Notulae* or "Notes on the Octateuch," an early collection of exegetical notes in a literal-historical vein starting with Genesis. Van Zwieten gives minimal evidence (although he lists further possibilities), but this opens up further material by Hugh specifically on creation. Hugh's *Notulae* supply his literal-historical interpretation of these few Old Testament books, yet this does not fully match his description of a prior historical reading of scripture as a whole, corresponding to his comprehensive doctrinal reading, the "other" meaning or allegory of *De sacramentis*. In the *Didascalicon*, he said that the historical reading of scripture would proceed from Genesis/Exodus and Joshua-Judges-Kings to the four Gospels and Acts, yet we do not have extant lecture notes on any such historical reading of the New Testament books. Perhaps they simply have not survived? What we do have, the *Notulae*, are particularly interesting for further insights into Hugh's interpretation of Genesis and can be correlated to his doctrinal interpretations of the same biblical accounts of creation in *De sacramentis*.

H. J. Pollitt has researched the *Notulae* especially for Hugh's use of prior sources, albeit without explicit quotation or attribution, such as Bede (who is named) and Augustine and Rabanus Maurus (who are not). Pollitt's opening sentence obliquely anticipated the argument developed later by van Zwieten, namely, that here we have what Hugh meant by a compendium of historical exegesis prior to the doctrinal reading of *De sacramentis*: "Hugh of St. Victor endeavored to equip the exegete for the higher task of allegorization by providing him with a series of glosses on the literal sense of the Octateuch."[46] The two groups of manuscripts (the larger confined to Genesis, Exodus, and Leviticus; the smaller including these and other books through I and II Kings) suggest "that the *Notulae* were collected by his pupils and represent his oral teaching."[47] The Migne printing (PL 175: 30–114) combines the manuscripts into the canonical order but with awkward duplications and omissions. Hugh may have revised some of this material, specifically on the Pentateuch, but never prepared the whole for publication, although Abbott Gilduin explicitly identifies the comments on Genesis for inclusion with *De scripturis*.

Hugh begins his *Notulae* on Genesis with reference to its title in Hebrew and Greek and then to Moses as the historian (and prophet) author. Then Hugh indicates part of his interpretive method, regarding the literal/historical sense: "the truth of the events and the form of the words."

> For just as we know the truth of the things [done] through the truth of the words, so also, vice versa, when we know the truth of the things we know more easily the truth of the words, for it is through this historical narration that we advance to the understanding of other things.[48]

Thus does Hugh's literal-historical sense contain its own "hermeneutical circle": through the letters and words, we understand the events narrated, yet through knowing these events (from other texts and other senses?), we also better understand the words of this text.

Here, juxtaposed to his comments on Genesis 1, are some general questions about creation, also taken up in *De sacramentis*: Was it all simultaneous or spread over six days? Was it raw matter first, then formed during those days? How should the six days be understood? This material bears a complicated relationship to the discussion of creation in *De sacramentis*. On the one hand, Hugh's summa in this case and in general adapts or just lifts whole sections from his own prior works. On the other hand, there is also a substantive difference between the literal-historical reading of Genesis in the *Notulae* and the (additional) doctrinal reading of the same texts in *De sacramentis*. For example, in the *Notulae*, Hugh notes that fish and birds were made together, from the waters, as the old hymn for the fifth day had it: "you assigned some to the abyss, but lifted some into the air."[49] In the *De sacramentis*, however, this text about fishes below and birds above yields, allegorically, a doctrinal truth about the human race: "While some are justly left below in that corruption in which they were born, others are raised above by the gift of grace to the lot of their heavenly country."[50] Another example of "the actual development of exegetical notions into theological argument," as isolated by van Zwieten,[51] concerns the waters above the firmament. Why they are not gathered into one place is an open question, on the literal-historical level of the *Notulae*, but he finds a theological reason in *De sacramentis*.

> This seems strange, that the waters . . . above heaven . . . are left diffused and spread out, as if the waters did not wish to be compressed or collected. What do you think this means, unless that "the charity of God is poured forth in our hearts by the Holy Ghost who is given to us" [Romans 5]? . . . Charity ought always to be spread out and extended.[52]

In these small samples, we can see Hugh's literal-historical exegesis confining itself to the words of Genesis and the sheer events of creation, but his "other" (allegorical) interpretation in *De sacramentis* then adds the doctrinal meaning.

The fuller discussion of simultaneity and yet six days provides a more complicated example. God certainly could have created everything at once, says Hugh in *De sacramentis*,[53] but chose to use the six-day format "for the instruction of and example for"[54] the rational creature who can learn something from this, namely, the angels originally and the human readers of scripture later. Hugh can also reconcile simultaneity with six days, both with scriptural and patristic support, by assigning simultaneity to the creation of all (raw) matter at once, and then the progression of six days to the granting of form to this original matter. This sense of sequence, of progress from unformed matter to the formed creation, is meant to teach that sheer being is only the start; the further goal is "beautiful being and happy being."[55] That the six days of Genesis teach the reader about spiritual progress is rather oblique in *De sacramentis* but more straightforward in the *Notulae*, showing that even there Hugh did not completely restrict himself to a literal-historical reading of the text. Further, the wording of this point in the *Notulae* shows that Hugh's overall distinction of creation and restoration is not so absolute. "It was for the repair of the human that God wished to distribute his work over six days,"[56] so that the human might learn to progress from plain being to blessed being. Hugh's overpowering interest in the repair or restoration of the human extends even to the interpretation of the six-day work of creation, namely, that God chose to spread out the creative forming of raw matter over specific intervals and sequential (historical!) steps, rather than a simultaneous creation, in order to teach humanity that there are sequential stages, or salvation history, to the work of restoration. Even the Genesis narrative of creation turns out to serve the repair or restoration of the human, Hugh's theological priority.

Thus, in parallel ways, Hugh's extant works show minimal interest both in creation by itself and also in the literal-historical sense by itself, although it is the foundation. These works show maximal interest in restoration and in the two senses of scripture that build upon the historical foundation, namely, the allegorical-doctrinal sense, as seen shortly in *De sacramentis*, and the tropological or spiritual (moral) sense, as evident at length in a wide array of works.

The allegorical-doctrinal and the moral-spiritual senses of scripture also reflect Hugh's historical interests, as Poirel has pointed out, since the doctrinal sense develops the relationships of events over time (as in the "typology" of other authors) and the tropological applies these historical events to oneself and what one should do *now*, in a continuation of such historical development.[57] This parallel preponderance of interest (in restoration and in the progression of scriptural senses) is actually the same priority for Hugh, within his integrative or holistic framework. The hermeneutical progression (from the literal-historical sense to the doctrinal/allegorical and especially from the doctrinal sense to the personal appropriation or the tropological or spiritual) is itself the progressive restoration of the human to the original intended state and indeed beyond that to final blessedness. Hermeneutic progress is progressive restoration or salvation. Building a house may be the metaphor, but *re*building the soul is the point. There may be other works of biblical exegesis further documenting Hugh's particular form of literal-historical interpretation (although many such works, especially homilies, are of disputed authenticity). Yet the weight of his emphasis is clearly on the doctrinal interpretation of scripture, as expressed in *De sacramentis*, to which we now turn in part II, and then especially on the personal or spiritual appropriation of history and doctrine, as seen in so many of his remaining works as presented in part III.

Part II

THE FRAMEWORK OF DOCTRINE

PREFACE AND PROLOGUE

In this book, I am presenting Hugh's corpus, first, according to his own overall pairing of God's works of creation and restoration and then according to his presentation of the biblical message of restoration according to a threefold interpretation: historical foundations, the (allegorical) framework of doctrine, and the tropological or spiritual finish. In this chapter, we move from foundation to framework. In Gregory the Great's homey image of constructing a house, first comes the foundation of history, as introduced in part I and to be reviewed shortly. Next comes the framework or structure of doctrinal truths, here in part II presented especially according to Hugh's massive masterwork *De sacramentis*. Finally, the finishing touches come in the spiritual (tropological) application of all this to one's own life, as in part III.

1. Preface

Hugh's own brief Preface to *De sacramentis* immediately presents an enormous textual challenge. This mature summation of his doctrinal theology, from the 1130s, incorporates substantial passages from his own previous works, as we have already noted. "I have incorporated some writings that from time to time I had composed previously, because it seemed to me an irksome, if not a superfluous task to express them in a new form."[1] Identifying the locations of these passages is not that difficult, but the version in *De sacramentis* is often a subtle revision of the earlier text, whether lightly or substantially, as Hugh himself wants the reader to know. "But afterwards, when I was incorporating these writings into the text of the present work, reason kept urging me to change certain things in them, in fact to add or take away certain things."[2] Naturally, his own revisions of prior texts as here presented in *De sacramentis*, concludes the Preface, should supersede and even correct any earlier versions. Thus Hugh not only quotes himself without attribution, sometimes at length, but also revises himself freely and creatively.[3] Neither the PL edition nor the English translation documents this major textual complication, leaving a first large task for a modern edition. Perhaps van den Eynde exaggerated the situation, but his comment on *De sacramentis* can indicate the extent of the editing challenge: "The largest and most famous of all the treatises of Hugh of Saint-Victor is in large measure nothing but a compilation and revision of material stemming from his own previous works."[4] By way of my own preface to *De sacramentis*, a few of these earlier works can be introduced, but this is only the first layer of textual sources Hugh used.

Adding to the complications of *De sacramentis* as a text is Hugh's incorporation of passages not only from his own prior works but also from other theologians, patristic and contemporary, sometimes named but often without any attribution at all. In this respect, Hugh nicely represents the overall concern of twelfth-century authors to synthesize their sources. As one example, for most of book 1, Hugh never mentions any of the Fathers, even when he is adapting Augustinian theology, yet suddenly (see later, regarding One, ten, vi) the bishop of Hippo makes an explicit appearance, as do Gregory the Great and the Venerable Bede. Here, it turns out, Hugh has incorporated into his text a letter he received from Bernard of Clairvaux, complete with patristic authorities! Bernard is the initial source, and the Fathers behind him. Hugh also uses the work of Isidore of Seville, Ivo of Chartres, and others, as Weisweiler and others documented long ago with respect to a dozen such sources. Sometimes, later in book 2, patristic sources were openly amassed but not fully digested, as regarding the Incarnation (book 2, part 1) or on marriage (book 2, part 11). When Augustine's *City of God* is repeatedly quoted at the very end of the work regarding the afterlife, it seems that Hugh did not himself finish his own text on these final topics.[5] Such are the challenges facing an editor of *De sacramentis*,[6] yet such specifics cannot all be documented here.

My goal here in part II on the doctrinal structure of *De sacramentis* is merely an initial acquaintance with the contents of the work, a synopsis of a *summa*. The sheer size and complexity of this work, along with its importance in the development of doctrinal theology, require this entire introduction to be selective and partial. In here introducing *De sacramentis*, my emphasis is on structure. First, what is the overarching outline or architecture of the work? The duplications with previous works can now be seen together, and in the specific order Hugh himself intended. Second, how does this one work fit into the structure or pattern of Hugh's corpus overall? Passages pertinent to these two structural questions, especially the internal order, are quoted in chapters 5 and 6. Yet for the doctrinal detail, nothing can substitute for reading Hugh's own classic directly, including his incorporations of prior material, beyond the synopsis offered here. Furthermore, for the full extent of his textual borrowings and revisions, we simply have to await the scholarly edition and then a new English translation.

When Hugh in his preface refers to works he had previously composed (or perhaps dictated), he undoubtedly meant at least his brief *Institutiones in Decalogum*, reused here regarding the Ten Commandments in book 1, part 12; his *Dialogue on the Sacraments of the Natural Law and the Written Law*; and a few other texts. Also of importance here is the *Sentences on Divinity*, which was actually a student record or "*Reportatio*" of his lectures. The *Dialogus* is entirely a sequence of brief and simple questions from a "disciple" with answers, usually straightforward, from the "master."

D: When did God make the world?

M: "In the beginning" (Genesis 1).

D: Where was the world made?

M: In God.

D: Whence was the world made?

M: From nothing.[7]

Such simple formulations regarding the first six days of creation are not taken over by *De sacramentis*, and the *Dialogus*, in fact, shows no signs of the larger creation-restoration framework. Yet when the *Dialogus* presents the creation and fall of human beings, its text is taken up in *De sacramentis*, often verbatim. For example, the woman was taken from the man's side, not from his head or feet, to show the partnership of love rather than domination or servitude.[8] From here on, the *Dialogue* briefly touches the same topics as *De sacramentis*, part 1, sometimes with the same wording, albeit briefly: creation of humanity, the fall, the dispute between God and the devil (in terms both judicial and military), the role of faith, the natural law, and the written law. As Weisweiler has documented, Hugh in *De sacramentis* has adopted and adapted his own prior composition, exactly as he announced in its preface.[9]

The other doctrinal overview before *De sacramentis* is a special case of student reporting.[10] One "Lawrence," perhaps of Westminster, wrote out Master Hugh's lectures "on divinity" for his own use and for his classmates, at their urging and with the master's approval, and not without Hugh's weekly review to see if anything was superfluous or omitted or badly put.[11] Only the prologue and first three parts of the *Sententiae de divinitate* have survived, exactly matching the topics and often the texts of the Prologue and first three parts of *De sacramentis*, book 1: On the Creation of the World, On the Primordial Causes, and (partially) On the Trinity.[12] Furthermore, its prologue, as Lawrence reported it, presented not only the triple sense of scripture (also in *On the Scriptures*) and the familiar pairing of God's works of creation in six days and restoration in six eras but also the exact same outline for twelve parts that we see in *De sacramentis*, book 1.[13] Here, too, Hugh has reworked his own material and, in effect, warned the reader to discount any earlier versions, such as Lawrence's work, even if it was an authorized report at the time. Nevertheless, the convergences and divergences of *De sacramentis* with the *Sententiae*, and also with *On the Scriptures*, are worth specialized study in their own right.

2. *De tribus diebus*

One of Hugh's earliest doctrinal works has recently received the most scholarly attention, and rightly so, for it is much more than a predecessor to *De sacramentis*. *De tribus diebus*, or "On the Three Days," has been edited and analyzed by Dominique Poirel, although the only full modern translation is in Dutch.[14] Although not long, more like an essay (thirty-five pages) than a book, this complex work is full—full of doctrinal themes such as creation and the Trinity, complete with implicit polemics especially with Abelard, and full of significance for Hugh's overall theological output, not merely as a draft for *De sacramentis*, and for later authors as well.[15]

Naturally, it starts with scripture. Keying off Romans 1.20, that the invisible things of God can be known through the created visible realm, Hugh begins:

> The invisible things of God are three: power, wisdom, and mercy. All things proceed from these three, all things consist in these three, all things are ruled through these three. Power creates, wisdom governs, mercy conserves. Yet these three, just as they are ineffably one in God, so they cannot be at all separated in operation. Power creates wisely through mercy; wisdom governs mercifully through power; mercy conserves powerfully through wisdom. The immensity of creatures manifests power; their beauty [manifests] wisdom; their usefulness, mercy.[16]

Although Trinitarian theology is clearly coming eventually, Hugh starts with creation, namely, how the invisible power, wisdom, and mercy (or goodness) of God are known, respectively, in his creatures' immensity (multitude and magnitude), beauty (placement, motion, species, and quality perceived by the senses), and usefulness (pleasing, apt, convenient, and necessary).[17] Each of these categories is then analyzed, as Hugh openly delights in the wonders of God's creation: "This entire sensible world is like a book written by the finger of God, that is, created by the divine might," in order to manifest and somehow signify the invisible wisdom of God.[18] Reading the "book of nature" in creation in general and in one's own body leads to the Creator, as seen in the many examples given. Hugh marvels at the gigantic and the miniature in the animal kingdom (from the boar's tusks to the moth's tiny teeth, the head of a horse versus that of a locust), as well as the odd and amazing, from crocodile and salamander to ant and spider. "These are all witnesses to the wisdom of God."[19] The sheer colors of the sky, the sun and moon and stars, all speak of God, not to mention gemstones and flowers, and the delights of the other senses.[20] Following his triadic outline, not only the power and wisdom but also the mercy of God is shown forth in the created realm specifically through the usefulness of creation extravagantly given to us beyond mere necessity.[21]

Having catalogued how the visible book of created nature points to the invisible Creator God, as St. Paul said, "we ought to consider now how or in what order one might ascend through them [the visible] to the invisible."[22] The starting point in the ascending order of knowledge is the category of wisdom, namely, in the beauty of creation. Hugh becomes more explicitly Augustinian and Trinitarian in this exposition, but there is a twist. First, as expected, comes the ascending order of knowledge, from the visible bodily creation through the invisible rational creature up to the wisdom of God. This ascent, however, is not the end but the beginning. "But now," following or imitating God's own order of creating, "we proceed returning [downward] first from the wisdom of God to the rational creature, then from the rational creature to the corporeal creature."[23] After we have ascended from the bodily creature to the rational creature and thence to the creator of both, having followed the order of knowledge or the "way of investigation," we can then recognize and follow the creator's own descent, the downward way of creating, from the invisible to the visible, from the rational creature to the bodily creature, in other words, back down to earth.[24] This is a complex and important point, a distinctively Victorine turn on spiritual or "mystical" experience. "What benefit is it to us if we recognize in God the height of majesty, yet collect from it no usefulness for ourselves?"[25] When we return from an intimate experience of contemplating the divine, what do we bring back with us from the region of light but some light to scatter our shadows? The familiar Victorine vocation of teaching and thereby helping others here applies the fruits of heavenly contemplation to the tasks of earthly service, specifically in terms of this essay's triad.

> If we there have seen power, let us bring the light of divine fear; if we there have seen wisdom let us bring the light of truth; if we there have seen mercy, let us bring the light of love. Power excites the torpid to fear; wisdom illuminates those blinded by the shadows of ignorance; mercy enflames the frigid by the warmth of love.[26]

The implication here, not fully developed as Hugh quickly moves on to the three days and divine Persons, is that lofty spiritual experience is turned into service or ministry for others, the sluggish and blind and cold.

Multiplying his triads, Hugh concludes this essay with more explicit Trinitarian and Christological emphases. The trio of power, wisdom, and mercy is linked with the first three days of the invisible creation, with fear and truth and love, and with the Trinity. "Power pertains to the Father, wisdom to the Son, and mercy to the Holy Spirit."[27] This is the kind of doctrinal summary that reappears in *De sacramentis*, albeit severely compressed.[28] Steadily more Christocentric, Hugh's poetic finale highlights the day(s) of salvation, the triduum of death, burial, and resurrection as the triune days of power, wisdom, and mercy, with the human counterparts of fear, truth, and love. The hint of eschatology turns homiletical as Christ's three days are applied to ourselves in conclusion. General doctrine yields to personal tropology.

> In the day of power, we die through fear; in the day of wisdom, we are buried from the noise of this world through contemplation of truth; in the day of mercy we rise again through love and desire for eternal goods.[29]

In summary, *De tribus diebus* reveals "Hugonian cosmology, theology, anthropology and spirituality."[30] It reflects a complex context of twelfth-century Trinitarian debate, especially with Abelard (as Poirel has shown), a brief compendium of doctrinal method from creation to creator to Christ's passion, and a poetic style that in fact inspired some medieval poetry.[31] Apparently revised by Hugh himself, it had wide circulation and influence.[32] Snippets were incorporated into *De sacramentis* but without the creative vitality of the original work. In his *Booklet on the Making of the Ark* (considered in chapter 8), Hugh's comment on Genesis 1 explicitly refers back to this tractate by name for more on how the immensity, the beauty, and the usefulness of creation pertain, respectively, to the power, wisdom, and mercy of the triune God.[33]

3. Prologue

The Prologue to *De sacramentis* immediately situates this work within Hugh's scriptural hermeneutics, as already indicated. Previously, he says, he wrote on the first sense of scripture, the historical; now he comes to the second level of instruction, the allegorical sense, by which he means the doctrinal lesson drawn from scripture, as we have seen.[34] Hugh's motivations here are explicitly and typically pedagogical. Once the foundation is firm, knowledge can be built up, step by orderly step.

> By this work they may firmly establish their minds on that foundation, so to speak, of the knowledge of faith, so that such other things as may be added to the structure by reading or hearing may remain unshaken. For I have compressed this brief *summa*, as it were, of all doctrine into one continuous work, that the mind may have something definite to which it may affix and conform its attention, lest it be carried away by

various volumes of writings and a diversity of readings without order or direction.[35]

Here Hugh is expressly the teacher, poised to outline a biblical structure that can accommodate further elaboration, and to do so in a linear order ("in one continuous work") so that his students and readers will not be carried off by topics or scriptural readings at random. As the whole Prologue makes clear, all of this concerns the subject matter of the Divine Scriptures, and Hugh's basic framework for understanding that subject matter is the familiar pairing of creation and restoration.

> The subject matter of all the Divine Scriptures is the works of man's restoration. For there are two works in which all that has been done is contained. The first is the work of foundation [creation]; the second is the work of restoration. The work of foundation is that whereby those things which were not came into being. The work of restoration is that whereby those things which had been impaired [ruined] were made better. Therefore, the work of foundation is the creation of the world with all its elements. The work of restoration is the Incarnation of the Word with all its sacraments, both those which have gone before from the beginning of time, and those which come after, even to the end of the world.[36]

Although it is familiar already from Hugh's previous works as introduced earlier, the restoration side of this pairing is here announced with the specific terminology of the Incarnation and sacraments. Hugh does not here pause to define these terms, preferring instead to invoke the Germanic martial imagery of the troops who precede and follow their warrior king. But it is clear that he means not the narrow definitions of Jesus' earthly life and the church's specific rituals but rather the entire history of salvation, the works and signs of the Incarnate Word from the fall to the finale.

The word *sacrament* later became so tightly bound to a specific set of rites that Hugh's title is often misunderstood, not least because he also covers "sacraments" in the more restricted sense, as we shall see. His own usage of the term *sacraments* is broad and varied. For now, his Prologue to *De sacramentis* establishes the basic subject matter. "Worldly or secular writings have as subject matter the works of foundation. Divine Scripture has as subject matter the works of restoration."[37] Here echoing his *On the Scriptures*, Hugh reviews his basic pairing of the six days of foundation with the (more sublime) six ages of restoration.

Nevertheless, as noted in chapter 4, a narrative of restoration presupposes a fall, and a fall presupposes a prior condition/creation, and this prior human condition must be situated within the creation of the whole world.

> First, therefore, [Sacred Scripture] deals with the subject matter of man's creation and original disposition; next with his misery in sin and punishment; then with his restoration and piety in the knowledge of truth and love of virtue; finally with his true homeland and the joy of heavenly happiness.[38]

Salvation history is Hugh's interest, and this entire treatise is his summary of the biblical doctrine of the history of salvation. Of the three senses of scripture (history, allegory, and tropology), it is the allegorical that pertains to this doctrinal overview of salvation history, for in it the biblical events (signified by the words) themselves signify other events, past or present or future. Hugh's summary of his hermeneutical theory and the liberal arts is here so compressed that the reader must refer to the *Didascalicon* and other works already introduced. As to this work, and what is yet to come, he explicitly identifies the restoration of the human with (allegorical) progress in right faith or teaching and also with (tropological) development of the right way of a spiritual life. "In these consist knowledge of truth and love of virtue; and this is the true restoration of man."[39] The current work concerns the doctrinal, the knowledge of the truth. The tropological, or the "moral of the story" for the good life, including what we might call spiritual practices, is explicitly developed in other works, and in part III. Because all of this pertains to scriptural interpretation, Hugh's Prologue ends with an identification of the biblical books with their names and categories, including "the Fathers" who amplified this same subject matter.[40]

After this crucial Prologue, the work itself is divided into two books, roughly into creation, fall, and the restoration of humanity before the Incarnation (book 1) and then the Incarnation and the time of grace through to the end and consummation of all (book 2). Hugh's clearest and most compact statement of this two-part outline is at the beginning of book 2:

> In the earlier part of this work I presented summarily the foundation [creation] of all things from the first beginning, together with the fall of man, and those things which were afterwards prepared for restoration, even to the coming of the Word. Now I would like to arrange in order those things which follow, even to the end and consummation of all. The time of grace. . . .[41]

Although this basic outline is clearly a matter of salvation history (including the literary sequences from the Old Testament to the New and to the Fathers), the specific order of topics within this outline is often detailed and complex.[42] The next two chapters trace the flow of the argument and sample Hugh's doctrinal theology.

5

DE SACRAMENTIS, BOOK ONE

*Part One: The Period of Six Days
in the Work of Foundation*

In a side comment prefatory to book 1 of *De sacramentis*,[1] Hugh combines a modest and prayerful spirit with an oblique reference to student requests, "prevailed upon by your frequent entreaty."[2] As at the outset of his initial Preface ("forced by the zeal of certain persons"[3]), Hugh's text sometimes retains allusions to his students as if in classroom dialogue. Indeed, he undertook the whole work, he says, "more on account of your insistence than on account of my own eagerness."[4] See also his "you say, but I say" or "do you understand what I say?"[5] That his students asked for this doctrinal overview may also be evident in an aside about vows. Hugh wryly admits that he has not yet kept his own vow. "You have demanded and I indeed am forced to pay what I have promised. Stealing a little leisure midst frequent occupations, I have briefly touched upon but not fully carried out what you asked."[6] The real substance of the start of book 1, however, concerns the challenge at hand and reminds the student reader that this work is all about the breadth and depth of sacred scripture: "I am truly entering upon an arduous and laborious task, not merely by compression to reduce to a compendium the whole content of Divine Scriptures, but also by explanation to bring to light the secrets of their profundity."[7] As teacher and author, Hugh stays true to this goal of compressing the broad biblical narrative and yet expounding its depth, not via the genre of commentaries but in letting the overall scriptural story of salvation be his guide: creation, fall, restoration centered on the Incarnation, the time of grace including the church and its rites, and to the end of this world and beyond.

First, as promised and as already previewed, comes the work of foundation in the six days. Hugh's concern to balance simultaneity with the daily intervals has already been discussed, along with specific doctrinal interpretations of the waters above and the relationship of fishes and birds.[8] Why light seems to precede the creation of the sun is another example of here adding doctrinal meaning to the literal-historical text of Genesis. The soul, in darkness, needs illumination (light), says Hugh, to distinguish virtues from vices, and then the sun of righteousness will begin to shine. This exegetical move he calls a "sacrament" or sometimes a "mystery," using a broad understanding of these related terms, before defining them, to indicate this doctrinal-allegorical interpretation of scripture.[9] Throughout, when Hugh draws the symbolic meanings out of the textual details of the six days, as traditionally done by Augustine and many others, he calls these doctrinal interpretations "sacraments," as seen in several texts and provided in chapter titles.[10] When he hurries on past other such details of the six days to provide a more general summary, he adds the language of "sacrament" to the familiar pairing of creation and restoration.

> There are very many other things that could have been said mystically regarding these days. But . . . we have proposed to treat in this work, in as far as the Lord will allow, of the sacrament of man's redemption, which was formed from the beginning in the work of restoration.[11]

Hugh next rehearses his definitions of the works of creation and the works of restoration, in six days and six ages, respectively, and again adds that the latter contains the "sacrament of redemption." Then he provides a fuller definition of the works of restoration that names the Incarnation and "sacraments" in the plural, along with a comprehensive historical sweep.

> We say that the works of restoration are the Incarnation of the Word, and those things which the Word with all His sacraments performed in the flesh and through the flesh, whether those sacraments which preceded from the beginning of the world to figure the Incarnation itself, or those which follow after, even to the end of the world, to announce and declare it.[12]

Thus the whole history of salvation is Hugh's subject, because it is the "whole sum of Divine Scriptures,"[13] wherein the "sacrament" or "mystery" of redemption includes the "sacraments" done by the Word before and after the Incarnation. Knowing that he must move on steadily to complete this ambitious task, Hugh quickly summarizes creation in general and announces a four-point agenda for what comes next: "So there are four points with which the subsequent discussion should deal in order, that is: first, why man was created; then, of what nature he was created; then how he fell; finally, moreover, how he was restored."[14] This quartet of headings holds up well for the middle part of book 1, although the final consideration of "restoration" naturally subdivides into many sections. The first point (why man was created) becomes a very complicated and extended treatment of God (part 2), of the Trinity (part 3), of God's will (part 4), and of the angels (part 5). The second point (of what nature man was created) is covered in part 6, and the third point (how man fell) in part 7. The fourth point (how man is restored) begins with part 8 on restoration in principle, but the topic quickly subdivides into the sacraments (part 9), faith (part 10), the natural law (part 11), and the written law (part 12). The *Didascalicon* had itemized this basic outline long before.[15]

   This four-point outline is thus of some initial help in orienting the reader to book 1, the narrative up to the Incarnation, but it is heavily loaded at the front, as will be apparent shortly. Furthermore, this outline is completely overloaded at the end where the category of "restoration" applies to the rest of book 1, until the Incarnation, and then to all of book 2, the Incarnation and the subsequent "time of grace" until the end.

   Ostensibly on his first point, "why humanity was created," the next four parts of *De sacramentis* (parts 2 through 5 of book 1) constitute a complex, perhaps even convoluted, section that stretches Hugh's outline almost to the breaking point. Briefly: the "cause of man's creation" is God (part 2), the Trinity (part 3) who by the divine Will (part 4) also created the angels (part 5). When he returns after these sixty columns (or pages) to his second point, "of what nature he was created" (part 6), Hugh is obliged to repeat the four-point outline that was set out so long before.[16]

   The doctrinal detail in this section is daunting, both in itself and also with respect to Hugh's unnamed sources, such as Augustine, and unnamed opponents, such as Peter Abelard. As Hugh acknowledged, some of this material also appears in other works, such as the trinity of power, wisdom, and will (or love or goodness) so characteristic of *De tribus diebus* and other works.[17] Here and throughout, small samples are no substitute for the rich detail of Hugh's own text. That the entire section reads increasingly like an excursus is perhaps inevitable, given Hugh's organizing principle. The works of creation and restoration presuppose a creator-restorer, of course, who is God. Yet these "works" of God pertain largely to the external divine activities toward the world rather than the internal divine relationships of the Triune Persons. Thus, the inner-Trinitarian concepts and terms can seem tangential. Furthermore, Hugh's announced topic is the restoration of humanity, meaning that he can include the angels only as a tangent to God as creator of all, both humans and angels. Here and elsewhere, we see Hugh attempting both to develop his announced theme of humanity's restoration and to include everything of significance in this summa of doctrine, such as creation, the creator, the inner triune relationships, and the creation of the angelic ranks. In this respect, Hugh's work creatively expands beyond a "treatise" that expounds one theme and ushers in the development of "systematic" theology, as advanced so brilliantly by the Parisian "schoolmen" of the next century. Theology in this sense of a comprehensive system has its own history, including Origen and Eriugena's *Periphyseon*; Hugh's *De sacramentis* holds a pivotal place in that history leading to such masterpieces as the *Summa theologiae* of Thomas Aquinas. What may seem like tangents on the formal level of Hugh's announced outline can also be appreciated as the uneven results of his imaginative development of a new genre of theological literature.

*Part Two: On the Cause of Man's
Creation, and on the Primordial Causes
of All Things*

In part 2, the cause of humanity's creation is the goodness of God, who also has (or rather is) the power and wisdom to fulfill this good creative will. God thus is power, wisdom, and will (or goodness). Here Hugh the Augustinian drastically abbreviates the theme of *De tribus diebus*, as discussed before: "The Catholic faith . . . assigned power to the Father, wisdom to the Son, and goodness to the Holy Ghost."[18] These three are one, and eternally so, yet they are known to us in our realm of chronological time where the divine wisdom also means *fore*knowledge and *pre*destination.[19]

Furthermore, and here Hugh quotes himself, the idea of "power" can lead to (Abelard's) confusion over omnipotence relative to providence, if our chronological limits are applied to God.[20]

Part Three: On the Trinity

In part 3, Hugh develops further how we know that God exists and believe that God is truly one and three, including the Trinitarian traces in ourselves as made in the image of power and wisdom and love, and the specific terminology of Father, Son, and Holy Ghost. Without any trace of attribution, all of this is notably Augustinian, including the starting point of self-awareness. While summing up this complex discussion, he also admits that human knowledge is partial: "From the beginning God tempered knowledge of Himself on the part of man, so that He would be neither wholly manifest nor wholly hidden," so that faith might be needed and assisted.[21]

Part Four: On the Will of God Which Is Eternal and One

Continuing his first point about the cause of man's creation, Hugh's part 4 specifies that "the first cause of all things is the will of the Creator."[22] God's "will," biblically, includes both what He made, which is good, and also what He permitted, namely, evil. This section, with extended discussion of the different manifestations of the divine will, including precepts and prohibitions, serves two strategic purposes within Hugh's overall structure. First, it opens up a context for free will, whether angelic or human, since God had arranged that there be both good and evil; indeed, "it was good that there be both good and evil," since "with these evils added, good things might be commended and become more beautiful through comparison with evil."[23] Within this context, the next parts take up the angels and the human, specifically on free will and the fall, and thus restoration, as befits Hugh's overall outline. Second, this section on the divine will also allows a logical (Platonic) sequence of subjects from the Creation-Cause to the divine mind's "primordial and invisible and uncreated causes of all things," as mentioned in earlier passages, to the invisible angelic creatures to the visible human ones. "After the first uncreated and invisible causes, therefore, our consideration will pass on and proceed to the angelic nature rational and invisible, then to the human nature visible and rational, about which it was first proposed to give full treatment."[24] Thus is space made in Hugh's outline for the angels.

Part Five: On the Creation of the Angels

Part 5 thus takes up the angelic realm, in accordance with the logical sequence just mentioned and yet also as an excursus from the overall topic of man's restoration. Within the overarching structure of humanity's salvation history, Hugh thus makes room for the eternal or celestial realm of the angels, even though they are not given any explicit place in the creation account of Genesis. As with Trinitarian theology, here, too, the Victorine's agenda to give systematic coverage to Christian doctrine puts a strain on his fundamentally historical structure regarding the work of restoration.

Furthermore, there seem to be other factors, and sources, for this interest in angelology. As mentioned, Hugh occasionally frames his work as responsive to student requests, and especially here in part 5. The entire topic (the nature of the angels, when they were created, of what nature, their number and orders and government) is introduced as a query posed by his students: "you now propose an inquiry into the nature of the angels. . . ."[25] This inquiry may take Hugh far afield, but like a good teacher, he will find the link to his real topic, namely, the issue of free will and fall. This section is also interesting for the sources not named, as with the earlier Augustinian trinities. Without attribution, Hugh here passes on some traditional angelology stemming from Gregory the Great, yet he elsewhere reflects a new interest in Dionysius the Areopagite. In fact, Hugh wrote an extensive commentary on the entire Dionysian treatise on the angels, *The Celestial Hierarchy*, as covered later, yet that treatise never appears in this section, even indirectly. The emphases here are not at all Dionysian, but rather on the initial creation of the angels (simultaneously with the new matter of original creation) and on four angelic properties: "first, a simple and immaterial substance; second, distinction of person; third, a rational form of wisdom and understanding, but fourth, the free power of inclining their will and choice either to good or to evil."[26] Hugh's emphasis prepares the way for his discussion of human free will and fall, namely, that God cannot be blamed for the evil that is chosen by free will, whether angelic or human, but that God's just will can order all things well. "For God is the orderer of evil wills, not the creator."[27] The rest of part 5 (the orders and numbers and names of the angels) is tangential to the larger outline of *De sacramentis*, but interesting for Hugh's angelology, as covered more specifically elsewhere regarding his commentary on the Dionysian *Celestial Hierarchy*.

Part Six: On the Creation of Man

Returning to his four-point outline, Hugh in part 6 takes up the second point, namely, of what nature humanity was created. Here Hugh masterfully adapts and compresses his own earlier explanation (*On the Vanity of the World*) that humans are both soul and mortal body so that they might long for future immortality.[28] "Thus God made man of a twofold substance, taking his body according to matter from the earth, but fashioning his soul without matter from nothing."[29] Discussing the human soul first by itself (chapters ii–xvii) and then as embodied, Hugh first identifies the biblical "image and likeness."

> Man was made to the image and likeness of God, because in the soul, which is the better part of man, or rather was man himself, was the image and likeness of God: image according to reason, likeness according to love; image according to understanding of truth, likeness according to love of virtue. . . .[30]

Hugh openly sets aside many questions about the definition and especially the origin of the soul, perhaps here alluding to the several Augustinian positions, abbreviating the issue to what the "Catholic Faith" holds, namely, that the original human soul was made from nothing when the body itself was formed: "it was made and associated with the body simultaneously by the Creator himself."[31] With the body comes the issue of free will, and yet human embodiment is a good thing. The human (rational soul) has a twofold sense, so that God is admired and loved not only internally from the invisible things but also externally through the visible things seen in the flesh. Flanked by the angels and by brute animals,

> Man was placed in a middle position . . . that he might go in and contemplate, and might go out and contemplate; that he might have wisdom within, the works of wisdom without, that he might contemplate both, and be refreshed from both, see and rejoice, love and praise.[32]

Inner contemplation is accompanied by physically seeing the external works created by wisdom.[33] The larger theme is human freedom of the will before sin, along with full knowledge of the Creator, of the self, and of what should be done. As embodied, the human can appreciate the lower goods of the visible and temporal world, as well as the higher goods of the invisible and eternal. Hugh seems to enjoy speculating, not asserting, what human life would have been like without sin. Children would be born, of course, because the union of male and female included the command (and blessing) to be fruitful and multiply, before sin, but what would such children be like?[34] So that all humans might know they are one and from one, a single human was first, but then the woman was made from man and from the side, not from the head or the foot.

> Now she was made from the side of man that it might be shown that she was created for association in love, lest perhaps, if she had been made from the head, she would seem to be preferred to man unto domination, or, if from the feet, to be subject unto slavery. Since, therefore, she was furnished to man neither as a mistress, nor a handmaid but as a companion, she had to be produced neither from the head nor the feet but from the side, in order that he might realize that she was to be placed beside him, whom he learned had been taken from his very side.[35]

Part Seven: On the Fall of the First Man

Part 7 brings book 1 of *De sacramentis* to Hugh's third point in the current quartet, namely, how humanity fell from this original state of creation. Here the envious devil plays a crucial role, but abruptly so, since he appears from nowhere. The earlier discussion had mentioned fallen angels or even evil angels but with no linkage to a specific individual, and no prior mention of the devil. Nevertheless, "he was envious that man should ascend there through obedience whence he himself had fallen through pride."[36] This wily enemy assumes another form, approaches humanity at its weaker point, and asks questions. The woman's first answer reveals her doubt and gives the devil his opening. God had said that if they ate of that tree, they would die; the woman said, "lest *perhaps* we die," and the devil took her doubts down another step of the fall, to flat denial: no, you shall not die.

> God affirmed, woman doubted, the devil denied. But by no means would the devil have presumed in the presence of woman to deny the word of

God, if he had not first found woman herself in doubt. Therefore she who doubted departed from Him who affirmed and approached him who denied. She herself, then, to some extent began malice, who gave to the tempter the boldness of iniquitous persuasion.[37]

The three vices in this original sin (namely, pride, avarice, and gluttony[38]) were shared dissimilarly by Adam and Eve, now given personal names for the first time, but the result is the same.

And so whatever blame there is in original sin, although dissimilarly, yet it redounds entirely to both; to her, indeed, because she sinned, to him because he consented to her sinning and made her sins his sin by consenting.[39]

Thereafter, humanity is beset by original sin, defined as "the corruption or vice which we take by birth through ignorance in the mind, through concupiscence in the flesh."[40] Theses two vices have partners: "Ignorance was the punishment of pride, concupiscence the effect of mortality. Thus four evils appear in man: pride, ignorance, mortality, concupiscence."[41] This part concludes with discussion of the transmission of original sin, but not specific sins, from generation to generation. All of this material, including elaborate distinctions too detailed to list here, is preparatory to the proper subject in scripture and thus of *De sacramentis*, namely, the restoration of humanity. Although it is preparatory, this discussion has been essential; the idea of restoration presupposes a fallen state, and the fall presupposes a prior state of original creation.

Part Eight: On the Restoration of Man

With part 8, Hugh formally completes his quartet of points introduced long before, yet actually launches into the overall subject of the rest of this entire work. Properly speaking, "Restoration" includes the Incarnation, eras of history, faith, and the sacraments (both in the general sense and also regarding specific sacramental rites). All of this now unfolds in *De sacramentis* according to its own outline as introduced in part 8. (As a preview of so much at once, part 8 seems to burst at the seams and should be read in its entirety; it can serve as a glimpse of the whole work and will be generously quoted here.)

"The first guilt of man was pride which was followed by a threefold punishment" and more guilt: mortality, concupiscence of the flesh, and ignorance of the mind.[42] So begins part 8, in severe abbreviation of the prior presentation on the fall. The divine mercy has arranged for humanity's restoration from this plight by providing the time and place for repentance and remedy.

> Therefore, three things occur here for consideration in the first place on the restoration of man: time, place, remedy. The time is the present life from the beginning of the world even to the end of the world. The place is this world. The remedy consists in three things: in faith, in the sacraments, in good works. The time is long, lest man be taken unprepared. The place is rough that the prevaricator may be punished. The remedy is efficacious that the weak may be healed.[43]

This compressed summary (even more so in the Latin original) is then explicated. As our (human) place, this world is poised strategically between heaven and paradise on the one hand and hell on the other.[44] The time is all of human history ever since the fall and on into the future, divided shortly into three.

> The first is the period of the natural law, the second the period of the written law, the third the period of grace. The first is from Adam even unto Moses, the second from Moses even unto Christ, the third from Christ even unto the end of the world.[45]

The triplex remedy (faith, the sacraments, and good works) takes longer to expound, indeed, the rest of De sacramentis, starting with parts 9 and 10 on the sacraments and faith. But first, Hugh inserts an explanation of why and how God chose to effect humanity's restoration/redemption in the first place. This section (chapters iv–x) on an imagined court case (God, the devil, and humanity) leading to the Incarnation seems awkwardly placed, especially since the overall historical outline reserves fuller discussion of Christ and the incarnation to the "time of grace" at the beginning of book 2. The courtroom language of guilt and debt and satisfaction borrows from contemporary discussions, especially Anselm of Canterbury, who is never mentioned even though a chapter title reads "Cur Deus homo" (vi). Humanity cannot pay the debt, so God provided a special Man who can, and more.

> Christ, then, by His birth paid man's debt to the Father, and by His death atoned for man's guilt, so that, when He Himself assumed death for man which He did not owe, man on account of Him might justly escape death which he owed.[46]

Why the God man? "And so God was made man that He might free man whom He had made, that He, the same, might be both Creator and Redeemer of man."[47] Since the entirety of humanity had been corrupted by sin and was due for damnation, there is no injustice if (only) some are saved through mercy, in familiar Augustinian terms.[48] God could have willed otherwise, not only regarding who should be saved but also doing it not by way of Incarnation at all. Again compressing his Christology and soteriology:

> On this account we truly declare that God could have accomplished the redemption of mankind even in a different manner if He had willed; however, it was more befitting our infirmity, that God should be made man and assuming the mortality of man for man should refashion man unto the hope of His immortality; thus man might no longer despair that he could ascend to the goods of Him whom he sees had descended to bear his evils, and humanity, glorified in God might be an example of glorification to men; in that He suffered they might see what they should return to Him, but in that He was glorified they might consider what they should expect from Him; He Himself might be the way in example and the truth in promise and the life in reward.[49]

After the anticipation of his fuller discussion of the Incarnation and the atonement, Hugh resumes his immediate sequence regarding the remedy God has provided from the beginning; namely, the sacraments.

> And so then from the very beginning of the world He proposed to man the sacraments of his salvation with which He might sign him with the expectation of future sanctification. . . .[50]

However, a *sacrament* is not yet defined, and the term is used loosely enough that the devil, too, has his "sacraments," albeit never itemized. The larger and very Hugonian point here is that from the beginning of this mortal life (first the time of the natural law and then the written law, before the Incarnation), "God at once prepared a remedy in His sacraments for restoring man . . . at different times and places for man's cure," whether before the law, under the law or under grace, using historical categories from Saint Paul and dear to Augustine.[51] But, using this medical language of sickness and remedy, why would any sacramental help be needed before sin brought on the illness? Hugh needs to account for the original institution of marriage, before the fall, as an exception to his overall program of expounding the sacraments as coterminous with restoration. Thus before proceeding to the definition and overall understanding of "sacraments" in part 9, the narrative here stops to insert a discussion of the first institution of marriage as an "office" before sin, as distinguished from its second institution as a remedy after sin.[52]

Part Nine: On the Institution
of the Sacraments

Part 9 finally provides some working definition to the title term, *sacraments*. Hugh sets out a fourfold outline for this part: definition, cause, matter, and division:

> First, what is a sacrament; second, why were sacraments instituted; third, what is the matter of each sacrament in which it is made and sanctified; fourth, how many kinds of sacraments are there . . . ?[53]

By preliminary and traditional definition, a *sacrament* is "the sign of a sacred thing."[54] Hugh is more specific, ruling out letters and statues and pictures, and avoiding an "empty" sign.

> A sacrament is a corporeal or material element set before the senses without, representing by similitude and signifying by institution and containing by sanctification some invisible and spiritual grace.[55]

In this influential definition, the corporeal element is related to the invisible grace in three ways: a (natural) similitude, a (dominical) institution, and a spiritual efficacy or "sanctification through which it contains that thing and is efficacious for conferring the same on those to be sanctified."[56] Thus a sacrament is a sign that also effects what it signifies. The example of baptism reveals the triple definition to be triune. The natural similitude of cleansing water comes from the Creator; the Savior "instituted visible water through the ablution of bodies to signify the invisible cleaning of souls through spiritual grace";[57] the "Dispenser's" part is put in St. Augustine's terms, yet without attribution: "the word of sanctification is added to the element and a sacrament is made."[58] In summary, using baptism to illustrate the three aspects: "visible water is a sacrament representing from similitude, signifying from institution, containing spiritual grace from sanctification."[59] Although Hugh quickly moves on from this definition to his second point (on why the sacraments were instituted), his tripartite definition is specified further in the sections to come, and in generations to come, in a gradual narrowing of the term *sacrament* from sacred sign in general to the specific rites of the church.

The sacraments, continues Hugh with his second point, were instituted for three reasons: humiliation, institution, and exercise.[60] If humanity fell away from God into the lower realm of the material, it is fitting that humans should now be consigned to the humiliation of needing the lower material things, in that God "offers salvation through them."[61] "The sacraments were also instituted on account of instruction . . . that the human mind may be instructed to recognize the invisible virtue."[62] Related to instruction is exercise, in that fallen humanity needs variety and change; thus God has provided various times and places and forms of worship as another reason for instituting the sacraments.[63]

To his second point, on the cause of the sacraments, Hugh then appends a discussion of the priest's role, lest anyone confuse the divine source of sanctification with the human ministry that dispenses it. The ruling imagery is medical:

> God the physician, man the sick person, the priest the minister or messenger, grace the antidote, the vessel the sacrament. The physician gives, the minister dispenses, the vessel preserves spiritual grace which heals the sick recipient. If, therefore, vases are the sacraments of spiritual grace, they do not heal from their own, since vases do not cure the sick but medicine does.[64]

This sharp distinction of external sacrament and internal grace, likened to a vase and the medicine it contains, also serves Hugh's further excursus on the sacraments as necessary regarding human obedience but optional regarding God's power to save without them. A polemic comes suddenly into focus, for some who think they are venerating the sacraments are actually dishonoring God. "You ascribe a necessity to sacraments and from the Author of sacraments you take away power and to Him you deny piety."[65] God could and can save otherwise, but since He has instituted the sacraments, human obedience is necessary.

Hugh's third point, on the "matter" of the sacraments, shows his further progression from a general to a specific understanding of sacraments. Generally speaking, sacraments can involve things or deeds or words, because fallen human life is made up of these externals. Yet "deeds," such as the sign of the cross, or "words," such as the invocation of the Trinity, are not

Hugh's proper subject in the way that "things" are, such as "the sacrament of baptism in water, the sacrament of unction in oil, the sacrament of the body and blood of Christ in bread and wine."[66] Hugh's discussion is centering on "sacraments" in the specific sense of churchly rites, but only gradually.

The next point (the fourth) distinguishes three kinds of sacraments: those necessary for salvation ("for example, the water of baptism and the receiving of the body and blood of Christ"), those "of benefit to sanctification" ("for example, the water of aspersion and the reception of ashes"), and those preparatory to the others, such as sacred orders or consecration.[67] Just when the reader might expect Hugh to discuss these and other specific sacraments in detail, perhaps identifying seven of them in particular or creating a category of "sacramentals," he backs off his division of the sacraments and opens up the large panorama of what is necessary for salvation before or after Christ, namely, "faith, sacraments, and good works."[68]

Part Ten: On Faith

This rather abrupt shift leads to a full discussion of faith in part 10, including both a catechetical overview of creation and restoration and also a specific understanding of faith as itself a sacrament. (Good works as a topic is picked up again tangentially at the end of part 11.) Part 10, "On Faith," is thus first an excursus off the subject of sacraments in the narrow sense and yet then comes back to the point, in explaining how faith itself can be understood as a sacrament. The first of Hugh's seven questions is simple: What is faith? His answer is traditional, from Hebrews 11: "the substance of things hoped for, the evidence of things that appear not."[69] Within his exegesis of this verse, Hugh concedes that God is *in*effable or *un*thinkable, a paragraph of apophatic, or negative, theology (note the negating prefixes) that is more conventional and Augustinian than specifically Dionysian. He briefly invokes his striking notion of the three eyes: the eye of the flesh can see in the physical sense, the eye of reason still "sees" but only partially or doubtfully, and the eye of contemplation can no longer, "after the shades of sin," see God and what is in God.[70] The Hebrews verse then yields to a more specific (and influential) definition, placing believers in between "conjecturers" and "knowers." "If any one wishes to note a full and general definition of faith, he can say that faith is a kind of certainty of the mind in things absent, established beyond opinion and short of knowledge."[71]

Faith, according to Hugh's second point or question, consists of "cognition and affection," meaning some knowledge and the willingness or credibility to believe.[72] Third, faith can grow in both respects. "Faith grows according to cognition, when it is instructed unto knowledge. It increases according to affection, when it is excited unto devotion and is strengthened unto constancy."[73] In considering the different kinds of behavior, Hugh invokes the dominical examples, for "the Lord showed manifestly that great affection in faith is more praiseworthy than great cognition."[74]

Fourth, what are the contents of faith? Here Hugh compresses his entire theology.

> First we were not and we were made; afterwards we perished and were redeemed; and by one both were done so that all our good was from one, and all in one, and all one. To the creator we owe that we are; to the Saviour, that we were restored. Therefore, these are the two things which as propositions of faith must be believed, Creator and Savior,

and whatever pertains to both.[75] This familiar pairing of faith's two parts is then explicitly named as the works of foundation and the works of restoration, the overarching structure of Hugh's theological system. "To the Creator pertain the works of foundation which were made in six days; to the Savior pertain the works of restoration which are being completed in six ages."[76] Full faith keeps these categories straight, whereas some confuse the creature for the Creator, and others "did not have faith in the Savior."[77] This capsule of Hugh's theology is further compressed into the Augustinian terms of "nature and grace" by the end of this paragraph. "The former we ought to believe, since through nature we were founded; the latter we ought to believe, since through grace we were restored."[78]

Hugh's fifth and sixth points on faith are interrelated: Has it changed over time, specifically, before and after the Incarnation, and what is its minimal core? Hugh takes care to oppose a static, timeless view of faith, as if those who preceded the Incarnation somehow had the same fullness of faith as those who followed it. He is here actually quoting at length a letter from Bernard of Clairvaux, without attribution.[79] Using Bernard, he for the first time introduces some patristic authorities into *De sacramentis*, namely, Augustine, Pope Gregory, and Bede.[80] Principally from the biblical sources, not the Fathers, Hugh advances Bernard's progressive or historical view of faith as developing or increasing over time. Adapting the Cistercian abbot's point, Hugh says that faith was the same faith, albeit lesser or greater. "And so faith increased in all through the times so that it was greater but was not changed so as to be different."[81] Before the law, God was known as Creator from whom salvation was also awaited, but only a few knew how; under the law, a Redeemer was expected, but only a few knew what kind; under grace, of course, this Redeemer is fully known and believed. Thus, the minimal faith, from the beginning, is "that there is one God, Creator of all things, Lord and Ruler of the Universe, that in truth He is not the author of evil, yet that He would be the Redeemer of those who in their evil sought and expected his mercy."[82] Before his seventh and final point, on faith as a sacrament, Hugh pauses for a recapitulation: "Therefore, true faith rests in two: Creator and Redeemer." Yet, "Creator and Redeemer are one, Creator as to Nature, Savior as to grace."[83] That such faith can be lesser or greater, and can increase, prepares the reader for Hugh's return to the sacramental question.

Part 10, on faith, culminates in an important discussion of faith and sacraments, here regarding faith itself as a sacrament in a special sense and then (in part 11 and beyond) on the sacraments of faith in the usual sense. Faith can be called a sacrament in light of Paul's expectant verse: "We see now through a glass [mirror] in a dark manner, but then face to face" (1 Corinthians 13). "What, therefore, we see now through the glass in a dark manner is the sacrament with respect to that which we shall see face to face in manifest contemplation."[84] Faith now points to a future face-to-face contemplation just as a sacrament points to a reality. "Faith, then, is the sacrament of future contemplation, and contemplation itself is the thing [res] and the virtue of the sacrament."[85] Thus is faith the beginning of the restoration toward full contemplation of the Creator and, in this unusual sense, a sacrament of that future contemplation.

Part Eleven: On the Natural Law

With this special linkage of faith and sacrament, Hugh can go back to his historical sequence regarding progressive restoration, moving from the natural law (part 11) to the written law (part 12). "After faith we must treat the sacraments of faith. Sacraments were instituted from the beginning for the restoration and guardianship of man, some under the natural law, some under the written law, some under grace."[86] This opening of part 11 contains both the work's title phrase, the "Sacraments of Faith," and also the triplex outline here unfolding. After a brief (and partial) presentation of sacraments under the natural law, Hugh moves to a fuller account of the sacraments and precepts of the written law (the Decalogue, in part 12) as the conclusion of the first book. "Under grace" applies to the Incarnation and thus to the second book.

In this historical sequence, "natural law" refers to the biblical era from the fall to Abrahamic circumcision and especially the Mosaic legislation. The sacraments of that era prefigure the later sacraments of grace, meaning that they are different in several ways. They are not themselves signs of invisible grace but rather the signs of the later visible sacramental signs; they were not necessary for salvation in the later sense; they were not efficacious until the Incarnation itself opened heaven.[87] These distinctions are mentioned only briefly and sometimes include sacraments under the written law; the whole of part 11, "On the Natural Law," is short and underdeveloped. Exactly what these sacraments are is only glimpsed in passing, as confirmed by a list elsewhere, namely, tithes, sacrifices, and oblations.[88] Only when part 12 refers back to these three do we learn that *sacrifices* refers to animals and *oblations* means "things," such as bread.[89] "Tithes," meanwhile, are considered briefly here in part 11 but, like oblations, only to illustrate the progressive (threefold) development of sacramental history. "Wherefore, first through oblation and afterwards through circumcision, finally through baptism it was ordained that the sacrament of expiation and justification be formed, since the form and likeness of the same cleansing is found obscurely indeed in the oblation, is expressed indeed more evidently in circumcision, but is declared manifestly through baptism."[90] Continuing this same theme of progressive revelation and thus sacramental development, Hugh calls the sacraments under the natural law (such as oblations) "a kind of shadow of the truth," those under the written law (circumcision) "a kind of image or figure of the truth," and those under grace (baptism) the very "body of truth," although they, too, will yield, eschatologically, to the spirit. "The first sacraments then were a shadow, the second an image, the third a body, after which in fourth place follows the truth of the spirit."[91]

Part 11's brief and uneven exposition of several topics at once culminates in an abrupt return to the topic of works, mentioned at the end of part 9 regarding faith, sacraments, and good works. The final paragraph of part 11 fulfills this mention by quick reference to works and the minimal precepts under the natural law (the Golden Rule) and by preview of the written law, specifically the second table of the Ten Commandments taken up in part 12.

Part Twelve: On the Written Law

The era of the written law, in Hugh's terms, begins with Abraham and the commandment to circumcise as preparatory to Moses and the Decalogue. The distinctive sign of Abrahamic circumcision is triplex: the bodily points to the spiritual present, when iniquity is cut away from the soul, and also to the future, when the body's corruption shall be laid aside. "The first then is in the flesh, the second in the mind, the third in the body."[92] Salvation history persistently frames Hugh's doctrinal theology, not only in this glimpse of past and present and future "circumcisions" but also in the historical sequence internal to this era of the written law, namely, that Abrahamic circumcision was preparatory to the Mosaic legislation. "The sacrament of circumcision was given before legislation and through it a certain preparation was made to accept the law."[93]

Under "the Written Law," Hugh presents primarily the precepts and secondarily the sacraments, where he also concedes a loose use of the term. The precepts (prohibitions or commands) are either permanent, specifically the Decalogue taken up first, or temporary ("movable").[94] The "immovable" precepts added to the natural law's Golden Rule are conventionally divided into the three of the first table regarding love of God and the seven of the second table regarding love of neighbor. These numbers contain a fitting symmetry for Hugh in that the initial trio of commandments befits faith in the Triune God and the seven precepts for daily life and love match the seven-day week. Furthermore, both tables include command and prohibition, both start out with fatherhood (whether divine or human), and the sum total of such faith and love is the complete number ten.[95] These numerical symmetries and hints of logical internal orders preview Hugh's forceful argument about the order of the Ten Commandments when he presents each.

Quoting wholesale from his own *Institutiones in Decalogum*,[96] Hugh begins his discussion of the Decalogue not with the first commandment of Exodus 20 but with a compact exegesis of Deuteronomy 6. The phrase "Hear, O Israel" demands obedience, "your God" suggests grace, "is one God" teaches truth, "him shalt thou adore" pertains to faith, "and him only shalt thou serve" pertains to good works.[97] With a side note on the difference between the adoration or service due to God and that due to humans, complete with the prior text's unusual invocation of the Greek terms versus Latin, this opening paragraph has effectively previewed the whole Decalogue.

Turning to the second precept, Hugh goes quickly past the simple literal meaning of not taking the Lord's name in vain, regarding false oaths or naming idols falsely, to the more complex "mystical" meaning regarding the Son as eternally God with the Father. "Therefore, what does it mean to say: 'Thou shalt not take the name of thy God in vain,' except just as you venerate and adore Him on this [one] account, because you were made by Him, so adore and venerate on this [other] account, because you were redeemed by Him."[98] Similarly, the third precept, "Keep holy the Sabbath day," is complicated by reference to several biblical Sabbaths, whether divine or human, external or internal.[99] In summary, "these, therefore, are the three precepts of the first table in which especially the love of God is commanded and the entire Trinity is ordered to be adored and cherished equally as one God."[100]

The seven precepts of the second table match the seven-day week of daily life and fittingly begin with paternal honor, regarding human beginnings, just as the first table began with honor to God the Father regarding our original foundation.[101] Brief comments follow on each of the remaining commandments, borrowing from a different prior text, with more detailed attention given to different forms of "false witness," namely, lies, false testimony, and perjury, along with oaths and vows.[102] Hugh's penchant for logical and historical order comes out in his summary of the ordering of these Ten Commandments, originally chapter 3 of the earlier *Institutiones in Decalogum*. First, God is to be adored (faith) and served (good works). After the faith of the heart comes confession of the mouth (the second commandment) and quiet time for both (the third). The second table regarding human life begins with honoring one's human source, including the promise of a long life for oneself (the fourth commandment), as then matched by respecting the life of the neighbor (fifth). The sixth, seventh, and eighth commandments prohibit diminishing our own lives through adultery or the lives of others through theft or deceit. The ninth and tenth prevent even the desire for any such diminishment, with the ninth regarding the neighbor's wife matching the sixth on adultery and the tenth on the neighbor's property matching the seventh on theft.[103]

After this forceful summary of the way the permanent precepts cohere, freely adapting his own prior work, Hugh moves but briefly to the movable or temporary precepts, here, too, framing dietary prohibitions not simply as historically transient but rather as developmentally symbolic of fuller revelations to come. Not eating meat with blood, for example, (loosely) prefigures "thou shall not kill," which is itself fulfilled in Jesus' further prohibition against anger.[104] Last, Hugh returns to the original question of sacraments under the law.

By the end of this book 1, leading up to the incarnational era "under grace" in book 2, Hugh's overall outline has been stretched considerably but stays basically intact, following the outline of salvation history. From creation and its cause in the will of God through the fall to the Restoration begun through sacraments before the law and under the law, Hugh's progressive or historical plan has survived the excursions into angelology, faith, and the Decalogue. At the end of book 1, he brings it back to the question of sacraments under the law, although the term applies only loosely here as in the prior section before the law. Hugh's three categories (remedy, obedience, and worship) do not clarify much here, because his examples are few. Having included Abrahamic circumcision "under the law," he can count it here, but otherwise his text gives only passing references to the tabernacle or vestments that preview future sacraments. The sacrifices and oblations before the law continued, of course, and are here further specified in several brief ways, including sins of omission or commission.[105] Otherwise, the first book here comes to a quiet end, as Hugh's considerable energies are next applied to the Incarnation, the sacramental life of the church, and the end of salvation history.

6

DE SACRAMENTIS, BOOK TWO

The brief Prologue to Hugh's second book of *De sacramentis* reminds the readers that this entire project stems from biblical interpretation and that with a deft phrase it can quickly turn theological, in this case, incarnational. Sacred scripture, repeats Hugh, has levels of meaning, for both the simple and the elevated. This harmony, not discord, means that great truths and lofty topics are juxtaposed to modest and simple things.

> Therefore, let no one wonder if after the great, and in the midst of the great sacraments of faith, mention is made of those things which in their own order seem inferior, since things that are one in truth are not at all abhorrent to each other. For God himself deigned to be humbled, descending to human things, that afterwards He might raise man up to the divine.[1]

With admirable brevity, this prefatory comment introduces both the whole of the second book (with its mixture of essential theology, major sacraments, and minor sacramentals) and also the immediate topic of the Incarnation in part 1. Hugh here previews his appropriation of classical Christology, that God became human so that the human might be raised up to the divine, and applies it to his literary purposes of introducing an immense array of material from the sublime to the mundane. This material also includes great stretches of text from the Fathers, unlike book 1, and often not even smoothly incorporated into the argument. In some cases, the literary significance is that traditional texts were here preserved and passed on to posterity, including to Peter Lombard's influential *Sentences*. In other cases, especially at the end of book 2, it seems that Hugh did not himself live to finish the work.[2]

Part One: On the Incarnation

Part 1 of the second book also begins with a preface applicable to the whole project.

> In the earlier part of this work I presented summarily the foundation of all things from the first beginning, together with the fall of man, and those things which were afterwards prepared for restoration, even to the coming of the Word. Now I would like to arrange in order those things which follow, even to the end and consummation of all.[3]

The familiar language of foundation (*conditio*) and restoration (*restauratio*) again supplies the contents of salvation history from the beginning to the end and consummation but as centered on the *adventus Verbi* or the advent "of the Son of God into the flesh."

Thus part 1 takes up, at length, the complex theological questions of the Incarnation. This part, "On the Incarnation of the Word," is the largest part of the whole work, yet it does not exhaust Hugh's Christology in general or his understanding of the Incarnation. The entirety of *De sacramentis* pertains to the Incarnation in the broad sense, for the whole "work of restoration is the Incarnation of the Word with all its sacraments, both those which have gone before from the beginning of time, and those which come after, even to the end of the world."[4] Nevertheless, this is the literary place and the salvation-history time for Hugh to address specific doctrinal questions, such as why it was fitting for the Son alone to become incarnate (chapters ii and iii). In chapter iv, Hugh uncharacteristically adds a battery of supportive patristic quotations, mostly from Augustine and Ambrose.[5] Passages from these "holy fathers" are introduced with literary humility relative to their great authority, but without being integrated into Hugh's argument. In fact, he did not even choose them individually but here took over a whole group of patristic quotations from an existing anthology (florilegium), albeit moving his beloved Augustine to the head of the list.[6] The end of this part 1 also quotes extensively from Augustine, without attribution, thus giving an early indication, confirmed by part 11 on marriage and by the final parts, that we here see Hugh's "working method" only partially completed; he gathered his sources but did not fully assimilate them into his own argument. In that sense, *De sacramentis* was unfinished.[7]

In any case, the narrative here just as abruptly switches back to Hugh's own exposition of the Incarnation: when the Word assumed human flesh, it cleansed the flesh of its original sin and yet took onto itself the punishment of that sin.[8] Opposing the early Greek heresy of Apollinaris (yet not by name), in that the Word assumed both "rational soul" and flesh, Hugh gives Western expression to the Greek patristic theme otherwise developed into *theosis*, or deification, namely, the reciprocal exchange of divinity and humanity. "From divinity itself humanity received through grace all that divinity had through nature."[9] While Hugh's text pursues several aspects of the Incarnation, such as Christ's growth in wisdom or merit in his (true) suffering (vi–vii), the theosis theme persists: "God took on humanity, man received divinity."[10]

The inner order of topics within this section is the credal sequence of the Christ events: conceived of the Holy Spirit (viii); Christ's "Union of Word, soul, and flesh" meant that he truly suffered (ix), died (x), and descended into hell (xi); yet in his resurrection he unites all humanity with himself (xii) and, according to his divinity, is everywhere, even as his ascended humanity is in heaven (xiii). Within the macro-chronological outline of salvation history as a whole, this part on Christology in particular is also historical, based on the specific sequential events of Christ's Incarnation, passion, and so on. Here, too, Hugh incorporates other material, his own and St. Augustine's. Chapter viii ("conceived of the Holy Spirit") is lifted whole from Hugh's letter-essay "On the Virginity of Mary."[11] The final chapter of this part (xiii: "That Christ according to Humanity Is Now in Heaven, according to Divinity Is Everywhere") is made up of verbatim excerpts from Augustine's letter to Dardenus.[12] The wealth of Christological tradition and Hugh's creative expression are passed over too quickly in my severe compression of his outline, but we thereby cut through the detail to his culminating concern for restoration, specifically, in the union of all humanity to the divine Word. The title to chapter xii can represent Hugh's Latin take on the theosis theme, his soteriology of the Incarnation. "That through the man united with the Word all who are His members are united with God."[13] Here Hugh juxtaposes language of mediation and union. "On this account then the Son of God was made man, so that between man and

God He might be a mediator of reconciliation and of peace."[14] And more than mediating between the diverse and even adverse (God and humanity), the Word in himself fully unites "us" and the Father:

> The Word and the Father were one in unity, since they were one in nature, and the Word himself wished to become one with us to make us one in Himself and through Himself and with Him [the Father] with whom He himself was one.[15]

Thus, the incarnational union of divine and human leads directly to the broader union of humanity with the incarnate Christ in the church, specifically in its sacramental life, as laid out in the rest of the second book. (My digest here leaves out many interesting aspects of Hugh's incarnational theology, including Jesus' compassion for others in a short work "On the Four Wills in Christ" and the cryptic reference to another work, "On the Soul of Christ," which the Deferrari translation attributes to Hugh instead of Augustine.[16])

Part Two: On the Unity of the Church

Part 2 of the second book thus moves smoothly from Christ as head to His body: "One head, many members."[17] The church is defined accordingly.

> Holy Church is the body of Christ vivified by one Spirit, united by one faith and sanctified. All of the faithful exist individually as members of the body, all one body on account of one spirit and one faith.[18]

As with a human body, these members vary most fundamentally in being on one side of the body or the other. "Now this aggregate [of Christians] embraces two orders, the laity and clerics, as it were, two sides of one body. For, as it were, on the left are laity who attend to the necessity of the present life."[19] Here "left" and "right" are not the condemnation and salvation of Matthew 25, but rather the good and better sides of the one body.

> Therefore, lay Christians who treat earthly things and the necessities of the earthly are the left part of the body of Christ. The clerics, indeed, since they dispense those things which pertain to the spiritual life are as it were, the right part of the body of Christ. But the whole body of Christ which is the universal Church consists of these two parts.[20]

After a bit of Greek etymology for *lay* and *cleric*, Hugh shifts the imagery from sides of the body to the (lower) body and the (higher) soul. Thus the earthly power stemming from the king has its own domain but must defer to the higher spiritual power of the "highest pontifex." Against the backdrop of the struggles over investiture attending the Gregorian reforms, this point is made with irenic brevity.

> Now the more worthy the spiritual life is than the earthly and the spirit than the body, so much does the spiritual power precede the earthly or the secular in honor and dignity.[21]

Hugh does not press the issue that "sacerdotal dignity still consecrates regal power,"[22] but it would loom large in later papal arguments.

Mentioning the "spiritual power" (orders, sacraments, precepts) but deferring it until part 3,[23] the Victorine closes this part with brief mention of earthly power, including how the church has earthly possessions and how the secular power distributes earthly justice.[24] This secular power, from king or emperor through dukes and counts and other magistrates, has its own "ornaments of dignity" such as rings and scepters and swords, but they are only mentioned in passing, with no hint of larger controversies.[25]

Part Three: On the Spiritual Power
(Ecclesiastical Orders)

As befits his overall subject, Hugh's text is more detailed and his borrowings more extensive regarding the "spiritual power" (part 3), namely, the ecclesiastical orders of clerics who administer the sacraments. "Spiritual power in the cleric is arranged with different grades and orders of dignity."[26] Like monks, all clerics share the same sign, the tonsure that crowns their head; "the baring of the head signifies the illumination of the mind."[27] After the tonsure that is applied to all clerics, "then follow seven promotions in grades, by which through spiritual power he ascends ever higher to carry on sacred things."[28] Hugh names these grades here, and then, quoting freely from Isidore of Seville and the more recent work of Ivo of Chartres, gives each one a subsequent chapter: porters, readers, exorcists, acolytes, subdeacons, deacons, and priests. The last grade is itself subdivided into priests, bishops, archbishops, primates and patriarchs, and the highest pontifex, the pope, "Father of fathers."

> This last is the principal and greatest successor of the apostolic see in the Roman Church, wherefore the Holy Church is accustomed to call him

especially "apostolic," to whom, presiding in the place of Peter, chief of
the Apostles, every ecclesiastical order should give obedience, who by
privilege of dignity has the keys of binding and loosening everything
upon earth.[29]

As he goes through each order, Hugh deftly combines extensive quotations
from Isidore's *De officiis ecclesiasticis* and Ivo's *De excellentia ordinum* and
Panormia. Via Hugh, this material from Ivo, a fellow canon who was bishop
of Chartres just before Hugh's arrival in Paris, passed on to Lombard's
Sentences and thus to extensive influence.[30] For each order, chapter by chapter, Hugh's composite text summarizes the office biblically, mentions what
objects are given at ordination and what is expected of the recipient, and
links the office to Christ's earthly activity. The porters or doorkeepers, to
take the first example, receive the keys and guard the doors, as Christ "the
door" cleansed the temple.[31] Readers receive a book of scripture readings
and the charge to read effectively, as Christ read the lesson from Isaiah (vi).
Exorcists supervise catechumens and, upon receiving a book of exorcisms
from the bishop, are ready to cast out unclean spirits just as Christ did (vii).
Acolytes or candlebearers receive a candelabrum at ordination, as Christ is
the light of the world (viii). The subdeacons who prepare the altar receive
the towel and basin used in ritual cleansing, as Christ washed and dried
his disciples' feet (ix). The deacons, initially the spiritual number of seven,
instruct the congregation, proclaim the gospel, and dispense the sacraments
that have been consecrated by priests (x). The diaconal office is full of assist-
ing duties, as symbolized by the stole or yoke they receive, especially in
reading the Gospels they receive from the hand of the bishop. Their model,
too, is Christ, who spoke and dispensed.

Last or highest are both the priests and presbyters, the successors of the
seventy disciples, and also the bishops, who are the successors of the apostles. On the one hand, they are all priests who share a ministry of "catechiz-
ing or of baptizing or of celebrating mass and of consecrating the body and
blood of Christ or of speaking in the church"; on the other hand, to the bishops as priests of a higher order belong "the ordination of clerics, the dedication of basilicas, the consecration of sacred chrism, the imposition of the
hand [confirmation] and the common benediction over the people."[32] Thus
their ordinations are similar and yet distinct, both derived from Christ's
office at the last supper and on the cross. Bishops should be ordained by a
"metropolitan" (xii), shortly identified with the office of archbishop, who

is also approved by the pope (xiii). As for "the highest pontiff," a special election and ordination is assumed: "since the apostolic see is preferred to all churches in the world, and it cannot have a metropolitan above it, the cardinal bishops without doubt perform the duty of the Metropolitan who conduct an elected priest to the apex of the apostolic column."[33]

After this apex, Hugh briefly itemizes the special offices of archdeacons (xvi), head chamberlain (xvii), and treasurer (xviii). Ordinations occur only on certain days (xix), at certain minimal ages (xx), with definite titles (xxi), and according to certain criteria (xxii), as "the fathers" have passed down to us, and these ordinations are meant to apply to a stable ministry in one place, as "the sacred canons" indicate.[34] Hugh's brevity here regarding his sources means that the large tradition of "fathers and canons" receives only this passing acknowledgment, even though part 3 as a whole is almost entirely taken over from such sources.[35]

Part Four: On Sacred Garments

Continuing the pattern of taking over prior texts, especially from Ivo of Chartres, part 4 interprets the sacred garments of the priesthood, old and new, starting with Aaron and including some specific items restricted to the "higher" priests, such as archbishops. Outer garments reflect inner qualities, according to a long exegetical tradition here appropriated but not acknowledged. Hugh is quoting an abridged version of Ivo of Chartres's sermon "On the Meanings of Priestly Vestments."[36] Leviticus 8, for example, itemizes some vestments, and the "new priesthood" of the church has made some adjustments. The "tunic of byssus" is a white linen garment that "signifies the cleanness of the ministers of God."[37] The girdle or belt tight around the loins signifies continence and chastity (iii), as do the "linen thigh-bandages" (iv). The interior sky-colored tunic signifies an inner heavenly cleanness (v). "The proper order follows: First, in the linen tunic and girdle and thigh-bandages cleanness of flesh is expressed; then, through the inner or hyacinthine tunic cleanness of heart is signified."[38] The "superhumeral" (over the shoulders) "signifies fortitude in work and patience in labour,"[39] but here the text starts to reveal some (theological) differences between the old priesthood of Leviticus and the new priesthood of the Christian church. The old superhumeral had precious stones and the names of the twelve patriarchs inscribed, but "our priesthood does not have the superhumeral similarly interwoven like the old, in as much as the Christian religion should be zealous for simple truth rather than for superstition."[40] The "rational" or logion is placed on the breast of the pontiff or higher priest "to show that there should be wisdom and discretion in his heart,"[41] as the miter or tiara on his head shows that "the minister who guides his life well adorns his head as Christ."[42] Of the items from the old priesthood, one is superseded entirely, according to a forceful but uncredited theological tradition: "The new priesthood does not have the golden plate. Instead the sign of the cross is now imprinted on the foreheads of the faithful, since the blood of the Gospel is more precious than the gold of the law."[43] Here Ivo's text openly quotes Jerome, but Hugh mentions neither.[44]

Further, the stole indicates the yoke of the Lord (x), the *planata* or *casula* (chasuble) signifies charity (xi), the napkin or maniple allows diligent purging (xii), and the broad *dalmatica* "signifies care of neighbors."[45] Sandals are firm and whole below but open above, to prevent pollution from earthly things but to stay open to know (and to share) the heavenly things (xiv). The pontiff carries a staff to indicate justice, wears a ring to represent the Church as bride of Christ (xv), and in the case of archbishops, uses the pallium as necklace to signify the fear and discipline of the Lord (xvi). To conclude this part, Hugh switches from Ivo's text to his own compact preview of the symbolic meanings of the sacred furnishings and vessels in a church, equally traditional in that the ideas come from the ninth-century Amalar of Metz. "The altar signifies the cross, the chalice the sepulchre, the dish [paten] the stone, the corporeal palla the muslin [cloth] with which the body of Christ was wrapped."[46]

Part Five: On the Dedication of a Church

With part 5, Hugh moves to sacraments more specifically, meaning rituals, starting with "the sacrament of the dedication of a church in which all other sacraments are celebrated."[47] Here he makes heavy use of Ivo of Chartres's fourth sermon, "On the Sacrament of the Dedication" of a church.[48] The church itself is baptized, so to speak, to symbolize baptismal regeneration unto salvation. "For what is expressed visibly in a figure in this house [of prayer] is exhibited entirely through invisible truth in the faithful soul."[49] Hugh emphasizes more than Ivo did how the biblical parallels of a building with the faithful pertain to particular features of a church's dedication.

Using Ivo's text, he first describes in considerable detail the various gestures, objects, and formulas used in the bishop's dedication of such a building to divine worship (ii), and then he supplies the symbolic meanings of these mysteries (iii). First, he provides the "letter" and the events and then the sense or symbolic interpretation. Basically, "a house to be dedicated is a soul to be sanctified."[50] Water is cleansing penance, salt is the divine word that chides and flavors, the twelve lamps are the apostles, and the pontiff (bishop), by his various gestures and movements, symbolizes Christ. Not just the building but also the furnishings to be used in other sacraments are all ritually dedicated, and interpreted, as seen long before Ivo in Amalar of Metz and many others.

> The altar is wiped with linen. The altar is Christ upon whom we offer to the Father the gift of our devotion. The linen is his flesh, brought by the beatings of the passion to the whiteness of incorruption, the incense the prayers of the saints. Now the oil demonstrates the grace of the Holy Spirit whose fullness preceded on the head; then participation flowed to the limbs.[51]

Since a church's dedication has already been likened to a baptism, Hugh has previewed the next part, on the "first" sacrament.

Part Six: On the Sacrament of Baptism

Part 6 continues the gradual specification of the concept and terminology of sacraments, now approaching the usage that became standard shortly after Hugh. "The sacrament of baptism is the first among all the sacraments upon which salvation is proven to rest."[52] The linkage to salvation itself is here supported biblically and later echoed in the introduction to the sacrament of the body and blood of Christ.[53] That salvation "depends on" (*constare*) a sacrament is said only of these two, in *De sacramentis*.

As he often does when beginning a major presentation or part, Hugh pedagogically previews the basic questions. What is baptism? Why and when was it established, especially relative to circumcision? What is the difference between the baptism of John and that of Christ? Is it absolutely necessary? This last question seems to interest Hugh in particular, but he also goes on to consider novices, catechumens, exorcism, godparents, and rebaptism.

Hugh's definition of *baptism* again invokes the Augustinian language of what makes a sacrament, but again without attribution.

> Baptism is the water sanctified by the word of God for washing away sins. For water alone can be an element; there cannot be a sacrament until word is added to the element and there be a sacrament.[54]

In this case, "the word" is explicitly the triune name of Matthew 28, not in rote repetition of the three names but in full faith in the one God who is Father, Son, and Holy Spirit, as Ambrose also taught.[55]

Relative to circumcision, baptism was instituted to be a clearer sign of overall purification.[56] Exactly when baptism was instituted and became obligatory involves the transitional time of John the Baptist, Christ's passion and precept to go and baptize, and the (brief) time needed for that precept to be spread "to all nations."[57] John's baptism may have had the same form, but the baptism Christ commands contains the power of the forgiveness of sins.[58]

After its full dominical institution, is baptism absolutely necessary for salvation? Hugh concedes that biblical tradition may seem clear on this necessity, especially John 3, but here as elsewhere, he seems concerned to distinguish, in principle, an inner faith that is in fact necessary from the outward action that is normal but not absolutely necessary. The classic example of exceptional circumstances concerns the martyrs who were baptized in blood before a water baptism was possible, not because blood literally contains water, but because of their faith and intention.[59] Similarly, apart from martyrdom, "to be baptized can be in the will, even when it is not in possibility," as Augustine also taught.[60] Hugh, again using Bernard of Clairvaux's letter, argues the point rather vigorously, against anonymous opponents probably including Abelard. "True faith and confession of the heart can fulfill the place of baptism in the moment of necessity. . . . If there were anyone who had these even without the visible sacrament of water he could not perish."[61]

Before taking up the specific sequence of items in the rite of baptism, Hugh pauses at the terminology of "the sacraments of the neophytes" or novices to incorporate the gist of Ivo of Chartres's sermon, *De sacramentis neophytorum.*[62] Specifically, Ivo and Hugh want those who are new in the faith to know that the faith is not new, but old, indeed, from the beginning, as are sacraments of the faith. Ivo and Hugh review the six eras or ages of restoration with their anticipatory "sacraments": Noah's ark, Abraham's ram, the Exodus, Jerusalem, the Babylonian captivity, and then Christ's climactic coming.[63] This sixth and last age of human history is likened to the sixth day of creation. Virtually quoting Ivo: "Finally in the sixth age, Christ was born of a virgin, just as on the sixth day the first man was moulded from virgin land."[64] Concluding this mini-excursus, Hugh's own summary of these six ages, with Christ's passion and commission, prompted the phrase in the work's overall title: "These are the sacraments of the Christian faith, founded from the beginning, to be believed [in faith], to be of benefit without end."[65]

Since Jesus said "teach and baptize" in that order, catechetical instruction is first, even if after mass conversions "Mother Church" had the providential dispensation to apply this order to children of the faithful who might otherwise die without "the sacrament of salvation."[66] Thus here, too, even for infants, the order is to catechize (hear), exorcise, and baptize for them "until they come to the years of understanding."[67] Baptismal exorcism is briefly itemized and lightly explained: the sign of the cross on the forehead and sense organs, salt, breath, and the opening of ears and nostrils.[68] The renunciation of Satan is made for the child, oil is applied, and the triune faith confessed. Thereafter, the threefold immersion reflects the name of the Trinity, the three-day death of Christ, and "the threefold cleansing of thought, speech, and operation."[69] The chrism, the white garment and head veil, and a lighted candle follow, although Hugh is extremely brief about all these ritual details.[70]

Saying the renunciations and confessions of faith, indeed, literally and symbolically holding the children up for baptism, are the "godparents," themselves baptized but not monastics; they are the "surety" or guarantees before God that these children will grow up to learn and keep the Creed and the Lord's Prayer, as in the traditional (patristic) texts collected by Ivo of Chartres.[71] The issue of rebaptism is solved by scripture ("one baptism") and tradition, since even those of old who had been baptized by heretical Arians were not rebaptized but rather received back by chrism in the East or the laying on of hands in the West, again using Ivo's collection of texts as a source.[72] Yet, correct form is not enough by itself without the right intention, according to Hugh's own emphasis. Just as there is no playacting or accidental consecration of bread and wine, so there is no unintentional baptism, for example, a triune invocation at the baths.[73] As the counterpart to his earlier distinction of inner intention and outward form (that baptism was not always necessary), here the distinction means that the outward form alone is not even the sacrament without the intention. "Behold, therefore, and consider that the work of the ministries of God should be rational and one should not forejudge on account of form alone where there is not intention of acting."[74]

Part Seven: On Confirmation

Having mentioned the ancient practice of anointing or the unction of chrism, along with the laying on of hands, instead of rebaptism, Hugh logically proceeds from baptism to confirmation as part 7. As Isidore of Seville had taught long before, the biblical practice of anointing or "christening" was expanded from Old Testament kings and priests to all who share the name of Christ; that is, all Christians receive the chrism of oil (infusion of grace) and balsam (the fragrance of good repute).[75] More specifically, "confirmation" is the imposition of hands, whereby the bishop signs the forehead with the unction of chrism. The two go together, baptism and this laying on of hands; "in the one case grace is attributed unto the remission of sins, in the other grace is given unto confirmation" or strengthening.[76] Even if an anointing might be done by a priest in case of emergencies, citing Pope Sylvester but by way of Amalar, the (unrepeatable) signing of the forehead is reserved for the bishop, at times of fasting, and should remain on the forehead unwashed for the Holy Spirit's seven days, as in the unacknowledged Amalar of Metz.[77]

Part Eight: On the Sacrament of the Body and Blood of Christ

Part 8 is not as long as the section on baptism (or the even longer part on marriage yet to come), but it is paired with the prior sacrament of initiation as "one of those upon which salvation principally depends."[78] The explicit language about salvation depending on certain sacraments back in book 1 is only applied to baptism and to this sacrament, which is furthermore unique because "from it is all sanctification."[79] Hugh gives a basic narrative definition and then addresses certain aspects of the subject:

> Our Lord Jesus Christ Himself instituted the sacrament of His body and blood when after the supper of the old pasch, changing the bread and wine into His own body and blood by divine power, He gave it to His apostles to be eaten and He ordered that after this they should do the same in commemoration of Him.[80]

The wording in this definition suggests several aspects worth pursuing, such as the nature of the "changing" (*transmutans*), but Hugh's narrative is driven by questions in his own time and by use of his own prior texts.

First, he poses a contemporary question, "whether at the supper Christ gave to his disciples his mortal or immortal body," and much prefers reverent modesty to an overconfident answer.[81] Nevertheless, if an answer must be made, Hugh argues biblically that Christ, while choosing mortality, could at the same time give his immortal body to the disciples, but not to Judas.[82] The paschal lamb was a prefiguring, but now the thing or substance (res) is itself received. Here Hugh again, as with baptism, distinguishes the sacrament (eating and drinking) from its substance (incorporation into Christ "through faith and love"). The latter is what counts.

> He who takes [receives] has the sacrament, he who believes and loves has the substance of the sacrament. Therefore, it is better for him who believes and loves, even if he cannot take and eat, than for him who takes and eats but does not believe nor love or if he believes but does not love.[83]

Immediately after this sharp distinction of the sacrament and its substance, Hugh appends an argument against those who might conclude from some biblical texts that the sacrament is "only" an image or figure, a likeness rather than the truth. "What then! Is the sacrament of the altar then not truth because it is a figure? Then neither is the death of Christ truth because it is a figure."[84] As, biblically, Christ's death and resurrection are both figures or images and truth at the same time, so, too, "why can the sacrament of the altar not be a likeness and truth? In one respect, indeed, a likeness; in another, truth."[85] Here, as elsewhere, Hugh reuses some material from an earlier work, in this case, his commentary on *The Celestial Hierarchy*, where Dionysius called this sacrament a figure.[86] Hugh draws careful distinctions between three sacramental components: "visible appearance [bread and wine], the truth of the body [of Christ], and virtue of spiritual grace."[87] In light of an old Carolingian debate, this allows him a middle way between extremes: on the one hand, the sacrament is not "only" a figure, because it is also truth; on the other hand, it is not mechanically or automatically participation or incorporation in Christ, because this "substance" of the sacrament (in faith and love) is distinct from receiving the bread and wine, as he has just argued and here repeats in summary of the whole *via media*.

> So the most divine Eucharist, which is treated visibly and corporally on the Altar, according to the appearance of bread and wine and according

to the truth of the body and blood of Christ, is a sacrament and a sign and an image of the invisible and spiritual participation with Jesus, which is being accomplished within the heart through faith and love.[88]

The integration of materials from the earlier Dionysian commentary then ends with further reflection on the physical and symbolic aspects of food and a glimpse at the Greek terminology, with a hint of theosis or deification:

> The Eucharist, that is good grace, is itself, of course, called the most divine and holy victim, since it makes divine and participants in divinity those people who partake of it in a worthy manner.[89]

At this point in part 8, literary linkages abound, not only to prior materials but also to later development in sacramental theology. The very next section discusses the change of the elements into the body and blood of Christ in terms that anticipate the full scholastic categories.

> Through the works of sanctification the true substance of bread and the true substance of wine are changed into the true body and blood of Christ, the appearance of bread and wine alone remaining, substance passing over (*transeunte*) into substance.[90]

This section repeats the language of "substance" so often, as distinct from "appearance," along with the language of "trans-" (*transeunte, transitionem, transitione*) and change (*convertitur* and *mutatam*), that the formulation of "transubstantiation" seems a natural outcome.

Referring next to the ritual action itself, Hugh gives the "mystic signi-fication" of the three portions of the body of Christ: Christ himself as the head, those united to him already beyond this life, and those still in this life of suffering and thus symbolically placed in the chalice.[91] Here Hugh also reflects a long tradition of sacramental allegory, famously represented on this very point by Amalar of Metz.[92] He hastens to head off any unseemly conclusions, as if the appearance of dividing the bread means that the body of Christ has really been "torn limb from limb," or then "gnawed to pieces," or some other apparently unworthy outcome.[93]

Specifically, "perhaps your thoughts again ask you what happens to the body of Christ after it has been taken and eaten."[94] Although Hugh implies that the question is impertinent, he nevertheless gives a careful answer, drawing a parallel between the Incarnation and sacrament. As Christ was corporally present for a time on earth yet thereafter in heaven at the right hand of the Father, to raise our attentions to his abiding spiritual presence, so also "in His sacrament now He comes temporarily to you and He is by means of it corporeally with you, that you through his corporeal presence may be raised to seek the spiritual and be assisted in finding it."[95] The corporeal presence in the sacrament applies as long as it is perceived (seen, touched, tasted) for the purpose of the spiritual result but not afterwards, as in idle speculation about digestion and so on.

> As long as the sense is affected corporeally, His corporeal presence is not taken away. But after the corporeal feeling in receiving fails, then the corporeal presence is not to be sought but the spiritual is to be retained; the dispensation is completed, the perfect sacrament remains as a virtue; Christ passes from mouth to heart.[96]

That Christ passes from mouth to heart and not to the stomach is reinforced by Augustine, namely, that sacramental eating does not change Christ into the believer in the way of ordinary food, but rather it changes the believer into Christ.[97] Otherwise, seek the corporeal presence of Christ in heaven.

Last, Hugh quotes yet another prior text, again without attribution, on the development of the "mass" from dominical institution through apostolic and patristic expansions; the naming of "missa" comes from both the trans*mission* or mediation of Christ and the priest and also the dis*missal* (but of the catechumens before the consecration of the bread and wine, not of everyone at the end of the service).[98]

Part Nine: On the (Minor) Sacraments and Sacred Things

With the next section, part 9, Hugh explicitly moves from the sacraments on which salvation depends to those sacraments and other sacred things that aid devotion, that is, objects like ashes and candles, gestures like the sign of the cross, and even special words like "Alleluia." All such items are sanctified by the word of God and done in the name of the Lord, that is, in faith.[99] Some of what Hugh inclusively calls "sacraments," here and elsewhere, will shortly be labeled "sacramentals," as when Peter Lombard, among others, specified the language of sacraments still further, indeed after studying at St. Victor.

The sprinkling of salted water signifies penitence and discretion, as credited to Pope Alexander, "fifth Pope after blessed Peter."[100] Ashes are received at the beginning of Lent as a recollection of mortality and a goad to devotion, remembering the original creation/foundation from Christ.[101] Palms and branches on the Sunday before Easter represent Christ's victory and our good works.[102] Pope Zozimus is credited, and Amalar of Metz used, regarding the Paschal candle of Holy Saturday as the catechumens are led to the waters by a new "pillar" representing Christ's humanity (wax) and divinity (fire).[103] Old Testament trumpets prefigured the church's bells, here borrowing from Amalar quite directly, and the biblical veils in the temple are represented now by curtains in the church.[104] Hugh says he cannot cover "the many other sacraments of the Church expressed by objects or deeds," but he pauses to comment briefly on the breath of exorcism, the sign of the cross, and kneeling.[105]

Moving from gestures to "sacraments set forth by the utterance of words only," the next chapter is largely a list of the texts of the Mass along with their biblical and some papal sources.[106] Weisweiler considers this material to stem especially from Amalar, along with Remigius of Auxerre.[107] The introit (antiphons from the Psalms) was established by Pope Celestine, the Collects come chiefly from Gelasius and Gregory, the angelic "Gloria" (Luke 2) was expanded by Hilary of Poitiers, the Fathers of the Council of Constantinople established that Creed, Pope Sixtus fixed the use of the Sanctus, Gelasius the *Te igitur*, and so on through popes Gregory, Leo, Felix, and Innocent.[108] Hugh adds a paragraph on texts used more generally: the *Gloria patri* comes from the Nicene bishops as translated and expanded by Jerome for Pope Damasus, the twelve Apostles dictated the twelve parts of the Apostles' Creed, and Athanasius contributed the *Quicumque vult* (Athanasian Creed).[109] Hugh never fully explains why these texts can also be called sacraments, but he rather thoroughly itemizes the traditional authority for many of them.

Last in this miscellany are "other sacred things in the Church, but not sacraments," in that they do not themselves effect grace or confer sanctification.[110] In theory, this includes anything that adorns a church, but Hugh is here more concerned with the tithes and possessions of the church in general, including money and property. These, too, belong to the church and cannot be taken away without sacrilege.[111] This turn of the subject to finances anticipates the next part.

Part Ten: On Simony

Part 10 is brief and oblique, especially in light of the Gregorian reform movement. "Simony is the desire to procure spiritual grace by money," specifically sacred orders.[112] Those who buy or sell ordination have indeed sinned, yet the ordinations performed by a "Simoniacus" are still valid when received innocently; here Hugh parallels Augustine's arguments about the Donatists, albeit without attribution: "a heretic or any other evil minister is evil, and yet is a minister, evil in that he has error or malice, a minister in that he has office."[113] At this point, the argument veers off from simony regarding orders to other fiscal abuses, such as the illicit selling of church property as already previewed.[114]

Part Eleven: On the Sacrament of Marriage

Part 11 of book 2, on marriage, is remarkably long, much longer than the treatments of baptism and the eucharist combined and matched in size only by the section on the Incarnation. It covers certain aspects in detail and quotes several prior texts at length without attribution.[115] Reflecting contemporary questions, it considers clandestine marriage (in secret) and the degrees of consanguinity as treated by popes and councils, that is, by canon law.[116] This special attention to marriage was previewed in book 1, when the general definition of sacraments regarding restoration after the fall needed to account for the exception of marriage before the fall.[117] There, Hugh integrated Augustinian arguments without attribution; here, he repeats them and adds others with copious quotations from Augustine's *On the Good of Marriage*, yet by way of unacknowledged use of tracts on marriage by the school of Anselm of Laon and William of Champeaux, according to Weisweiler.

In summary, God's institution of marriage is twofold:

> One before sin for office, the other after sin for remedy; the first, that nature might be multiplied; the second, that nature might be supported and vice checked.[118]

The former finds its biblical parallel in the union of Christ and the church yet with no further amplification from Hugh; the latter involves the ambiguous details of human sin, which the rest of part 11 explores at length and with frequent insertion of other texts.

By definition, adding "legitimate" to (Isidore's) traditional wording, "marriage is legitimate consent, that is, between legitimate persons and legitimately made on the part of male and female, to observe an individual association in life,"[119] even if some unknown hindrance such as consanguinity later comes to light. The marriage begins upon this consent, not upon the prior promise (engagement) to consent or upon the subsequent joining of the flesh.[120] It begins upon this consent even if done in secret, although this exceptional circumstance is fraught with perils, as a hypothetical case illustrates at length.[121] Hugh's detail here even includes a full and fervent prayer for use by anyone caught in the dilemma of choosing the lesser of sins.

After the definition of marriage, including its parameters of validity, Hugh considers the three blessings (or goods) of marriage, citing Augustine along the way, but in fact by way of his intermediate texts: faith (faithful exclusivity of relations), hope (of children), and the sacramental blessing on the permanence of the bond, with or without faithfulness or children. These three goods mitigate the lust that clings to this life, "so that carnal concupiscence becomes at least conjugal chastity."[122] The blessing or good of hope for children is twice worded in the same compact and elegant way: that such children be "expected devoutly, received lovingly, nourished religiously."[123] These blessings or goods are separable from marriage itself, for it endures despite infidelity or childlessness; even among unbelievers, as Augustine traditionally says and as treated more fully shortly, there can be the sacrament of marriage but not its sanctity or virtue, which is reserved for the Church.[124] Augustine is also cited, again by way of the unacknowledged intermediaries, on lust within marriage, which is likened to overeating, and on (excusing) Abrahamic polygamy.[125]

Just because a marriage could be dissolved in exceptional extremity does not mean that it was not a real marriage, any more than false reception of baptism or of the body of Christ would mean that those sacraments were not true and efficacious in themselves.[126] Yet those who abandon their religious vows of celibacy to enter into vows of conjugal union should not be considered legitimately married, even if Augustine appears to endorse this concession biblically.[127] Here Hugh genuinely wrestles with Augustinian authority and yet, invoking the change of historical context and for the sake of avoiding a chaos of vows, differs with the Bishop of Hippo, since "now times are different and something different is fitting or necessary for human salvation."[128] With similar Augustinian argumentation, Hugh wades through the convoluted cases of unbelievers, those who marry each other or believers, those who come in or out of the faith, or in or out of marital vows.[129]

The longest section in this long part on marriage is lifted from Ivo of Chartres's *Panormia*, concerning consanguinity (blood relations), along with affinity (in-law relations, by marriage) and spiritual kinship (baptismal godparent-godchild). It spells out the details of the degrees of consanguinity wherein marriage is prohibited and appends the testimonies of several popes and other various authorities, exactly as Ivo did.[130] Similarly, the definitions of affinity and spiritual kinship (whereby marriage is prohibited to in-laws, godparents, and godchildren) are also set out with authoritative citations, as in Ivo's *Panormia* and also preserved afterward in the Gratian Decretum.[131] Finally, as if to underline the earlier emphasis on marriage as conscious consent, a ceremony marred by fraud, such as the substitution of one person for another, is not a valid marriage because it lacks consent or intention.[132]

Part Twelve: On Vows

Hugh's next part, on vows, offers his typically thorough treatment. Yet, atypically, there is no discussion here, or earlier, of any sacramental dimension to vows.[133] Hugh opens with unusual personal levity in admitting that he has not yet paid his own vow in giving his reader-students what he had promised, as mentioned earlier regarding glimpses of original lectures.[134]

Beyond a generic promise, a proper vow is an obligation before God and thus a debt to be paid.[135] The vows of fools, perverse or illicit or indiscreet, are not to be kept.[136] Of good and proper vows before God, anything involving one's soul or life cannot be changed by way of substitutions, for nothing can compensate for them.[137] "All other vows admit change according to place and time and cause," such as forms of money or place of work, except that if a vowed virginity cannot be paid, only penitent humility can substitute for it.[138]

Part Thirteen: On Vices and Virtues

As with part 12 on vows, part 13 on the vices and virtues leading to love for neighbor and especially for God also makes no mention of sacraments or the sacramental-incarnational works of restoration that mark book 2 as a whole. There is no explicit linkage or transition or overarching rationale in the order of these several parts from simony (10) to marriage (11) to vows (12) to vices and virtues (13) to the next part on confession (14). They cohere, regarding the Christian life in the age of grace between the Incarnation and the end, but they could be in almost any order as self-contained presentations (some of them taken from previous contexts).

The vices (inclinations or weaknesses toward specific sinful acts) are traditionally seven principal vices, called "capital" as the heads or sources of others.[139] In the orderly hands of Hugh the teacher, and lifted from his little letter on septets, they have a logical sequence:

> Pride takes God from man; envy takes his neighbour; anger takes himself; despair scourges him when [thus] despoiled; covetousness ejects him when scourged; gluttony seduces him when ejected; lust subjects him to slavery when seduced.[140]

Thumbnail definitions follow, along with the routine distinction of venial and mortal sins.

The virtues (healthy capacities and inclinations toward acts of justice) are likewise seven: humility, clemency, remorse, desire for justice, mercy, cleanness of heart, peace of mind.[141] Yet what Hugh develops for the rest of part 13 is not this septet but rather the "two movements of the heart by which the rational soul is impelled to do everything which it does. One is fear; the other, love."[142] Fear (yielding to a superior) can be evil (a servile fear and mundane fear) or good (initial fear and filial fear) once it is combined with love (charity).[143]

"Charity" dominates the rest of part 13, by far the bulk of the section that is ostensibly on all vices and virtues. In biblical (and Augustinian) terms, charity is twofold: love of God (for God's own sake because God is our good) and love for the neighbor (on account of God, since with the neighbor we seek God and God's goodness and justice and truth).[144] A third precept (love thyself) would be superfluous, since sin leads to the wrong (excess) love of the body and to love one's soul is to love its good, which is God.[145]

Echoing Bernard of Clairvaux and opposing some anonymous "wise men," Hugh labels as "mercenary" any love for God for the sake of a reward except that God Himself is desired and sought, "not anything from Him but Himself, that is, freely."[146]

How much to love God and neighbor? Loving God "with thy whole heart and mind and soul" (Matthew 22) means "as much as you are able," and this effort will lead to yet higher loving, as Hugh turns hortatory, perhaps homiletical: "that is, with your whole intellect and your whole affection and your whole memory."[147] "To love thy neighbor as thyself" (also Matthew 22) is fulfilled when "that good which we desire for ourselves we also desire truly for him" with no need to quantify love for multiple neighbors.[148] To summarize the two precepts of charity:

> First, concerning love of God in whom man truly loves himself; second, concerning love of neighbor in whom he loves his neighbour as himself.[149]

Once possessed, charity, say some, can never be lost, citing 1 Corinthians 13. Hugh mounts a vigorous polemic against such a view, since St. Paul only meant that in the next life we will no longer need earthly faith and hope, but we will always have love.[150] With further exegetical polemics and invocations of Augustine, Hugh seems concerned to counter the (mis)understanding of the "perseverance of the saints," as if it meant that no one ever lost a saving love for God once it was truly possessed.[151] Apparently some wanted to define *charity* as the kind of love for God that perseveres to the end, whereas for Hugh *love* and *charity* mean the same thing, and it can be lost.[152] With King David and Simon Peter as disputed case studies, this biblical polemic against unnamed opponents is lively and extensive, especially on the relationship between perseverance and true charity or love for God.[153]

Part Fourteen: On Confession

Part 14, "On Confession and Penance and the Remission of Sins," begins a sequence of topics that unfolds through the rest of book 2 and thus to the end of *De sacramentis*. Confession leads to anointing (the brief part 15), followed by death (part 16) and the afterlife (parts 17 and 18), although the contents of these last parts are largely quotations from Augustine.

The abrupt opening and drawn-out conclusion of part 14 both suggest a lively polemic with unnamed opponents, perhaps in a prior essay. "Great is the malice of man," begins Hugh, with an immediate frontal assault on those who claim that there is no command from the Lord to confess one's sins to another, as if silent tearful confession to God were enough.[154] On the one hand, Hugh concedes that Christ never ordered confession, but for a reason: "Christ wished that your confession should rise from yourself that it might not seem as if extorted or forced."[155] On the other hand, James said, "Confess your sins to another: pray one for another, that you may be saved."[156] So that "the humility of confession may aid the tears of contrition," the right order is "first there should be weeping, afterwards confessing."[157]

Inner penance leads to outer correction or satisfaction, the fruit of penance, although it would be hard to know how much is enough ("It is better that you do more than less") without the exterior measurement.[158] If the measure is mistaken or the earthly life too short, there is still hope. "For even after death there is a certain fire called purgatorial, where they are purged and cleansed who began to correct themselves in the world but did not complete the task."[159] The brief reference to purgatorial fire, filled out in later parts, emphasizes not punishment but a cleansing unto salvation, citing 1 Corinthians 3: "Indeed you will burn until the combustible material which you carry shall have been consumed. But you will be saved, since there has remained in you the foundation of God's charity."[160]

Both the Epistle to the Hebrews (6 and 10) and St. Jerome seem to say that to repeat penance is impossible for those who have fallen again, but according to Hugh, "it is impossible for them, but not for God," who wishes to aid by grace unto repentance.[161] As to a deathbed repentance, if genuine: "better late than never," although risky and without time for satisfaction.[162] It all comes down to a good will; "the entire merit is in the will," which naturally results in good work.[163] It is the good will that counts, even if the resources of time or money (Zacchaeus and the widow with two mites) be unequal. "There are two things: the will and the work of the will. God weighs the will; man judges the work."[164]

Returning at some length to oppose those who believe that inner confession to God is enough, Hugh shows that his emphasis on the will or intention by no means excludes the ministry of the priests. God's forgiveness comes normally (and biblically) by means of human mediation, indeed fittingly so, since the proud sinner needs to yield humbly to a mediator.[165] Finally, at curious length, Hugh addresses those who think that once a sin is forgiven, it cannot return, as if a second homicide would not be condemned because the first was forgiven. But "when blame returned, punishment also returned."[166]

Part Fifteen: On the Anointing of the Sick

The brief part 15 distinguishes this oil from the "oil of the principal chrism," meaning the ointment of oil and balsam used in baptisms and confirmations and for kings and bishops.[167] "The sacrament of the anointing of the sick" stems from James 5, for healing of body and alleviation of the soul.[168] Unlike the baptismal anointing (or confirmation or ordination), this sacrament, like prayer itself, can and should be repeated as there is need. As with the sacrament of the body of Christ, "so he who has received the sacrament of unction, if it should be necessary and cause or devotion demand, is not forbidden rationally from receiving it again."[169] Although no mention is made of a final or extreme unction before death, Hugh's sequence of parts leads next to the dying and the afterlife.

Part Sixteen: On the Dying

"On the Dying or on the Goal/End [*finis*] of Humanity" is the PL title of part 16, in anticipated parallel to part 17, "On the Goal/End of This World" (*De Fine Saeculi*). From the end of 16 through most of 17 and 18, the large blocks of quotations from Gregory the Great and especially Augustine suggest that Hugh did not complete his own writing on the subject, as confirmed by the absence of this material in the summary of *De sacramentis* by Odo of Lucca just before Hugh died.[170]

  "Blessed are those who die in the Lord," meaning in faith and hope and charity even if small.[171] Where or how the soul departs from the body is not for us to know fully. "This one thing we know, that when the soul recedes the body dies and the very separation of the soul is the death of the body."[172] Visions or even purported experiences of the soul in the next life without the body may still be narrated in corporeal or bodily terms, simply because such narration now depends on our corporeal state.[173] How can bodiless souls be corporeally punished by scriptural fire? Hugh flatly admits that he does not know how, but he believes it nevertheless, because "Sacred Scripture, the teacher of our faith, tells us this."[174] Similarly, scripture assigns corporeal places for corporeal punishments, with the place of torments "down" and heaven called "up," "since blame also presses downward and justice raises upward."[175] Hugh remains tentative about any actual locations, such as under the earth, including purgatory, where the flawed just are temporarily purged.[176] The specific torments of hell may be more than fire, such as the scriptural worm "of conscience," but how such corporeal factors could possibly affect bodiless souls remains a mystery, as Augustine said regarding the "hidden abodes" of the afterlife. "How incorporeal spirits or souls freed from bodies can be tormented by fire, the authority not only of Christian faith but of Holy Scripture does not explain."[177]

Upon mention of Augustine and his *Enchiridion* regarding fire and punishment, this part begins to assemble extensive quotations from the bishop of Hippo, especially *The City of God*, and from Gregory the Great on the same theme (with minimal editorial indications in PL or Deferrari). These texts reinforce the points about punishments for the wicked and other issues of the afterlife. For example, Augustine's *Enchiridion*, referenced earlier regarding the afterlife's hidden abodes, is now quoted directly from that same section regarding prayers for the dead, which are of value only for those whose lives merit such help.[178] Similarly, the interesting passage citing Vergil and confessing the difficulty of the whole subject is entirely a quotation from *The City of God*,[179] just as Gregory the Great is also quoted directly on the effects of prayers and sacrifices for the dead.[180] Finally, whether the departed souls hear our specific prayers is also more than we can know or need to know. "For how can we who can neither grasp nor investigate that knowledge which they have about us be certain in our knowledge about them?"[181]

Part Seventeen: On the End of the World

Part 17 is comprised almost entirely of quotations from Augustine, heavily but not exclusively from *The City of God*, with a dash of Gregory the Great. Perhaps Hugh himself collected these sources, or found them already gathered together, yet did not live to write his own text, or perhaps they were gathered together after he died. Scattered points are made in a rough and hurried sequence: we cannot know when the end will happen, except after the gospel is preached globally (i); Satan shall then be freed (ii–iii) to mount the last persecution of the church (iv) for three years and six months (v). Elijah will return to help convert the Jews (vi), and Christ shall come to judge the good and the evil, although they will not behold Him equally (vii). The dead shall be raised, just and unjust (viii), in an instant (ix–x) to join the living, who are likewise transformed (xi–xii). All of this leads to various questions about the resurrection of the body, as famously discussed by Augustine at the end of *The City of God*.

To some, the very idea of the resurrection of the body seems impossible, given that bones turn to dust, but nature itself gives witness, says Hugh, or rather Gregory the Great, in the daily return of the sun and the yearly return of green growth.[182] Yet particular questions abound, starting (as did Augustine) with aborted fetuses and deformed infants.[183] In general, with paraphrase and unacknowledged quotations from Augustine, the body will be raised unblemished and fully formed according to the ideal of Christ, namely, at thirty years old.[184] The wicked, too, will be raised, but to punishment,[185] as God, along with our conscience, will judge all our works, "whether good or bad."[186] God's judgment may seem hidden or even unjust for now but will be turn out to be most just, again incorporating passages from *The City of God*.[187]

*Part Eighteen: On the State
of the Future Life*

Consonant with the pattern already established, part 18 closes *De sacramentis* with reference to the afterlife, including the vision of God, by way of direct quotations from *The City of God*. "On the State of the Future Life" first revisits the various eternal punishments for the wicked and how knowing about them benefits the just.[188] "Therefore, while bad angels and men remain in eternal punishment, the saints will then know more fully what a blessing grace has brought them," although their prayers can no longer help the lost.[189]

The subject turns decisively from eternal punishment to the vision of God. "If you ask whether God can be seen, I reply: He can."[190] God has been seen already, by some, not as He is but as He wished to appear; yet, in the future, will He not be seen as He is (1 John 3)?[191] Hugh's own answer is fuller in other works, on contemplating God, as presented in the next chapter, but *De sacramentis* continues to quote St. Augustine. After a distinction between seeing and believing,[192] the specific discussion of seeing God resumes with a direct quotation about Elisha from *The City of God*.[193] The sequence of quotations lurches from "whether our thoughts there will be changeable"[194] to that great "joy where there will be no evil, where no good will lie hidden."[195] This quotation from *The City of God* is followed by a longer one from the same chapter and with an acknowledgment: "The same one says in the same work."[196] After a pithy summary of heaven's triple blessing ("Our being there will not have death; our knowing there will not have error; our loving there will not have offense"),[197] the very end of *De sacramentis* quotes the conclusions of *The City of God*, even naming "that city . . . freed from all evil, filled with all good," where the saints will be free of all evils.[198] The eloquent doxology that concludes the work is actually Augustine's: "There we shall call and we shall see; we shall see and we shall love; we shall love and we shall praise. Behold what will be in the end without end!"[199] Fittingly for these last parts, the finale is not in Hugh's own words but elegantly chosen from *The City of God*, whether by Hugh himself or by someone who finished his work for him. The need for a critical edition identifying those passages taken from Hugh's own earlier works and from traditional sources is especially obvious at the end of *De sacramentis*.

Summary

As a whole, *De sacramentis* occupies a central place in Hugh's corpus both in general terms and also within the specific triad of biblical interpretation. As he said at the outset, after the historical reading of scripture comes this allegorical reading, namely, the doctrinal summary drawn from scripture. After the foundation, in other words, comes the framework. To move from historical facts to doctrinal truths is substantial progress. The third and final or highest level, the finish, is that of the moral of the story, the personal or spiritual appropriation, sometimes called the tropological sense, and abundantly represented in Hugh's spiritual writings yet to be sampled. Thus the doctrinal level of the *De sacramentis* is pivotal or central, between the literal-historical level such as Hugh's partial biblical commentaries on the one hand and his numerous essays or treatises of meditation and contemplation on the other hand. This very process of biblical interpretation is presented as the dynamic progress of building on a foundation and ascending (being restored) toward the goal of God.

As to contents, Hugh is explicit about the overarching theme of the restoration of humanity to the image of God and that the notion of restoration presupposes a prior foundation or creation, as well as a fall. Thus book 1 begins with that foundation and creation (parts 1 and 2) by the triune God (3) whose will (4) created the angels (5) and humanity (6). After the fall (7), the restoration (8) begins and unfolds by ways of the sacred signs/sacraments (9) and faith (10), first during the time of natural law (11) and then under the written law (12). Book 2 continues the historical progression through the time of grace, specifically the incarnation (1) and the church (2), including the clergy (3) with their garments (4) and the church building (5). In this church, baptism (6) leads to confirmation (7) and the "Sacrament of the Body and Blood of Christ" (8). Other sacraments (9) and loosely related topics are covered: simony (10), marriage (11), vows (12), and vices and virtues (13). Book 2 closes with the sequence of confession (14), anointing the sick (15), the end/death of man (16), the end and judgment of this world (17), and the future world of seeing and enjoying God (18). After the foundation regarding creation (and fall), Hugh's design for *De sacramentis* follows the salvation history of restoration quite faithfully, with a few digressions. That many sections of book 2 are quotations from prior sources, as became common in the twelfth and thirteenth centuries, does not detract from the contribution of the outline itself.

Yet this overarching order can be misleading in one respect. From the modern point of view regarding literary analysis, *De sacramentis* seems to be "about" the restoration of humanity as a discrete topic, as if neutrally observed. But, from within Hugh's hermeneutical and spiritual point of view, this process of moving through the doctrinal meaning of scripture is itself part of the restoration of humanity, as personally experienced. Hugh's "brief summa" of doctrine, as he calls it, is the central phase of restorative progress toward God, as eloquently suggested by the concluding passages from Augustine on the final blessedness of seeing and enjoying God. The meditations and contemplations comprising that final approach to the divine, the third and highest level of scriptural reading, are the subject of our next part.

Part III

THE SPIRITUAL FINALE

TROPOLOGICAL (SPIRITUAL) ESSAYS

Hugh's corpus features a great many works, large and small, of the meditative and contemplative sort that moderns might call "spirituality." Since these are usually meditations or contemplations of scripture, they, too, find their overall place within Hugh's biblical hermeneutics. Among so many and such diverse works, there is no necessary sequence for our presentation, such as the pedagogical order we followed regarding the first works in Gilduin's edition. We can sample some of them as an introduction and just mention others. But the size and importance of the treatise on *Noah's Ark*, with related works, make it central. Here Hugh explicitly named his emphasis as the spiritual interpretation of the ark, after brief consideration of its literal historical meaning and its allegorical doctrinal sense. The culmination and personal experience suggested in *The Soliloquy* (*de Arrha Animae*) make it a fitting finale. Otherwise, these many spiritual essays, which are mostly available in modern editions and (largely French) translation, do not fall into a specific sequence.

As a group, however, Hugh's works of scriptural meditation and contemplation occupy a definite place in his literary output, just as meditation and contemplation have a specific place in the framework of his thought. The *Didascalicon* specified that "the fruit of sacred reading" was that it first instructs the mind with knowledge, pertaining to history and allegory as we have seen regarding the doctrinal framework of the *De sacramentis*, and then "it adorns the mind in morals," which "has to do with tropology."[1]

Although "morals" in English may seem narrowly concerned with ethics or morality in the modern sense, Hugh fills out what he means by this way of life and thus what tropology is all about: after study or instruction come meditation and prayer, working toward a culminating contemplation.[2] The tropological or moral sense of scripture pertains to a spiritual way of life, specifically in prayer and meditation and contemplation, along with some consideration of virtues and vices in general (see *On the Formation of Novices* in chapter 3). Just as the allegorical turned out to mean the framework of doctrinal, so the tropological or moral sense of scripture turns out to mean spiritual. It is by meditation and contemplation that the building or house is finished or adorned in the third and final phase of interpreting and appropriating the biblical message, after a doctrinal framework has been (allegorically) built on the foundation of the literal-historical sense. The moral sense of scripture is thus the moral of the story, that is, the personal application of the biblical message to the whole of one's own (spiritual) life, rather than just to the one part of life later called morality. In this respect, Hugh and other medievals continued an ancient tradition, in that "philosophy" led to a total way of life.

Thus Hugh's meditative and contemplative works of biblical interpretation correlate to the third and highest sense of scripture, the tropological sense that culminates the process of building, or rather restoring, the edifice of the human in the image of God. Not only the traditional, especially Gregorian, image of a building but also the traditional and Gregorian example of the book of Job reinforce this affiliation of the spiritual writings with the moral or tropological sense. As presented before, and as heard often at Saint Victor, the book of Job is not just literally the story of a historical man named Job. It allegorically and doctrinally signifies Christ in his descent into our miseries and also signifies "any penitent soul" who meditates and laments.[3] This last meaning of the text, it turns out, is the tropological or moral sense, explicitly indicating repentance and meditation as to "what should be done" by us, based on "what has been done" in Christ as presignified in the literal story of Job. If morality is what should be done, then what Hugh and other medievals meant by this is not social behavior in the later sense of ethics but rather repentance and prayer, meditation and contemplation. The tropological is thus the culminating moral of the story, and Hugh's many essays of scriptural meditation and contemplation find their proper placement after the historical and the doctrinal. Noah's ark supplies a much more detailed example of the same pattern: literally-historically, it was a big ship; allegorically-doctrinally, it represents the church; tropologically-spiritually, it is one's own heart or soul as the home God is building within. As such contemplation culminates in the final approach to God, the process of restoration itself is nearing its end. The interpretive move from historical facts to doctrinal knowledge and especially the personal move from doctrine to a spiritual way of life represent the progress of God's work of restoration, restoring the human to the fullness of the image of God. In this respect, biblical interpretation is not merely *about* God's restorative work, it is itself that work of restoration.

1. Prayer and Love

Of the numerous shorter essays of spiritual meditation, several have been recently edited and translated into French. Following the general instruction for Victorine novices presented earlier, they fittingly begin with prayer and love.[4] "On the Power of Praying" (*De virtute orandi*) shows Hugh's pedagogical patterns: he explains scripture, anticipates questions, classifies different types of prayer, and above all, encourages or even forms his readers and hearers toward an inner disposition of their affection and love for God. Originally addressed to the abbot of Hamersleben and again mentioning Hugh's uncle, this little treatise on prayer found a wide diffusion, especially within the later *Devotio moderna*.[5] The different types of prayer, all related to our misery and to God's mercy, are systematically itemized and classified,[6] with an emphasis on the inner posture of opening and directing one's affections and love toward God. With a "pedagogical progression," Hugh links prayer requests and the specific external words of prayer to an inner affection and fervent love for God that goes beyond words.[7] "Let us show outwardly by words that we have within us an affection of devotion toward God."[8] The Psalms and corporate liturgical prayers all aim at the same inner results; "the entire power of praying is in the affections of piety."[9] Through the literal words and the knowledge built on this textual foundation comes the spiritual finale of an affection that is aflame for God, a fervent love that goes beyond all words, even the words of prayer.[10] It is this love that inspires Hugh's most rhapsodic praise, specifically in the next essay and at the end of his *Soliloquy*.

De laude caritatis, "In Praise of Love," is one of Hugh's shortest yet most powerful essays. Reflecting an Augustinian heritage, Hugh's several texts on love are part of a twelfth-century explosion of literature on this theme, both biblical-theological and courtly. Affectionately addressed to one Peter, this brief tractate praises love with conceptual rigor and poetic rhapsody. Human love for God ascends, as the saints have shown us; God's love for us descends, as seen in Christ. Paragraphs 1 through 9 show the way up, while paragraphs 11 through 16 chart the way down, and in both cases, the way is love: "Whose way? The human way to God and God's way to humans."[11] Paragraph 10 is at the pivotal pinnacle of this praise for love and matches Bernard's more famous fervor. It is here shared in its poetic entirety.

> O blessed way, you alone know the exchange of our salvation. You lead God down to humanity, you guide humanity up to God. He descends when he comes to us, we ascend when we go to him. Yet neither he nor we could pass one to the other except through you. You are the mediator, reconciling adversaries, associating the separated, somehow equalizing the disparate. Humbling God, raising us; drawing him down to the depths, raising us up to the heights, yet such that his descent is not abject but merciful, and our ascent is not proud but glorious. Thus you have a great power, o Love! You alone can draw God down from heaven to earth. O how strong are your chains by which God can be bound, and bound humanity breaks the chains of sin. I do not know if I could say anything in greater praise of you than this: you draw God down from heaven, and you raise humanity from earth to heaven. Your power is so great that through you God is humbled even unto this, and humanity is exalted even unto this.[12]

Of course, concludes Hugh, such effusive praise for love is really praise for God, since "God is love."[13] Other essays treat the same theme, sometimes at exegetical length, but rarely with such direct and compact force.

2. Mary and the Canticle

A second recent volume of Hugh's works presents his handful of known meditations on Mary, in an edition of the Latin texts and an annotated French translation. The abbey gave special attention to Mary, including her Assumption, as seen later in Adam of St. Victor.[14] Yet, as volume editor Bernadette Jollès notes, these essays of biblical exposition are not specifically about Mary in her unique role, with one exception, but rather about

Mary as an exemplar for all the faithful and about her Son in particular as Lord and Savior.[15] They thus function, loosely, as a tropological interpretation of certain biblical texts, in that the moral of the story of Mary pertains to the spiritual lives of all Hugh's readers as believers in Christ. Besides the *Magnificat*, of course, the *Song of Songs* also received Hugh's spiritual interpretation in these essays (*Super Canticum Mariae* and *Pro Assumptione Virginis*) and in other writings about the divine bridegroom and the human soul as bride, specifically in *De amore sponsi ad sponsam*, also introduced in this section.

The one Marian text that is not a biblical meditation of general spiritual application is an explicitly polemical argument about Mary's unique combination of perpetual virginity with marriage and motherhood. *On the Virginity of the Blessed Mary* (*De beatae Mariae virginitate*) is Hugh's reply to a bishop's appeal for help against an irreverent challenge.[16] In short, if Mary retained her virginity, and if the definition of marriage includes sexual relations, was Mary really Joseph's wife? In reply, the ever-virgin Mary was really married, true virgin and true wife, because the definition of marriage does not require marital relations when both partners agree to abstain. Hugh quotes and explains the traditional (patristic) saying "It is not coitus but consent that makes a marriage."[17] Typically, the Victorine's exposition expands to touch on creation and election, nature and grace, being and being blessed,[18] before going on to his briefer concluding points, including the role of the Holy Spirit: as Mary conceived without pleasure so she gave birth without pain, and remained a virgin.[19] Appended is a curious corollary, or rather a refutation of the idea that allowing a celibate marriage could lead, absurdly, to spiritual unions of two men or two women, since there must be a basic difference involved.[20]

In Hugh's exposition of the *Magnificat* (*Super Canticum Mariae*), he moves quickly to the "mysteries" of the spiritual understanding of these familiar words.[21] After a quick review of the historical context of Mary and Gabriel, then Mary and Elizabeth, Hugh devotes his full attention to Mary's opening words as to their spiritual significance—in sum, how to relate "My soul magnifies the Lord" to "My spirit exults in God my savior." Soul (*anima*) and spirit (*spiritus*), magnify and exult, Lord and Savior—these words were revealed to the Virgin and thus to us, says Hugh, in exactly this order. First, *soul* and *magnify* and *Lord* indicate the realm of powerful majesty and fear; then, *spirit* and *exults* and *my savior* point to mercy and goodness and love, to abbreviate Hugh's exposition severely.[22] Not that there are finally two realms, because "the catholic faith" affirms the unity of subject, called *soul* relative to the body and *spirit* relative to itself.[23] Similarly, and within this same exposition, holding the majesty of the creator Lord faithfully together with the mercy of the (restoring) Savior God is essential to Hugh's overall synthesis of creation and restoration. All of this is not specifically Mariology but rather tropology, that is, the spiritual lessons from Mary's words for the life of faith in the Creator and Restorer. Such is the moral of the *Magnificat*.

Subsequent phrases from the *Magnificat* receive less and less commentary from Hugh, although he reused two significant passages in *De sacramentis*. "He who is mighty" (*qui potens est*) prompted Hugh to a complex excursus about God's omnipotence (does God have the power to make better than He makes?) directed straight at Abelard and reused in *De sacramentis* word for word.[24] Similarly, the itemizing of four fears ("mercy to those who fear him") is repeated exactly in *De sacramentis*: servile, mundane, initial, and filial.[25] Remaining phrases of Mary's Canticle receive less comment, although in the same general vein, for human pride and the divine promises apply to everyone's spiritual life.

There was another canticle, of course. Amid all of the earlier and contemporary interest in the Song of Songs, Hugh, too, tried his hand, not in a commentary or set of sermons like Bernard, but rather, initially in reply to a monastic request, with some comments on those particular verses that were used in the liturgical office for "The Assumption of the Virgin," starting with *Pro Assumptione Virginis* and including "The Love of the Bridegroom toward the Bride." In Hugh's masterful hands, as Jollès points out, these phrases pertain to Mary initially, but then largely to all the faithful; working only with certain phrases and for "fraternal edification" makes for a lighter work, admits Hugh.[26] "You are all fair, my love; there is no flaw in you" (Song 4.7) says the bridegroom Christ to the beloved, who is both bride and mother, his virgin mother Mary *and* the virgin mother church; such marvels prompt Hugh's burst of praise to the Son and Bridegroom, who himself gives birth: "First, your beloved the virgin mother Mary birthed you, then your beloved the virgin mother church was borne from you! Coming in the flesh, you were made the son of your bride-mother who was also a virgin in the body; dying in the flesh, you were made the father of your bride who was a virgin in the faith."[27] From here on, Hugh's comments are more and more concerned with Christ and the soul, rather than Mary or the church. Honey and milk (Song 4.11) are Christ's divinity and humanity;[28]

"happy is the *soul* who hears that 'winter is past'" (Song 2.11).[29] Steadily the emphasis is on how we should all "taste and see" (Psalm 34.8) because the "flowers that appear on the earth" (Song 2.12) all derive their beauty from the tree of life who is Christ, although Hugh does return to Mary herself in conclusion.[30] Overall, Hugh's comments on these verses from the Song of Songs do not emphasize Mary, never mention her Assumption directly, and instead develop via poetic association the theme of love between the bridegroom Christ and the bridal soul,[31] as also seen elsewhere in Hugh and, of course, in many other authors.

Elsewhere, Hugh developed another set of spiritual comments on a portion of the Canticle (Song 4.4–6) that was an antiphon for the office of the Assumption of the Blessed Virgin, indeed, using the exact liturgical text,[32] yet without any reference to Mary at all. *De amore sponsi ad sponsam* ("On the Love of the Bridegroom toward the Bride"), also known as the *Eulogium sponsi et sponsae*, moves directly to the spiritual interpretation of the bridegroom as God and the bride as the soul, including the bridal gifts (*arra*) discussed more fully in Hugh's *Soliloquy*.[33] What moderns usually call allegory (for example, myrrh as the bitterness of the body's mortification) is Hugh's tropology, the moral of this song for one's own soul: in the end, it is the soul that ascends from incontinence to chastity, from indulgent pleasure to parsimony, from the many to the one, namely, to be united to God.[34]

The same pattern holds true for the last and briefest material in the second (Marian) volume of Hugh's works, principally a homily on Isaiah 11 (*Egredietur virga*; "There shall come forth a shoot") that also integrates verses from the Song of Songs.[35] Playing on the pun of *virga-virgo*, Hugh starts off with the virgin Mary as the "shoot" (*virga*), and her son (*Filius*) as the flower (*flos*) but moves immediately to general spiritual lessons, again the moral of the story, about the straight shoot as rectitude giving birth to the flower as beauty and blessing.[36] From there, Hugh makes a quick transition to the "shoot-let" (*virgula*) or column of smoke in Song 3.6 and continues his tropological lessons about the spiritual life: rectitude and beauty, justice and glory, prosperity and adversity, chastity and humility, and so on. The homily concludes with Mary, the example, relative to Christ, the remedy: "In this the Son is greater than the mother, because by his passion he took away the sins of the world; it was not the mother but the son who died for the redemption of the world. . . . Blessed shoot who produced such a flower! Through Mary Christ is given, and through Christ salvation is given."[37]

Jollès's volume of Hugh's Marian writings concludes with another poetic paragraph (*Maria porta*) that is probably homiletical and certainly a fitting spiritual finish, at least to this tropological group of writings about Mary.

> Mary is the door, Christ the entrance, the Father the hidden [interior]. Mary is a human, Christ human and God, the Father God. Through Mary to Christ, through Christ to God. In Mary is pity, in the Father majesty, in Christ pity and majesty: pity out of compassion for the [human] race, majesty by the excellence of deity. Mary is the star, Christ the sun; thus are sinners consoled by Mary as if at night, and the righteous are illuminated by Christ as if by day. Therefore, if you, preparing to pray, fear to approach Christ, look to Mary. There you will not find what you fear, but you will see your own race. This is the first pity by which the supreme majesty that may still frighten you is tempered. Here you will be encouraged and nourished, until you are consoled and crowned.[38]

3. Others

Another handful of brief spiritual essays is available in a modern Latin edition and French translation, besides the dozens of miscellany in the older Migne collection (including some not by Hugh at all).[39] Roger Baron presented six authentic *opuscules spirituels*, often found together in the manuscript tradition, that can be noted briefly here in three pairs: "On Meditation" and "On the Word of God," "On the Five Septets" and the related "Seven Gifts of the Holy Spirit," and "Of the Nature of Love" (as the published English translation puts it) coupled with "What Should Be Truly Loved."[40]

Meditation, for Hugh, is a broad category encompassing the admiring consideration of creation, the careful triplex reading of sacred scripture, and the circumspect examination of one's own life. ("Contemplation" directly of God is reserved for the next life.) Creation is barely mentioned, and scripture's three considerations are listed quickly in the familiar terms of history, allegory, and tropology, with the last pointing directly to Hugh's main interest here.[41] The tropological lesson of scripture (that is, what should be done or avoided, what pertains to instruction or exhortation or consolation or fear, in short, a spiritual way of life) leads to and then undergirds the third and longest discussion of meditation, the meditation *in moribus*, meaning, one's way of life, itself divided into three categories: affections, thoughts, and deeds.[42] This discussion is not about morals or mores in the modern senses of ethics or customs but rather about the believer's way of life, a life of pure thoughts, good intentions, inner conscience and outer reputation, influences divine or diabolical, all with spiritual goals and obstacles. In fact, parts of this text closely parallel Hugh's guidance for Victorine novices regarding their religious way of life.[43]

On the Word of God (*De Verbo Dei*) is a compressed example of Hugh's synthetic virtuosity.[44] Starting with scripture, especially Hebrews 4 on the living word of God that penetrates soul and spirit, joint and marrow, thoughts and intentions, Hugh himself penetrates to the heart of the matter with his spiritual interpretation and application. He quickly weaves together scriptural words and the incarnate Word, soul and spirit, thoughts of the mind and intentions of the heart, the three "eyes" (of the flesh, of the heart, of God), and the exterior word of preaching and the interior word of inspiration. This last item is itself double, in familiar terms: "through nature and through grace, through nature when it inspires in those who have been created a knowledge of the good, through grace when it suggests to those who have been restored a love of the good."[45] As the apostle (Hebrews) goes on to speak of Christ and priesthood, so, too, does Hugh's homiletical exposition, masterfully but briefly.

In two very brief essays, "five septets" preoccupied Hugh, in apparent answer to a query: the seven vices, the seven petitions of the Lord's Prayer, the seven gifts of the Holy Spirit, the seven virtues, and the seven beatitudes.[46] The correlations are somewhat forced but occasionally ingenious, as with gluttony or especially pride as the first vice: it is countered by the first petition ("hallowed by *thy* name"), the first of the Spirit's gifts ("fear of the Lord"), the first virtue (humility), and so forth.[47] More important than the specific correlations is the general treatment of the vices as ailments or wounds of the human patient, with God the physician applying the remedies unto health and blessing.[48] Hugh's insightful paragraph on the sequence of vices (how pride and envy and anger lead to despair, avarice, gluttony, and lust) was repeated in *De sacramentis*.[49]

Hugh's brief *Of the Nature of Love*, with its even shorter companion *What Should Be Truly Loved*, shows both his Augustinian lineage and his own distinctive features. The former essay, on disordered love/cupidity for the world and ordered love/charity for God, is available in English translation, such that Hugh's debt to Augustine regarding love for God, the neighbor, and the world can there be read directly.[50] It is in the continuation, according to many manuscripts, that Hugh points us from the general

Augustinian language of the restless heart to his major example of the ark, a stable ship of faith upon the restless seas of this world. *What Should Be Truly Loved* says that we can more readily understand this ark and the flood, spiritually speaking, if we remember God's works of creation and restoration, but it does not make the linkage explicit.[51] For the full connection of the familiar framework of creation and restoration to the major biblical example of the ark, we need to turn to Hugh's largest and most important work of spiritual exegesis, *Noah's Ark*.

8

ARK TREATISES

1. *Noah's Ark*

Hugh's central "spiritual" work is *Noah's Ark*. With his propaedeutic *Didascalicon* and the doctrinal *De sacramentis*, it is one of his three most important books overall and serves as the pivot for other works on the ark theme. With it (*De archa Noe* in the modern edition) comes a *Booklet on the Making of the Ark* (*Libellus de formatione arche*)[1] referring to a complex diagram that physically exists nowhere except in modern renditions, along with a dialogue on the theme of flood and ark, *On the Vanity of the World* (*De vanitate mundi*).

Noah's Ark concerns one main question, with this ark serving as a massive biblical example including extensive details along the way. The Augustinian question ponders the restlessness of the human heart; the Victorine answer invokes God's works of creation and restoration: insofar as we wrongly love the works of creation, we will be forever distracted and even swept away by this flooded world, yet when we reintegrate our thoughts according to the order of God's works of restoration, we will safely abide in a vessel of spiritual wisdom centered on the Author of creation and restoration.[2] Because the master example is biblical, this treatise also gives the fullest extant case of Hugh's scriptural interpretation of one passage, specifically the literal-historical ark of Noah, the doctrinal-allegorical (typological) ark of the church, and the spiritual-tropological ark of the soul as the moral of the biblical story for Hugh's hearers and readers.

Book One

The four books of *Noah's Ark* unfold in a complex but coherent way as guided by the initial question, expanding the biblical example into minute detail and occasionally mentioning a pedagogical visual aid. Amid the twists and turns of the text, it is easy to forget that this biblical ark is but an illustration of Hugh's spiritual theme of the restless and the stable, the raging flood and the heart at home with God. This theme, says Hugh at the outset, emerged in discussions with the brothers, from a *collatio, in conventu*.

> We began with one accord to marvel at the instability and restlessness of the human heart, and to sigh over it. And the brethren earnestly entreated that they might be shown the cause of these unstable movements in man's heart, and further particularly begged to be taught if such a serious evil as this could be countered by any skill or by the practice of some discipline.[3]

Master Hugh, their teacher, becomes our author, with the common Augustinian starting point of the restless heart. His poetic eloquence is mostly lost in any synopsis of the basic thematic progression but can perhaps be glimpsed in translated samples.

The problem began when the first human no longer "remained one in the love of the One" but craved transient earthly objects and thus became subject to "movement without stability . . . toil without rest, travel without arrival," in sum, the disease and restlessness of the heart until it again rests in God through the restoration of its proper love for God.[4] To attain this love for God who will stabilize our restless hearts, we need to know Him; to know God, as when someone visits another person's house, we need to visit God's house: "the whole world, the church, each faithful soul."[5] Hugh moves from the general (world) to the specific (church) to the intimate (soul). The faithful are not only in the house of God, they *are* that house, where God dwells both by knowledge as to the structure of faith and also by love as to the adorning finish, in an echo of Gregory the Great's analogy of building a house.

> Now, therefore, enter your inmost heart, and make a dwelling-place for God. Make Him a temple, make Him a house, make Him a pavilion,

Make Him an ark of the covenant, make Him an ark of the flood; no matter what you call it, it is all one house of God.[6]

Although Hugh has here broached the theme of Noah's ark as the structure of the soul, he does not pursue this one example without first bursting into praise that God is "everything to you," and thus any one of many (biblical) images could also be developed: the house of God, the city of the King, the body of Christ, the bride of the Lamb, heaven, sun, moon, ship, vine, manger, garden, rose, door, dove, pearl, scepter and throne, table and bread, and spouse and mother, among dozens more.[7] Whatever the image, the Word was made flesh so that humanity might be raised, that is, restored in the full love for God that gives the heart rest at last.[8]

After this poetic preamble, Hugh proceeds to his chosen exemplar of this spiritual edifice, namely, Noah's ark, with a depiction for the student's outer eye, complete with specific colors and figures, so that the inner soul might be formed accordingly. References to a specific visual aid, completely consistent with Hugh's pedagogical purposes, are complicated by the companion *Libellus* to be considered later. In the sequence of *Noah's Ark* as a treatise, this first mention of a diagram is not about a small central square, as in the *Libellus*, but about the larger whole wherein the ark as the church and thus as the body of Christ is framed by Christ's whole person, head and members, as beheld in Isaiah 6. Hugh explicitly says that "in a visible form" he has depicted the whole first so that his hearers and readers will better understand what will be said later about the parts.[9]

"The Lord, sitting upon a throne, high and lifted up," with "the whole earth full of His glory" and "two seraphim standing" were given visual expression and exegetical interpretation. The seraphim, for example, with their three pairs of wings, signify scripture in its three senses (history, allegory, and tropology), each one pairing love of God with love of neighbor.[10] In that they cover the Lord's head and feet,[11] they show that we cannot know God's beginning before the creation of the world or God's end after the consummation of the age, but we can know the era of the church in Christ's body in this age. "This is the ark, of which we have set out to speak; and it reaches from the head to the feet, because through successive generations, Holy Church reaches from the beginning to the end."[12] Thus the ark as the historical church, the body of Christ, is framed by the protective arms of the Lord who will guide it as if through the flood into a safe harbor of eternal rest.[13]

As Hugh concentrates on the ark within the larger picture, he identifies several arks, or rather several meanings to the Genesis 6 passage, as already hinted. First is the (literal-historical) vessel Noah made with wood and pitch; the second is the (typological-allegorical) signification of the church as a later historical reality; the third is the "ark of wisdom" built in our hearts by meditation, the particular subject to be discussed most fully.[14]

Literally-historically, Noah's ark was a big boat, of a certain size and composition, and with specific features such as a door and a window. Hugh names but disapproves of Origen's speculation on the shape of the ark but works with what the "doctores" have taught about several of its features, such as the various levels (stories) or the placement of the door.[15] The specific biblical dimensions (three hundred cubits long, fifty cubits wide, and thirty cubits high) interested Hugh greatly, first on the literal level regarding the "great discipline of geometry" (measurements of hypotenuse and so on by the author of *Practical Geometry*)[16] and then for the symbolic meanings of these numbers.

Insofar as the biblical ark prefigures the ark of the church (as Noah prefigures Christ, according to the allegorical-typological meaning), the length of three hundred cubits indicates the three periods of this age (natural law, written law, and grace), the breadth of fifty indicates the full breadth of membership, and the height of thirty cubits stands (circuitously) for the biblical books.[17] That the ark gets narrower near the top of its stories, even unto a single cubit (Genesis 6.16), means that there are fewer people at the higher levels of the spiritual life and Christ at the pinnacle of all.[18] That the ark took one hundred years to build correlates temporally, and theologically, to the church's redemption in the period of grace.[19] Coming back to the measurements, the ark's proportions are those of a human body, as befits the ark as the body of Christ, and the specific numbers have other significations as well.[20] Of the several features of the ark considered allegorically, that is, as the church, Hugh here gives the most attention to the stories or levels: three in this life (carnal, sensual, spiritual) and two in the next (souls before the resurrection, souls reunited with risen bodies), starting with the lowest level where animal dung matches the life of the flesh and the carnal will.[21] The *Libellus* supplies much more detail along this (allegorical) line of the ark as the corporate story of God's people. From one (aerial) viewpoint, movement from stern to center to bow is the history of humanity, from Adam through the patriarchs to Christ and Peter's successors. From another viewpoint, the ark shows how individuals can rise up from the floodwaters through successive steps and decks to the peak that is Christ.

To conclude book 1, Hugh begins the move to his proper subject, the ark of wisdom within.

> But to speak now in terms of tropology [*moraliter*], whoever makes it his endeavour to cut himself off from the enjoyment of this world and cultivate the virtues, must with the assistance of God's grace erect within himself a building of virtues three hundred cubits long in faith of Holy Trinity, fifty cubits wide in charity, and thirty cubits high in the hope that is in Christ, a building long in good works and wide in love and lofty in desire.[22]

Explicating these measurements and other features of the ark in terms of the soul is the agenda for book 2.

Book Two

Hugh completes his transition from the allegorical (typological) treatment of the ark as a prototype of the church to the tropological discussion of the soul's "ark of wisdom" by moving from the exterior realm of a historical thing (res), namely, the church, to the interior realm of thought where past, present, and future come together. Indeed, the right thoughts, useful and chaste, are the timbers we need to build our inner ark.[23] The "pitch" or bitumen we use to cover these thoughtful planks inside and out is charity, "outside, so that you may show gentleness, and inside, that you not lose charity."[24] Following the sequence of Genesis 6, Hugh moves from "timbers" and "pitch" to the measurements of our inner ark and then to the spiritual door and window. Building on his earlier comments, the "length" of three hundred cubits is our consideration of the marvelous salvation history God is working from beginning to end; the width is wideness of heart in contemplating the lives of the faithful, and the height corresponds to the high knowledge of the scriptures (and, shortly, the height of Christ himself).[25]

The "door" and "window" receive more thorough exposition under a recapitulation of the whole point.

> As we have said before, the ark of the flood is the secret place of our own heart, in which we must hide from the tumult of this world. But because the feebleness of our condition itself prevents our staying long in the silence of inward contemplation, we have a way out by the door and

window. The door denotes the way out through action, the window the way out through thought. The door is below, the window above, because actions pertain to the body and thoughts to the soul.[26]

Actions of the body (going out the door) are of four kinds, correlated to the unclean and clean animals (lustful or necessary actions of the body) and to Noah and Ham (humble or vain activities in the church).[27]

Similarly, there are four ways we exit (through the window) in contemplation, a rather complex quartet that includes the raven who never came back and the dove who brought an olive branch back in the window. First, when we contemplate created things in themselves, we find them empty and should hold such vanity in contempt; second, when we consider such mutable creatures in the eternal mind of the Creator, we praise God.[28] Third, we can contemplate the ways God uses created things like air, water, and earth, as quoted before under Hugh's doctrine of creation.[29] Fourth, we can contemplate such useful creations as ways to satisfy our lusts and then, like the raven, "never want to come back again to the ark of conscience."[30] Yet in the other three kinds of contemplation, the soul returns with specific benefits, like the dove who came back with the olive branch in leaf.[31]

Ascending up through the stories of our inner ark to its singular pinnacle occupies Hugh at some length, indeed for the rest of book 2 and all of book 3. Right thoughts lead "up" to useful actions and then to internalized virtues, especially the love that is God. "So in the first story there is knowledge, in the second works, and in the third virtue, and at the top the reward of virtue, Jesus Christ our Lord."[32] In Genesis, the ark's roof peaked at a single cubit square, thirty cubits high; Hugh concludes that there could have been a pillar in the middle of the ark, on which everything depended: "This is the tree of life which was planted in the midst of paradise, namely, our Lord Jesus Christ, set up in the midst of His Church for all believers alike as the reward of work, the End of the journey, and the victor's crown."[33] This tree of life, this Christological column at the center of things, receives continual exposition, indeed the whole of book 3. Hugh first interweaves the ascent to this peak from the four corners of the ark, representing the four corners of earthly ills. "The cold of the east [northeast] is the swelling of pride, the cold of the west [northwest] is the blindness of ignorance."[34] Amid considerable detail, and even more in the *Libellus*, the point is to ascend from these depths to the peak that is Christ, who "puts down pride and enlightens blindness. . . . Let the proud give ear to His reproof and be humbled. Let the blind listen to His teaching with their mind, and be enlightened. . . . Let us go up."[35] Let us go up with joy, exhorts Hugh with picturesque language for the ascent and the summit. The first ascent is from the (northeast) swelling of pride, the second from (southwest) fleshly concupiscence; the third is from the (northwest) blindness of ignorance, "for when through abstinence and the practice of discipline we have extinguished in ourselves the passions of the flesh, we shall be free to give ourselves up gladly to meditation, and to the teaching of Divine Scripture."[36]

Although the *Libellus* supplies extensive detail about these four ascents of thirty steps each,[37] Hugh here keeps his hortatory eye on the pinnacle of the Christological pillar. "Thirty cubits high" means both the Divine Scripture, as he said before, and also Christ, regardless of whether there was literally a pillar there, because "the whole Divine Scripture is one Book, and that one Book is Christ."[38] This Christ-pillar is both the "Book of Life according to the humanity that He has taken" as the exemplar, and also "the Tree of Life in respect of His divinity" as the remedy.[39] Hugh signals that he wants to meditate awhile on the multiple meanings of "book" and "tree," of words and the Word.[40] To understand his rapid succession of three books, three words, three trees, and three paradises, we need to keep in mind Hugh's triplex biblical hermeneutics: first the literal-historical meaning, then the typological-allegorical doctrine, and then the tropological-spiritual application. The whole section aims at appreciating the spiritual tree of life, which is about to receive a full book of its own. The first tree was a material tree in an earthly garden; the second tree is Christ in his humanity planted in the midst of the churchly garden of faith; the third tree of life is the wisdom of God planted invisibly in the hearts of the saints.[41] The idea of a Christ column in the middle of the ark has led Hugh to a spiritual tree of life, the planting of wisdom in human hearts that develops by fifteen specific steps, each one worthy of separate exposition.

This, therefore, is the tree of life indeed, the word of the Father, the wisdom of God in the highest, which in the hearts of the saints, as in an unseen paradise,

is sown in fear,
watered by grace,
dies through grief,
takes root by faith,

buds by devotion,
shoots up through compunction,
grows by longing,
is strengthened by charity,
grows green by hope,
puts out its leaves and spreads its branches through caution,
flowers through discipline,
bears fruit through virtue,
ripens through patience,
is harvested by death,
and feeds by contemplation.[42]

Before launching into his extended commentary on each phase of this tree's life span via each phrase for the soul's spiritual development, Hugh pauses to close book 2 on the spiritual ark of wisdom. He will come back to the building of this inner house of God in book 4, after his eloquent excursus (book 3) on the growth of the spiritual tree of wisdom within the human heart.

Book Three

We have shown at the end of the preceding book, under the figure of a tree, how wisdom comes to be and grows in us. The stages of its growth, which we previously compressed into a brief summary, we shall now explain fully and in detail.[43]

Book 3 is a tour de force, pressing the analogy of a plant's life cycle as the growth of wisdom within the human heart in fifteen biblical steps. In a separable excursus from the ark theme, its Christ pillar has become the tree of wisdom in the personalized, almost existential, sense of one's own faith journey. (How this pillar also centers the church on every level is an allegorical point taken up later, in the *Libellus*.) As a masterpiece combining a horticultural paradigm with scriptural imagery and insights on faith development, it needs to be read in full to appreciate its rich detail. For example, that wisdom is first planted or "sown in fear" correlates to two biblical starting points: "the fear of the Lord is the beginning of wisdom" and the first beatitude about the "poor in spirit."[44] God graciously waters the seed and makes it sprout (III, iii; cf. Isaiah 55.10), and thus the seed itself dies (through grief) even as it germinates (III, iv; cf. John 12.24).

Unbelievers are rooted in this world's transient goods, and those of shallow-rooted faith cannot withstand temptation, but others "through faith and love are rooted and grounded in God."[45] Germinating in devotion, the heart's wisdom "shoots up through compunction" (III, vi and vii, naming the field parable(s) of Matthew 13). Hugh summarizes the first six stages, drawing a parallel to Abraham's faith journey and thus our own: "We, therefore, get us out of our country by fear, and out of our kindred by grace and out of our father's house by grief; we follow the Lord through faith and devotion, and after that at the sixth stage our promised land is shown us through compunction."[46] Seventh is upward growth through longing, and eighth is the strengthening of wisdom through charity. Here Hugh pauses for a (loose) correlation of these first eight steps to the eight beatitudes.[47] Greening through hope (III, x), "the tree of wisdom [tenthly] 'puts out its leaves and spreads its branches through caution,'" whether upward in contemplation or outward in action.[48] Here Hugh pauses to warn the contemplatives against proud disdain for others and to offer extensive spiritual direction about relating generously to all kinds of people, about fear(s), anxiety, necessity, and attraction.[49] Amid this homiletical digression, Hugh confirms that God's gracious work of restoration "not only repairs that which has been destroyed, but also over and above adds that which formerly we lacked . . . [and thus] so restores us that we seem to have fallen not to our destruction, but for our further growth."[50] That the spiritual finish of the work of restoration exceeds God's original work of creation is often implicit in Hugh's works, as in *The Soliloquy* (to be treated later), but rarely so explicit as here.

The final stages are treated briefly: the tree of wisdom "flowers through discipline" in the [outer] beauty of good works (III, xii), "bears fruit through [inner] virtue (III, xiii), "ripens through patience" and perseverance (III, xiv), "is harvested by death" as brought to the king's banquet (III, xv), and there "feeds by contemplation" (III, xvi), a phrase that receives no more commentary than a quotation from Psalm 16.11. In conclusion, it is the "mystery" of numbers that interests Hugh: fifteen stages means the seven of this (Old Testament) life and eight of the eternal life promised in the New Testament; fifteen doubled in love for God and neighbor makes thirty, the fullness of Christ's maturity (Ephesians 4.13), and the two Sabbath septets are joined by the eighth and central stage of charity.[51] Not only this numerical postscript but also the entire horticultural metaphor and spiritual exposition in book 3 are admittedly a digression.

But now, in following up the explanation of subordinate matters, we have strayed somewhat far from the subject that we took in hand. . . . Now therefore, let us return to our subject, and pursue the matter of the construction of the ark of wisdom.[52]

Book Four

After the Christ-column tree of life turned into book 3's extended metaphor for the growth of wisdom in the human heart, Hugh's return to his main subject first emphasizes not the specific features of the ark as a static object, as back in book 2, but rather as the larger spiritual-theological concepts implied in the building of an inner ark as a dynamic process, for the final book 4. The specific terminology used in the transition to book 4, and later as well, makes the point: "let us pursue the *construction* of the ark of wisdom" and "we wish to speak about the *building* of the house of God."[53] In book 4, Hugh's emphasis on the dynamic activities of God building this ark in us leads to his fullest theological expression of the spiritual themes mentioned at the outset, namely, the restless heart and its final peace. The deep background of the original "works of creation" and historical "works of restoration" becomes central and is then explicitly invoked to answer the original question of why the heart seems adrift on unstable seas and how it can find an abiding home at last.

To specify the place for building this ark and the materials to be used, he writes: "the place is the heart of man, and the material is pure thoughts."[54] Here, signaling a tone for all of book 4, Hugh's teaching turns fervently hortatory. God "wants to dwell in your own heart—extend and enlarge that!"[55] Continuing his forceful direct address, Hugh reassures "you" that God will teach you how to build this house in your heart as He taught Noah, Moses, Solomon, and Paul the Apostle; so "call upon Him, love Him, . . . and He Himself will come to you and teach you."[56]

Beyond the location and material and cobuilder, Hugh turns to the "how" of constructing this ark, namely, the order and arrangement of our thoughts. Rather than chase after the infinity of earthly goods and vain thoughts, we need a pattern to lead us up from this vale of tears toward the simple unity and true simplicity that is God, just as the ark rises out of the depths to its peak of a single cubit.[57] This gradual progress from the world's multiple distractions to the supreme stability that is the contemplation of God is fully named in familiar terms as "reparation" or "restoration."[58]

These are the "works of restoration" that are paired, commonly and here again, with the "works of creation." Hugh first reviews, yet again, these paired works of God, the original creation and the incarnational restoration, but then adds that the former was for all whereas the latter is for the elect only: "He who created all has not redeemed them all, but saves some in His mercy and condemns others in His justice."[59] This Augustinian complication delays Hugh only slightly, but he must account for grace and free will, and especially for God's partial self-revelation, unto belief or unbelief: "So He makes Himself known that faith may be fostered; and He continues hidden lest unbelief be overcome. He remains hidden, that faith may be proved; He makes Himself known, that unbelief may be convinced."[60] That is why God has always spoken "with the few, occasionally, darkly, and in secret."[61] That God speaks "in secret" or "in hiding" is illustrated by the bridegroom calling the bride upward in the *Song of Songs*, as in Hugh's other works.[62] That God speaks "darkly" or "obscurely" fires the faithful with greater longing and protects the truth from unbelievers.[63] That God speaks seldom and with only a few, namely, the elect, is explained more slowly by way of salvation history. After the fall, humanity was so distracted by external plurality that God's loving purpose in redemption needed to start with the focal point of one people, one place, one Savior, yet for the sake of all.[64] Hugh's summary of this selectivity (the restoration of some) reconnects his theological narrative to the example of the ark:

> So, then, when God by speaking with the few (and that but seldom) draws our hearts [minds] to unity and by speaking darkly and in secret draws them upwards to Himself, what else is He doing—if I may so say—but producing in our hearts the form of an invisible ark?[65]

Yet at this point, nearing the end of his treatise, Hugh's interest is not on the details of the ark but rather on the larger concepts being illustrated, specifically the (six-day) works of the creation of all things and the (six-era) works of the healing or restoration of humanity. The "reprobate," even the philosophers of the Gentiles, are distracted by the transient visible creatures; but the elect, including the philosophers among the Christians, meditate upon the merciful Creator's invisible work of eternal restoration.[66] The language of ascent "through the visible to the invisible" triggers a broad summary statement, nearing the point of the whole work:

> By visible things the reprobate fall from those that are invisible; but by the visible the elect climb up to the invisible. You must understand,

however, that the visible things from which the elect mount up are different from those by means of which they do so. They mount up *from* the works of creation, *by means of* those of restoration, *to* the Author of creation and of restoration. But those ascents must be conceived not outwardly but inwardly, as taking place by means of steps within the heart, which go from strength to strength.[67]

This familiar overarching perspective on creation and restoration serves to reframe the extended example of Noah's ark and to make Hugh's overall point. As an ark once floated above the floodwaters, so in the human heart there is also an ark, namely, faith in Christ, that rises above the inner flood of lusts; concupiscence always flows downward, toward the transient creatures, whereas faith rises up to perpetual good.[68] "Everyone, then, is subject to a kind of flood of concupiscence in his own heart, from which nobody can be released save by the ark of faith."[69] Playing with this imagery, Hugh specifies three options: first, those who have a flood of lusts but no ark are the unbelievers; second, those who are awash in the tides of this life and know about the ark but are not in it are the lukewarm believers, who may even come to church but then think more of Saturn and Hercules or "Plato and Aristotle, than of Christ and His saints" ("what is the use of knowing the truth and loving what is false?"); third are the true believers who not only have an ark but also live in it.[70] The rest of the treatise develops what it means to live in the ark, the "spiritual ark which is our faith" and which rises above worldly lusts.[71] In each heart, there is both a flood of persistent concupiscence for the created world and yet also a saving ship of faith.[72]

> Concupiscence has to do with the works of creation, and faith with those of restoration; for by inordinate love for created things we are weakened by concupiscence, and by devout belief in the works of restoration we are made steadfast through faith.[73]

With this Augustinian distinction between God's creation that is good in itself and our disordered lust for it that keeps us from the higher goods and from the good Creator himself, Hugh finally answers his original question about the restless heart and explains how his framework of creation and restoration applies to the extended exegesis of Noah's ark as a "spiritual house of wisdom."

This one passage holds the whole work together:

> We have now, I think, shown sufficiently clearly the origin of the infinite distraction of our thoughts from which we suffer—that is, from the

world and from the lust of it, from the works of creation. Again we have
shown by what means our thoughts can be reintegrated—that is, by the
works of restoration. And because, as we said above, there can be no
order where there is no limit, it remains for us now, having left the work
of creation behind us, to seek out the order of our thoughts where they
are bounded—that is, in the works of restoration. For this is the matter
that we previously proposed for investigation—namely, what the order
of our thoughts should be, if they are to enable us to build in ourselves
the spiritual house of wisdom.[74]

The Augustinian query initially posed by the assembled brethren—how
can the restless heart find stability at last?—has received its Hugonian
answer: by turning from disordered lust for the distractions of creation to
the orderly pattern in God's works of restoration, as from the flood into
the ark.

Turning, then, from the works of creation, as from a flood beneath us
from which we have emerged, let us begin to treat the works of restoration, and with them go, as it were, into the ark.[75]

Going into the works of restoration, as into the ark, means first a reprise of
the basic definition of those works: "all the things that have been done, or
that still must be done, for the restoration of man, from the beginning of the
world until the end of the age."[76] Turning from chaotic concupiscence to
God's orderly plan of salvation history means noticing an order in several
dimensions. The order of dignity pertains to higher and lower, as in the
stories of the ark; the order of place and time is the providential progression from earliest times in the eastern realm of Eden and Assyria, then to
the Greeks, and in later times to the Romans on the western end of Hugh's
world.[77] Egypt and Babylon are also situated in this context, exegetically,
geographically, etymologically, and especially historically, as befits the
chronological sequence to the works of restoration.[78] Biblical passages can
be applied, as Hugh explicitly multiplies his exposition. Indeed, the different senses of scripture also pertain to this ark, these works of restoration:

In these three measurements the whole divine Scripture is contained.
For history measures the length of the ark, because the order of time
consists in the succession of events. Allegory measures the breadth of the
ark, because the fellowship of faithful people consists in their sharing
in the mysteries. Tropology measures the height of the ark, because the
worth of merits increases with advance in virtue.[79]

The height of this ark of God's restoration also involves successive steps (stories) and thus a dynamic historical progression. Quickly naming various aspects of restoration, Hugh itemizes a group of triadic levels: shadow, body, spirit; figure, actuality, truth; prefigurations, visible sacraments, invisible graces; for example, (crossing) the Red Sea, baptism, and the washing away of sins.[80] Rapidly multiplying the triads, the narrative here begins to parallel the diagram regarding the three stories or levels, as to increasing height (dignity) and length (history): humans, angels, God; faith, hope, love; right thought, wise meditation, pure contemplation; knowledge, discipline, goodness; and nature, written law, grace.[81]

Such multiple namings of the three stories, as if going around their four sides, might seem labyrinthine, even with a diagram, as Hugh seems to admit in conclusion.

> What then is this ark, about which we have said so many things and in which so many different paths of knowledge are contained? You do not think it is a maze [labyrinth], I hope? For it is not a maze [*labor-intus*], nor is there toil [*labor*] within [*intus*], but rest (within).[82]

The ark, as more fully envisioned in the *Libellus*, may have seemed like a complicated labyrinth, but Hugh plays on the word to assure his hearers and readers that it is not "labor-in-there" but "rest-in-there" and joy and peace.

Time to sum up. "What, then, is the ark like?" It is a storehouse of every delight, specifically all the works of restoration in all of history, in the mysteries of the sacraments (doctrine), and in the tropological sense of spirituality.

> There all the works of restoration are contained in all their fullness, from the world's beginning to its end; and therein is represented the condition of the universal Church. Into it is woven the story of events, in it are found the mysteries of the sacraments, and there are set out the stages of affections, thoughts, meditations, contemplations, good works, virtues and rewards. There we are shown what we ought to believe, and do, and hope.[83]

From stern to bow, the ark represents the history of salvation. From side to side, it stands for the whole people of God. From bottomless seas to its peak, it shows the soul what steps to take. In all three dimensions, Christ is central. Seeing it whole, as if stepping back and appreciating a complex panorama all at once, is like a glimpse of simultaneous eternity rather than the transient past, present, and future, concludes Hugh.[84] There is, after all, another world. "In this world men run after and applaud vain shows, but in that world they are occupied with inner silence, and the pure in heart rejoice in the sight [contemplation] of the truth."[85]

With "contemplation of the truth," Hugh has reached the pinnacle of his ark, although he has yet more to say about the ark diagram and motif and also about the supreme encounter with the divine. The point of *De archa Noe* was to steer the restless student soul into the stable home of God's saving works of restoration; an advanced soul's further spiritual experience of loving God (almost) beyond words is reserved for his soliloquy *De arrha anime*, "On the Betrothal Gift of the Soul." For now, Hugh concludes this treatise and brings up the diagram.

> I meant to speak but briefly, but I confess to you that I am pleased to have much to say; and perhaps there was still more which I might have said, had I not been afraid of wearying you. And now, then, as we promised, we must put before you the pattern of our ark. Thus you may learn from an external form, which we have visibly depicted, what you ought to do interiorly, and when you have impressed the form of this pattern on your heart, you may rejoice that the house of God has been built within you.[86]

Even before we engage the complexities of the *Libellus* ("On the Making of the Ark"), this concluding reference to an exterior depiction needs to be paired with Hugh's comment at the outset of *Noah's Ark*, namely, that the whole image with its colors and figures was visible from the beginning, the ark as the churchly body of Christ, head and members.[87] Such consistent references to a visible diagram make it all the more puzzling that no such visual representation of the ark or any part thereof exists in any medieval form, but only in modern conjectures. But for the full picture, with its staggering detail, we turn to the companion work.

2. *The Making of the Ark*

The *Booklet on the Making of the Ark* raises many questions, both about the hundreds of details envisioned and also about the nature of this text itself: does it stem from rough student notes rather than Hugh's own expert hand, and (especially) why is it that none of the scores of manuscripts contain any diagram at all?[88] What such a massive and intricate diagram might have looked like has been partially rendered by Grover Zinn, Patrice Sicard (first in his monograph and more fully as appended to his edition of the text), and also by Conrad Rudolph, who disputes some of Sicard's conclusions.[89] A brief introduction to the work here cannot possibly cover all the details of the text, the modern diagrams, or the attendant arguments. It can, however, summarize the *Booklet*'s contents, sample some representative passages, highlight some of the spiritual teachings about the ark that were not developed in *Noah's Ark* itself, and in conclusion mention the debate about a physical diagram.

The title, to start with, has been demystified by editor Sicard, since there never was any warrant for the Migne name, "The Mystical Ark of Noah" (*De arca Noe mystica*), and it has led to unfortunate confusion.[90] The manuscripts give various titles, or none. The most frequent name, *Libellus de formatione arche*, means the "making" of the ark neither by Noah nor in the spiritual sense of God building a home in the heart, but rather the "drawing" or "painting" of an ark-diagram, as evident in the alternative titles.[91] Indeed the entire narrative is put in the first person active (I draw, I make, I color, I paint), just as Hugh wrote in *Noah's Ark* that "I have depicted . . . in a form that you can see," an exemplar "which we have depicted externally."[92]

Saving for later the puzzle that no such depiction survives, we can sample this pattern in the quick way that the text starts, with no preamble: "First, I find the center of the plane on which I want to draw the Ark, and there I fix a point. Around this point I make a small square" like one biblical cubit.[93] This small square occupies Hugh at some length: a cross that is centered and gilded, an alpha and omega, a Greek chi and a sigma for *Ch*ristos, and a lamb. "What else could this picture say to you, if not that Christ is the Beginning and the End, the Bearer of the Old Law and of the New? . . . He was sacrificed on the cross for the sins of man, like a meek lamb."[94] This initial cubit square, including its symbolic colors, is the central Christ column in the middle of the rectangular ark, originally three hundred cubits long and fifty wide, as already mentioned in *Noah's Ark*. Drawing a large representative rectangle as if viewing the ark from straight above, Hugh includes two proportionately smaller rectangles to indicate the stories (rooms or decks) built upon this base, all centered on the middle cubit, which is the Christ pillar at the heart of the ark.[95] The text explains "what could not be represented in a plane," namely, that this square cubit is the top of the column erected from the floor of the ark up (30 cubits) to the peak.[96] As already expounded in *Noah's Ark*,

The column is Christ; its southern side (which signifies His divinity) is called the Tree of Life, and therefore it is colored green; its northern side (which signified His humanity) is called the Book of Life and is colored blue. The Ark leans on this column, and the Church leans on Christ, since it surely would be unable to stand without His support.[97]

In *Noah's Ark*, this Christ column was mostly interpreted tropologically, namely, its peak as one's spiritual goal and the tree imagery as the soul's inner growth of wisdom. Here in the *Libellus*, the emphasis is allegorically on Christ and the whole church, from top to bottom: the Christ column runs through each level, distributing different gifts perhaps but centering one and all, from the lofty to the lowly. Even if we cannot rise above the lowest level, exhorts Hugh,

> Let us not lose hope, but let us come together as one through faith in His name, and let us be at least in the first room and as one with the Church. Let us keep our faith inviolate, and Christ himself will come to us and stand in our midst, celebrating with us our good effort, prepared to help us and to lift us up higher, so that He may be One in all, and One amid all, and One above all, the Lord Jesus Christ.[98]

This rare glimpse inside the ark to the Christ column centering each level of the church provides an allegorical supplement to the tropology of *Noah's Ark*.

Similarly, the next section adds detail to the allegory of the ark as the history of God's people from Adam through Christ to Hugh's present, with space left for the future. Regarding the central band or line down the length of the ark viewed from above: from the top down to the middle cubit column are the generations from Adam to the Incarnation; from the Christ column further down to the bottom are Peter's successors.[99] At the top, the A in Adam's name also indicates east (Anatole), thus orienting the whole image; from Seth down to Jacob the names are listed vertically for the first era, and then the twelve patriarchs are not only named (horizontally) but also pictured, "which the Greeks customarily call 'icons.'"[100] Then, continuing down the line, come the names of each generation from Judah to Joseph, with an inscription: "to this point the first Adam according to the flesh."[101] "Next, after the column, in the same [horizontal] line, I put Peter first, and around him on his right and left the other apostles with their icons," a faithful dozen to balance the patriarchs of the law named and pictured above the column.[102] From Peter downward come all the names of his successors from Clement to Honorius II, who was pope from 1124 to 1130, thus dating this work.[103]

The six eras of human history are here mentioned, as in *The Chronicles*, complete with specific durations, but the text gives more attention (and coloration) to the three theological periods: from the top down to the patriarchs is the era of natural law, from the row of patriarchs to the incarnational column is that of the written law, and "the third part, from the column downward, i.e. from the Incarnation of the Word to the end of the world, is the time of grace."[104] Three bands of color on the exterior borders of the ark, to the far left and right of the vertical center line with all its names, indicate the kinds of people living in these eras. To summarize a complex passage, the color green dominates the (upper) era of natural law, in this case meaning concupiscence, then it almost disappears under the restraints of the written law, but it reemerges somewhat under the mercy of grace. Yellow is the color of the written law, and purple the color for men of grace; these two colors dominate their own eras but are not absent in the others, for "if we look carefully, we find all three sorts of men in each of these times."[105]

Next, Hugh puts on labels for these eras and men, among other details. Top to bottom, he writes on the right side, "Its length was three hundred cubits" and on the left, the names of these three eras; similarly, "fifty cubits was its breadth" is explained by the label "the community of all the faithful under one head, Christ," Jew and Gentile, male and female.[106]

The three rectangular rooms, or stories or decks, are then inscribed on all four sides. Viewed from one side, the ark would carry ascending labels of faith, hope, and charity; from another side, knowledge, discipline, and goodness; from a third side, nature, law, and grace; finally, right, useful, and necessary.

> This last division harmonizes with each of the others thus: faith is right, hope is useful, charity is necessary; likewise, knowledge is right, discipline is useful, goodness is necessary; likewise, nature is right, law is useful, grace is necessary.[107]

Remarkably, there are still more ascending triads of labels for these three stories: married, continent, virgins; those who use or flee or forget the world; those who crawl/repent, those who walk, those who fly.[108]

All these names, icons, colors, and labels might seem enough to overwhelm a diagram already, but the largest dosage of detail is in the next section on the steps that lead up from the four corners through the three decks or stories to the peak. For starters: ascending from the northeast ("cold of the east") corner of pride, one moves through fear, grief, and love; from the southwest corner of concupiscence, through patience, mercy, and remorse; the climb from the northwest corner of ignorance passes through thought, meditation, and contemplation; finally, from the southeast "fervor of the spirit, the first room is temperance, the second, wisdom, the third, strength."[109] These twelve ladders have ten steps each, making 120 rungs that receive yet further detail, such as thirty biblical books listed on the northeast and northwest ascents, specific verses inscribed on various ladders, and a profusion of symbolic numbers as well as three different colors.[110]

At this point, just when a single diagram would seem impossibly cluttered, the text returns to the overall themes of the four ascents, reviewing each triple ladder but also listing the four *descents* of the fall into such predicaments as pride, lust, and ignorance. The ascents are thus actually *returns* from dispersed corners, with echoes of restoration. The "first man" fell.

> And in this fashion he spread through the four parts of the world and was dispersed. When he is gathered and [re-]called together, first from the four parts of the world he approaches the Ark, which is the Church, and ascending upward from there he gathers himself into a whole little by little, until he reaches the highest point. But where he first fell, he first ascends, that is, from the cold of the east, and then he treads upon the head of the serpent, that is, pride. Next he ascends from the warmth of the west, and there he treads upon the belly of the serpent, that is, lust. Next he ascends from the cold of the west and there he treads upon the chest of the serpent, that is, ignorance. Next he returns to the warmth of the east, where he was first created, and, ascending from there, he presses the whole coiled serpent down.[111]

This rehearsal of fall and restoration is further illustrated with the symbols of the four evangelists, the Book of Life and the Tree of Life, personifications of Fear, Grief, Love, and many other symbols.[112] In one very Hugonian example, the ascent from ignorance up through thought and meditation to contemplation is illustrated by a figure ignorantly breaking a jar (the soul), one thinking about the pieces and meditatively collecting them, and then "on the third ladder, Contemplation is drawn, like a smith, joining the pieces, . . . melting [the soul] with the fire of divine love, [and] pours it back into the mint of divine likeness to be formed anew."[113] This ascent is thus the reintegration and restoration of the soul, Hugh's major theme. The text repeats yet again these four ascents, each through three stages, noting that much more could be said and thereby confirming their important place in the overall scheme.[114]

The ark's window and door allow exits in thoughts and deeds, of four types each, as Hugh says he has already discussed in *Noah's Ark*. As the Christ column is two-sided, so, too, the door can be seen from two sides: on the north side, where the Book of Life stands for the humanity of Christ, the (closed) door is the faith by which we have already passed from unbelief into the Church; toward the south, where the Tree of Life indicates the glory to come, the door is ever open toward that future.[115]

Last, regarding features of the ark itself before expanding the picture to the world and universe around it, Hugh returns to his extrabiblical interest in the "little rooms" or exterior receptacles that allowed otters or seals to be in the water now and then.[116] Although scripture does not supply such detail, Hugh imagines six of them, matching three cities on each side of the River Jordan, which thus also cuts through the middle of the ark in the likeness of baptism, "the end of the law and the beginning of grace."[117] Apart from their specific symbolic locations, these "little rooms" or cubicles find their proper (penitential) place within the overall image of the ark of the Church, as here summarized.

> The Ark signifies the Church; the flood, the lust of this world. The animals, which go back and forth repeatedly from the Ark to the water and from the water to the Ark, signify the weak people and the fleshly people in the Church, who often slip by sin into the desire of this world. For these people the remedy of repentance is prepared, like little rooms in the spiritual Ark, that is, in the Holy Church.[118]

Recalling the world outside the ark leads to mention of Babylon and Egypt with their geographical locations, relative to central Jerusalem, in a "map of the world."[119] Although the text first itemizes the (forty-two!) biblical places charting the path "from the Egypt of the natural law through the desert of the written law to the promised land of grace,"[120] it is the map of the world around the ark that commands attention.

The final section of the *Libellus* is no longer about the ark in itself ("that is enough"), but rather about the still wider context of the physical world and spiritual universe around it.[121] In quick succession (and with little interpretation) come the map of the world already mentioned, with Paradise and Inferno; a circle of the four seasons personified as a singing boy (spring), a flower-scattering youth (summer), a man sniffing a fruit (fall), and an old man eating it (winter); the twelve winds by name in four triads; the twelve months and the "twelve signs of the Zodiac. . . . This arrangement signifies the grand rationale and working of nature, and the whole vault of the heavens is finished."[122] That the course of history here matches a movement in geography (from eastern antiquity to western modernity) is called a "marvelous arrangement," phrasing that is perhaps more indicative of a student reporter than of Hugh's self-congratulation.[123]

Although it thus surrounds and dwarfs the central ark, this universe of earth and ether and air is itself embraced by the still larger figure of Christ in majesty, as in Isaiah's vision invoked at the start of *Noah's Ark*.[124] Christ's arms "embrace all things," from the winds and seasons to the ark itself, and point to the Kingdom of Heaven on his right and eternal fire on his left.[125] From Christ's mouth descends a sextet of small circles indicating the six days of creation leading up to humanity, namely, the ark of human history here receiving its final summary:

> In this way, the word proceeds from the mouth of the Majesty, and the whole series of creation follows, and the whole expanse of the Ark reaches from the beginning of the world up to the end of time, having places here and there, hills, rivers, forts, and towns, Egypt to the south, and to the north Babylon.[126]

Last, and again without much interpretation, two seraphim are drawn, as in Isaiah 6, and then the nine ranks of angels who number ninety-nine after the angelic fall and who "contemplate the face of the Majesty . . . to which man was added, as the one-hundredth sheep, and the city above was completed."[127] This final reference to "painting" the seraphim and other angels reminds the reader of the overall narrative about externally drawing, painting, arranging, and inscribing the ark in its global context of salvation history, all for an inner spiritual purpose, as Hugh summarizes in conclusion.

> I have said these things about the drawing [*figuratione*] of our Ark, so that if it please anyone to gaze inwardly upon the elegance of the Lord's house and His miracles, which are without number, he might at the same time rouse his emotion [*affectum*] with this exemplar. Blessed be God forever. Amen.[128]

So ends the compact yet complex *Libellus*, although much more should be (and has been) said about it.

Whether there ever really was such an extensive physical diagram cannot be decided here, although the arguments must be mentioned. On the one hand, the entire narrative is all about making such a material representation, a process mentioned often in *Noah's Ark*. Hugh's point here in concluding the *Libellus* is one he also made early on in *Noah's Ark*, namely, about an external visible form and an internal tropological effect, indeed, the spiritual goal of God's restorative works: "Now the figure of this spiritual building which I am going to present to you is Noah's Ark. This your eye shall see outwardly, so that your soul may be fashioned to its likeness inwardly."[129] The plain meaning to this frequent talk of outward depiction and inward formation is that Hugh's teaching method, perhaps also for other lectures besides those preserved in *Noah's Ark*, included a physical drawing of some kind. Twelfth-century texts did sometimes include illustrations, famously and prominently in Hildegard of Bingen and also in William of Conches.[130] On the other hand, as thoughtful scholars have argued, the overwhelming detail envisioned and especially the utter absence in the dozens of extant manuscripts of any such drawing (or even of a partial diagram, such as the central cubit) together suggest another possibility. Perhaps this was entirely a way of teaching without any materiality at all, a rhetorical strategy to stimulate the imagination and feed the memory such that the ark was "externally" envisioned by the hearers and readers for the sake of inward learning but was never physically drawn?[131] This interpretation of the texts is forceful, perhaps forced, but it does square with the manuscript evidence of not a single extant medieval diagram of any kind. Editor Sicard and Grover Zinn have separately suggested a middle way between these two possibilities: perhaps Hugh himself had a large visual aid of some kind, such as a wall painting or a set of parchment sheets, but not in a permanent form.[132] When copies of *Noah's Ark* were requested, the impracticality of copying the diagram suggested a written description instead, namely, the *Libellus* itself as a substitute. Thus Hugh, in this appealing conjecture, had a physical diagram, later lost forever, but subsequent copies of *Noah's Ark* and the *Libellus* never did have accompanying diagrams. Furthermore, perhaps the *Libellus*, as Conrad Rudolph argues, came later from composite student notes of Hugh's comments rather than from his own hand. Rudolph has briefly summarized the debate, including the two versions of the *Libellus*, and has promised a full treatment with his own rendition of the diagram itself.[133]

3. Related Texts

The *Libellus* also leads the reader to other texts, or at least to questions about them. It refers not only back to texts already done, namely, *Noah's Ark* and *De tribus diebus*,[134] but also forward to a work Hugh is "thinking about doing." After itemizing the forty-two biblical stations from Egypt through the desert to the promised land, Hugh suggests further exposition of both the mysterious names (in Numbers 33) and also the theological transition from natural law to written law to grace:

> I will pursue what needs to be said about the interpretation and the significance of these stations at more length, perhaps, in another work, which I am thinking about writing about this same Ark, and also, why the natural law is compared to Egypt, the written law, to the desert, and grace, to the promised land, and what sort of path leads from the first through the second to the third.[135]

As tantalizing as another ark treatise might be, exegetically and theologically, there is no sign that Hugh completed such a work, and the entire paragraph even disappears from the later (shorter) version of the *Libellus*.

More complicated is the possibility that the *Libellus* refers not merely to a "map of the world" within the diagram but to another work entirely, a *Descriptio mappe mundi*, as Patrick Gautier Dalché has recently argued, and others before him. The text says, regarding the locations of Babylon and Egypt relative to Jerusalem, that "this will later be clarified in the description of the map of the world."[136] The printed translation ("from the drawing of the map of the world") gives no indication or annotation that another project might be meant, but Gautier Dalché has edited, annotated, and argued thoroughly for such a work, whether directly by Hugh or at least a student report of Hugh's geographical teaching.[137] The text is largely a long list of place names, but the introductory paragraph shows typical Hugonian traces of style, pedagogy, and exegesis.[138] The work may indeed stem from Hugh's encyclopedic productivity, perhaps indirectly from student notes, but it pertains more to the earlier foundations of pedagogy rather than the "spiritual finish" of tropology featured in *Noah's Ark*, our main point in this chapter.

The overall theme of the world's flux and the soul's home, with the imagery of flood and ark on the canvas of creation and restoration, also figures prominently in another full-scale work, *On the Vanity of the World*. Hugh repeats his basic teachings, in a lively dialogue, with vivid examples, all aimed directly at the spiritual finale of encountering God.[139] Reason and the Soul (functionally, a teacher and an inquirer) converse about the vanity of the world, looking past several scenes of superficial and temporary happiness by contemplating (truly seeing) their eventual ruin. First in view is a luxury cruise with orchestra and fine dining on a sun-washed deck amid frolicking schools of fish, but only until a furious storm ruins everything, and the shipwrecked wretches become fish food themselves. Vanity, and vanity of vanities.[140] Hugh's rich rhetoric does not yet name the flood or an ark, but he is just getting started. A second vision watches a fine caravan of traders as it is ambushed and devastated, a third notices that a rich farmstead leads to worries and selfish evils, and a fourth sees how a happy wedding becomes a miserable marriage.[141] Each dramatic vignette trades on the flow of time, the flux of this world's vain decline. The fifth and final example is a school, more directly out of Hugh's experience and leading straight to his point. On the surface, all is well: young and old learn and grow in grammar and logic, mathematics and music, geometry and botany, "the qualities and properties of everything."[142] Yet this, too, is vanity, when vain and obstinate men "search out the natures of things while they remain in ignorance of the One who is the Author and Maker of themselves and of all things alike. Yet they do not inquire after Him—as though without God truth might be found or happiness possessed."[143] The journey of human learning must arrive at the divine destination, or else the "learned" are even more lost and miserable than the shipwrecked and the ambushed. Thus comes Hugh to his spiritual finish, in that the whole ark imagery is finally about encountering God.

Vivid vignettes have set the stage in book 1; the spiritual lesson, the heart of the work, is book 2. The very transience of this world, as just seen so dramatically, points to the flow of time: from the past, yet toward what future, what goal? While this mutable world lamentably plunges downward as if in a flood, where is our "safer dwelling" for an inward and upward approach to the immutable God who abides on high?[144] The entire Augustinian discussion about lower distractions and inner/higher unity is familiar from *Noah's Ark*, yet with certain new touches and sometimes a greater emphasis on the final spiritual goal of finding rest in God. From base dispersions, inner unity leads higher to the immutable divine.

Thus the soul ascends from this infinite distraction which is below; and, as was said, the more it is collected into one the more it is raised on high until it arrives at the true and unique immutability which is with God, where it may rest for a change.[145]

Moving to the explicit imagery of a flood below, and upon it "a special sort of ark in the human heart," Hugh gives several new roles for God above, namely, "at once the helmsman who steers the ark of man's heart that rides there on the heaving ocean, the anchor that holds it, and the haven that receives it."[146] The "saving wood" of the ark is the "way of salvation," but how do we enter it and ascend to God?[147] Using the visible example of height, the point is really the invisible interior.

To ascend to God means, therefore, to enter into oneself, and not only to enter into oneself, but in some ineffable manner to penetrate even into one's depths.[148]

The original dignity of the human creature was lost, but it is the internal that is near and supreme and eternal, whereas the external is weak and distant and transient. To turn from the world "below" to God "above" is to turn within, and to return to oneself is to meditate on "the things that pertain to one's salvation," specifically, the works of creation and the works of restoration.[149] Hugh reviews these basic categories, this time in explicit connection to the flood and the ark. "The elect emerge from the works of creation flowing down below as if from a shipwreck, and carried up through the works of restoration, that is, the sacraments of their salvation, as if on a certain saving ark."[150] With these basics reviewed, "ponder and meditate unceasingly upon the mysteries [*sacramenta*] of your restoration and the blessings of God's loving kindness to you, and you have entered into the ark," with its historical length of three eras, its allegorical breadth of all believers, and its tropological scriptural height. But as Hugh says himself, these things have been treated more fully in another book on the ark and should not be repeated here.[151]

What should be noted here, continues Hugh, is the spiritual goal for all this, namely, "that we should enter this saving dwelling . . . and find therein those delights of God's sweetness that He keeps hid for those who love Him."[152] The more intimate and affective language of sweet delights is here briefly reinforced by way of the Canticle's bride with her King, but quickly disappears again. To make the general point about living comfortably in that ark or home where all "will contemplate God's wonders and . . . praise

Him in His works," Hugh paints another word picture, this time of how a son dwells happily on the family manor.[153] Some details here, such as finding birds' nests and bringing the fledglings home, suggest that this lively vignette is informed by Hugh's own memories, even with the didactic allegory briefly appended.[154]

As book 2 closes, the teacher offers to become a tour guide through this house, "the works of our restoration from the beginning of the world" in the east to its consummation in the west, namely, the rooms and levels within this long and broad and high ark, and we "will not cease until we come to the King's throne."[155] Books 3 and 4 then offer a detailed journey through such salvation history, from the creation of Adam (reprised in *De sacramentis* One, six, i)[156] and the patriarchs through Christ and the saints and fathers, but it never seems to arrive at the "King's throne" as promised. The dialogue partners marvel at these works of God throughout history,[157] but the narrative remains preparatory. The "sweetness" of divine delights and the final stop at the King's own throne are never directly discussed, at least not in the ark treatises, which largely chart the approach to such climactic goals. There is, however, one further treatise where the spiritual finish is quite directly and personally revealed.

THE FINAL *SOLILOQUY*

Hugh's *Soliloquy*, *De arrha anime*, is a fitting climax to our overview of his major works, specifically for the way that the foundation of history and the framework of doctrine here culminate in a spiritual finish. Judging by the number of manuscripts, more than three hundred, it was his most popular work. Like a precious gemstone with various facets, the *Soliloquy* reflects several aspects of Hugh's life and work in review: his original Augustinian foundations, a lifelong exposition of salvation history both corporate and individual, the focus on love by way of the *Song of Songs*, and his pedagogical exposition of scripture as history, (allegorical) doctrine, and tropology regarding the soul's ascent and final goal. On the last point, this late essay also adds something distinctive to Hugh's corpus. The ark treatises and other spiritual writings led the soul on its ascent toward its destination but stopped short of the peak; the *Soliloquy* reflects the ecstatic completion of this itinerary, insofar as it is possible in this life. Master Hugh's last lesson is that amid this earthly journey we receive a down payment on the future gift of eternal life with God, an engagement gift that promises and indeed inaugurates the full blessings of that intimate relationship.

1. Prologue

As a cover letter, Hugh's brief "Prologue" reveals a context, introduces the fuller title, and deftly previews his theme. "To our beloved Brother G. [Gunther] and to the other servants of Christ at Hamersleben. . . ."[1] As noted at the outset, Hugh probably spent some formative early years at this Augustinian community in Saxony. That he sends his essay and greetings to a "Brother G.," and then to brothers B and A and the others, suggests the time frame of 1139, when Gunther may have functioned as prior. The *Soliloquy* is thus one of Hugh's final works, and its title and content equally reflect his spiritual home with the Augustinians. I am sending you, he writes, a "soliloquy on love," on where to seek true love and heavenly joys so that the heart may find its rest.[2]

Augustine wrote not only on these themes but also a *Soliloquy* that seems to have been Hugh's model; the bishop of Hippo also wrote precisely on the theme and terminology of the soul's *arrha*. The idea of an internal dialogue, a soliloquy in this case between Hugh as the teacher and his own soul as the learner, stems from Augustine's *Soliloquy*, although there may also have been intervening examples. The Victorine's revival of the genre received massive circulation and inspired many later examples.[3] When Hugh further specifies the title of this soliloquy as "The Soul's *Arrha*," he invokes a complex biblical and Augustinian heritage, with a medieval development. The Pauline "*arrabon*" (2 Corinthians 1.22 and 5.5, Ephesians 1.14) is like a down payment or firstfruits of what is coming; the Holy Spirit is the initial gift now or "guarantee" of the full gift yet to come. Augustine carefully distinguished this *arrha* as the real beginning of the gift, over against a pledge (*pignus*, as in Jerome's translation) that merely substitutes now for a future gift; further, Augustine himself associated this language with the betrothal gift of the *Song*'s nuptials,[4] a sort of bridal gift or perhaps even an engagement ring, whereby the groom starts giving the bride all that is his. By Hugh's time, this terminology had lost most of the fiscal overtones of down payments or earnest money and had become wedded to the bridal imagery. "The *Arrha* of the Soul" thus means the special gift to the bride that is the beginning of the groom's gift of himself. When Hugh concludes his prologue by diplomatically explaining that his own gift of this essay is both for his dearest brother especially and also for the others communally, he subtly previews his theme that the divine gift is both for each individual soul and also for the communal others.[5]

2. *Soliloquy*

Apart from the "Prologue," which Hugh may have written last of all as a cover letter with its "Farewell," the *Soliloquy* itself begins with a private inner question: "Tell me, my soul, what is it that you love above all things?"[6] Love is essential to life, but what should we love? The soul's cautious reply pleases "Hugh," since this world is fleeting, so the search is on for a lovable beauty greater than these temporal goods. "Why do you not esteem [love] yourself instead," asks Hugh of the soul, "you who in your comeliness surpass the grace and beauty of all visible things?"[7] This is not solitary self-love but rather the realization that there is someone else who sees you more clearly than you see yourself, whose high evaluation and powerful love will prevail. Hugh tells his soul, "you have a betrothed, but you do not know it."[8] This husband, this bridegroom who loves you and thus reveals that you are lovely and lovable, is sending gifts, and so Hugh comes to his title phrase.

> As yet he [the bridegroom] has not wished to present himself to you, but he has sent his gifts and given the pledge money [*arrha*], the bond of his love and the sign of his fervor.[9]

What is this *arrha*, this down payment, this lavish engagement gift from the great giver to his beloved bride? "And so I shall tell you so that you may know what your betrothed has given you. Look at the universe and consider whether there is anything in it which does not serve you."[10] For starters, nature itself, the seas and the seasons, is there for your pleasure and your need, an open gift from a hidden giver, the *arrha* of the groom, blessings from the Lord.[11] This is rightly ordered (Augustinian) love, to love the gifts not in themselves but as given, to realize that one's own soul is also thus beloved and gifted, to love the Giver above all.[12] The soul is inflamed by such sweet words, kindled in ardor for the bridegroom, yet hesitates. "But my devotion suffers this wrong, for though I love him only I am not his only delight." The pledge [*arrha*] of his love is shared by not only bestial men but also even the beasts themselves, who all receive the same sunlight and air and life itself.[13] Here "Hugh" is, typically, a patient teacher, who has already hinted at this original concern in the prologue. This groom gives three kinds of gifts: some to all the living, some to special groups, some to individuals. "Does your lover then honor you the less because he has bestowed certain of his gifts on everyone as well as you?"[14] The common gifts of creation and human society should occasion thanksgiving, not jealousy. The soul is partially persuaded, at least about lower creation, yet within the human circle, why should everyone, believers and unbelievers alike, even criminals and the impure, all share in these gifts of life?[15] Here Hugh needs to invoke a "divine dispensation" whereby even the evil serve the good, at least by negative example.[16] As for sharing the groom's gift with other good and faithful recipients, this company is itself a gift of the Creator. "Indeed it would be blessed to enjoy this love alone, but it is much more blessed to delight in it in the company of the many good men in this life."[17]

At this pedagogical point, with the "soul" and the readers catching on, Hugh teaches a more advanced lesson about the love that is both communal and singular. Such spiritual love becomes more singular for each precisely when it is shared with all. Your groom's love cannot be lessened by division.

> He is present to each one as he is to all. . . . Such love is unique, yet not private, singular yet not solitary, shared but not divided, both communal and singular . . . sweet and eternal.[18]

The soul, now a more advanced student, appreciates the idea but presses the question in more learned terms: how can this chaste groom be present to each individual beloved as to all, "in affect and in effect," namely, in inner affection and in manifest reality?[19]

The underlying question here, explains Hugh to the soul, is whether you will appreciate the groom's gifts as not only common to all the living, such as sunlight and air, and special to humankind such as faith and wisdom, but also singular to yourself, just as Peter, Paul, and John had distinctive gifts.[20] This would seem to leave a teacher no recourse but individual tutorials on discerning one's own singular gifts, but Hugh masterfully zeros in on any honest reader's realization of God's gifts and the personal appreciation of them. The language is evocative, affective, and effective, to personalize the point. First of all, *you* exist. "There was once a time when you did not exist and in order that you might come into being, you received this as a gift from him. . . . In truth, your existence is a wholly gratuitous gift."[21] Here Hugh the teacher joins the student soul in marveling at this great and good gift, and in praising and thanking such a Giver, yet there is even more. "But He has given more for we have received not merely existence but a beautiful and fair existence." And yet more:

> But the bounty of the Divine Bestower could not be stayed here. He has given us something more, for He has raised us to the level of his own

likeness. As He took us to himself in his love, so He also wished to make us like himself.[22]

For such gifts so lovingly bestowed, the soul can only love in return. Beyond sheer existence and life, there are still further gifts, wisdom within and the senses without. "How exalted and glorious you have been made, my Soul," robed and bejeweled as befits entrance into the bridal chamber of the celestial king.[23]

Even without individualizing the gift, Hugh's heightened rhetoric evokes a personal response and then turns a corner.

> You had much to rejoice in and you ought to have guarded your treasure closely in order not to destroy or defile this incomparable gift, nor to disfigure such great beauty.... Yet, consider what you have done, my Soul. You have deserted your Lover and have squandered your affections on others.[24]

Showered by the bridal gifts of creation itself, what have you done with the creator-groom's generosity? You fell away, like a harlot! As the soul tries to hide or at least cover the shame that has been exposed, we realize that Hugh is telling the human story of creation, Eden's blessings, and the fall.[25] This history is being retold and personalized for what comes next, "to make you more vividly aware of your obligations to Him who both created you when you were not and also redeemed you when you were lost," and thus the corner is quickly turned from creation to restoration. "Your lover [bridegroom], who appeared so sublime when He created [*conderet*] you, permitted himself to be humbled when He redeemed [*repararet*] you."[26] The power of the original creator becomes the mercy of the incarnate restorer, one and the same lover, coming down to lift you up, restoring what you lost: "He came down among men, took on their mortality, suffered His passion, conquered death, and restored mankind."[27] The works of creation and works of restoration do not need to be rehearsed in full, being so explicit throughout Hugh's works, but their connection to the language of the *arrha*-gift is helpfully specified in the *Eulogium*: the communal *arrha* is in the creation of nature, the special *arrha* in our restoration by grace.[28]

Hugh's passionate rhetoric renders the soul briefly speechless, for the groom's grace abounds just as if you had never fallen; in fact, "He promises you blessings even greater than before."[29] At this, the soul exults ("O happy fault!") that the fall has led to such love: "In His innocence He died for me, in whom there was certainly nothing to love."[30] But why? "If you should seek the cause for this you would find no other reason than the free and gratuitous charity of your Savior. He as your Espoused, your Lover, your Redeemer, and your God," concludes the Augustinian master, "selected and foredestined you."[31]

Convinced, the soul has a different kind of question: why, then, the delay? Why can't I come into the lover's arms now? Because you need to be cleansed, clothed and adorned, in sum, to prepare yourself.[32] The necessity of extensive bridal preparations leads to the biblical exemplum of King Assuerus or Ahasuerus in Esther 2, complete with historical, allegorical, and tropological meaning. In short, it is not enough to realize that you are among the first elect, those called together by order of the king; you must also undergo thorough cleansing and preparation to be the one selected by the royal will. When King Ahasuerus was spurned by Queen Vashti and sought a new bride, his ministers gathered many together for lengthy preparation and adornment before he chose one of them. This, says Hugh, is a "useful example."[33] Having presented its literal historical sense, such as six months for anointing and then six months for makeup, the interpretation turns to other senses of the passage. "Let us consider therefore, if this example can be adapted to the matter which concerns us here."[34] Hugh's treatises do not offer many compact examples of a scripture's historical, allegorical, and tropological meanings, as we have seen with respect to Job and Noah's ark, but the pattern is predictable. Allegorically, the text points to another King, indeed, the son of the high King, who sought a worthy wife; when He was spurned by Judea, then His ministers, "namely the apostles," brought prospective mates into the church to be anointed and patiently prepared so that when they came into the presence of this King they might become his elect, not the reprobate.[35] From the (allegorical) doctrine of Christ and the church in general, the expositor turns to tropology, the moral of the story for you: "Look, therefore, where you are and you will realize what you ought to do."[36] The bridegroom has brought you to the place where the ointments and nourishments are available. Therefore, "prepare yourself as is needful for a spouse [bride] of a King, a spouse of the King of Heaven, a spouse of the immortal Lover [bridegroom]."[37]

The soul is newly anxious to do the right thing; converted toward the right love, she begs, she pleads to know the particulars of how to prepare herself to please Him.[38] Hugh tells her what to do, spiritually interpreting the room of preparation as the church, and the king's bridal chamber as the heavenly Jerusalem yet to come. Everything has been provided by His love: the cleansing waters of baptism, the chrism and anointing oils of the Holy Spirit, the nourishment of the body and blood of Christ, the garments of good works, and the fragrance of the virtues. If you are soiled again, your tears and contrition can refresh you. "See how on every side you are aided by the divine plan! You had not and you received; you wasted . . . and it is restored to you. You will never be utterly abandoned and thus you know how greatly you are esteemed by your Lover."[39] The exemplum has led to the moral, and the exhortation reaches its climax.

> Pray that in His mercy He will cleanse you if any sins now remain in you, that in His benignity He will perfect whatever spark of virtue you may possess, and that He will bring you to Himself in the way He has ordained. What more can I say to you?[40]

As often with Hugh, the one more word is "charity." "Such is the love of God for us, that everything which our human frailty endures is disposed in His great benevolence for our welfare."[41]

3. Confession

At this point, the *Soliloquy* introduces a *Confessio* to sum up everything, equally Augustinian in that it is partially a confession of sin and mostly a rapturous confession of praise. As Hugh's most personal testimony, apparently about himself and his own spiritual experience, here it is generously quoted to let him speak in conclusion for himself. In the prologue, Hugh spoke to his brothers; in the soliloquy, "Hugh" spoke to his soul, a pattern resumed shortly, with a difference; in the confession, Hugh first speaks to God, in Augustinian tones.

> I confess to You your mercies, my Lord and my God, because You have not deserted me, O Sweetness of my life and Light of my eyes. What shall I return to You for all You have given me? You wish me to love You; yet how shall I love you and how greatly shall I love You? Who am I that I should love You? And yet I shall [love You], my Lord and my Strength, my Support, my Refuge, my Liberator, my God, my Helper, my Protector, the Pledge of my Salvation, and my Surety. What more can I say? You are my Lord and my God.[42]

Incorporating the Psalms (116 and 18 especially), as did the bishop of Hippo, Hugh has turned from soliloquy to the kind of pure prayer he commended in "The Power of Praying" mentioned earlier.[43]

When Hugh then addresses his soul, it is not so much a pedagogical dialogue ("I" teaching "you") but that "we" should singularly love God, as He has been our singular (not communal) lover.

> My Soul, what shall we do for our Lord God, from whom we have received so many great blessings? He certainly was not satisfied to grant us the same goods which He gave to others. Even in our trials and misdeeds we have recognized Him as our particular [singular] Lover, and so we should love him utterly [singularly], in good times and bad.[44]

The recurrent theme of a singular love and gift relative to general blessings will come back once again as the soul resolves its questions for good, but first "Hugh" gives a personal testimony. This extraordinary paragraph resonates not only with Hugh's observations about the life of learning in the *Didascalicon* but also with everything we can conclude about his character and spiritual life from all the writings we have sampled. It sounds genuinely autobiographical:

> You have so endowed me, O Lord, to recognize You and understand better than many others the revelations of your secrets. You have left my contemporaries in the darkness of ignorance, but in me You have infused the light of wisdom. You have granted that I know You more truly, love You more purely, believe in You more surely, and pursue You more ardently. You have given me many gifts: keen senses, an able intellect, good memory, fluent speech, a pleasing manner of discourse, ability to persuade, talent in my work, a pleasant personality in discussion, progress in studies, success in my enterprises, comfort in adversity, and wisdom in prosperity. Wherever I have applied myself, there your favor and mercy have preceded me. Often when I seemed about to falter, You suddenly came to my help. When I was lost, You led me back to the way; when I was in ignorance, You taught me; when I sinned You took me up. In sadness You consoled me, in despair You comforted me. If I fell, You raised me up; if I stood erect, You sustained me. [When I went away, You led me back; when I came back, You received me.] All these and many other things You have done for me, O Lord. It will be sweet always to think of them, always to speak of them, ever to give thanks for them. In this way I shall praise You and love You, O Lord God, for all Your blessings.[45]

From someone else, the opening comparisons with others would sound vain or proud, yet Hugh's insightful writings and wise pedagogy back him up and undergird the rest of this spiritual testimony of praise and thanks and love.

Turning back to his soul and back to the *arrha* theme, "Hugh" initiates the final soliloquy exchange.

> Behold, my Soul, you have your earnest money [*arrha*] and because of it you can recognize your Spouse. Keep yourself untouched, undefiled, pure, and without stain for Him. If once you were a harlot, now you have become a virgin, for His love has been pleased to give back to sinners their spotlessness and to preserve for the innocent their chastity. Never forget, therefore, how much mercy He has shown you and how greatly you are loved by Him, for you know that His blessing has never failed you.[46]

Upon hearing this exhortation, and indeed the full confession of praise just quoted in its entirety (albeit in four parts), the soul's recurring question about how the bridegroom's love can be singular *and* communal is resolved.

> Truly I confess that His love is worthily called singular, for although it bestows itself upon many, it embraces each one individually. It is certainly a good and wonderful blessing, for it is the common possession of all and the complete delight of each one. It watches over all and fulfills the desires of each one; it is everywhere present, takes care of everyone, and yet is equally provident for the individual.[47]

It can even seem that I am His only love, confesses the soul, that He is always and only devoted to me, fully attuned to my every thought and deed. Yet the Lover's singular devotion, so longed for, also brings the soul a fearful realization: "How many are the faults for which I blush in His sight and on account of which I am greatly fearful of offending him."[48] Now it is the soul's turn for an inner soliloquy to address its stains: "Go! Depart, and offend no longer the eyes of my Beloved. . . . From Him I have learned that I ought to remove you, and now I know how I shall do this."

The soul has come so far and learned so much that "something wonderful is happening to us," says Hugh as he sums up how they have talked through several issues.[49] First, even from the "Prologue," came the issue of singular and communal love.

> You said, for example, that an individual love and one held in common with others were mutually impossible. But then that love has been shown

to be more truly marvelous because it is at once held in common by many and yet in an especial way bestowed on each one.[50]

Next came the issue of the delay, with the biblical moral.

Again, you said that you were not perfectly loved because you had heard that you were chosen for His regimen of preparation, but you had not yet seen yourself taken to His chambers; yet here too His love for you has been revealed to be even greater because your self-reform is patiently awaited by Him.[51]

Last, wondered the soul, could He really love me with my shameful lingering faults?

If, therefore, He deigned to love you when you were wholly repulsive and possessed no attraction, how much more does He now desire you, now that you are beginning to be beautiful and to put aside your former vileness?[52]

There is only one more question, a testimony of a wholly different order, the experiential query that secured Hugh's place in the flowering of medieval mysticism.

I now ask that you kindly answer this last question. What is that sweetness which sometimes touches my consciousness, and so forcefully and pleasantly moves me that I begin somehow to be wholly taken out of myself [a memetipsa abalienari] and in some way to be transported? Suddenly I am renewed and am become totally different, and I experience a well-being beyond my ability to describe. My senses are exhilarated, all the misery of past sorrows falls away, my mind is exultant, and my perception enlightened. My heart also is cheered and my desires are pleased. Now I see myself in some other place, I know not where, and as it were I hold someone within me in the embraces of love. Who it is I do not know, and yet I struggle with great effort to retain Him in my possession and never lose Him. My mind somehow fights in a pleasurable way lest He ever depart, for it desires to be always in his embrace. And as if it would find in Him the fulfillment of all its desires, it hopes for nothing more, seeks nothing beyond, wishes always to be like this, completely and ineffably rejoicing. Is that one my Beloved? Say, I ask you, that I may know whether He is that one; then if He should come to me again, I will beseech Him not to depart but to remain forever.[53]

Jacob wrestled with an angel; Bernard of Clairvaux once reported a similar fleeting experience of the divine presence;[54] Richard of St. Victor developed this language of ecstatic alienation from self for generations of spiritual writers to come.

Yet, here our focus remains on Hugh, for with these concluding lines we come, after all the pedagogical context, historical foundation, and doctrinal framework, to the spiritual finish. Hugh answers the soul's query, and the soul is content with the finale.

> Certainly that one who comes to you is your Beloved. But He comes hidden, unseen, and imperceptible. He comes to touch you, not to be seen by you; to admonish you, not to be beheld. He comes not to give Himself entirely, but to present Himself to your awareness [taste]; not to fulfill your desires, but to gain your affection. He offers the first and certain signs of His love, not the plenitude of its perfect fulfillment! In this especially is there evidence of the pledge [*arrha*] of your espousal, for he who in the future will permit himself to be contemplated and possessed by you forever now presents Himself to you that you may know how well-disposed He is. Meanwhile you are consoled in His absence, since by His visits you are continually refreshed lest you grow weak. My soul, we have now said many things; but after all these words I ask you to acknowledge Him only, love Him only, pursue Him only, take Him only, and possess Him only.

> *His soul:* This is my wish and my desire, and I seek this with all my heart.[55]

APPENDIX: HUGH AND DIONYSIUS

The *Commentary* on
The Celestial Hierarchy

An introduction to Hugh's major works cannot cover his entire corpus, even if some of his many smaller works have here been clustered around the *Didascalicon, De sacramentis*, and the ark treatises. Yet there is still so much more: so much biblical exposition, so much miscellany, so many sermons, albeit often of disputed authorship. And Pseudo-Hugh would be a topic all its own. But one more major work does deserve separate attention, for Hugh wrote a long commentary, one of his longest works overall, on the first (Pseudo-) Dionysian treatise, *The Celestial Hierarchy*.[1] It is here relegated to an appendix because it lacks the characteristic Hugonian themes that this book used to organize the Victorine's works.

A bit of patristic and Parisian background is needed. Long before Hugh, a venerable tradition held that the Dionysius of Acts 17 (the Areopagite Athenian converted by St. Paul's sermon about the "unknown God") became a bishop, wrote several theological treatises (*The Celestial Hierarchy, The Ecclesiastical Hierarchy, The Divine Names*, and *The Mystical Theology*), and later ended his life in Paris as a missionary martyr. He thus became the decapitated Saint Denis whose (royal) abbey dominated the north side of Paris. Peter Abelard doubted whether this particular Dionysius ever came to Paris, and modern scholarship has shown that the real authorship of these works dates from the early sixth century. But to Hugh and to his predecessors, as well as contemporaries (including Abelard) and successors, the Dionysian corpus was the first of the Fathers.[2] In the ninth century, a Byzantine emperor had given a Greek manuscript of Dionysius to the Frankish court so devoted to Saint Denis. As shortly translated into Latin by Abbot Hilduin and then by John the Scot (Eriugena), this manuscript, still extant, begins with *The Celestial Hierarchy*. Eriugena himself wrote a commentary on this first Dionysian treatise, and his encounter with the Areopagite's thought permeates his overall corpus.[3] Between Eriugena in the ninth century and Hugh, only a few authors took (minor) notice of Dionysius, but interest picked up in the twelfth century, especially in Chartres and Paris.[4] When in the *Didascalicon* Hugh itemized the Fathers such as Augustine or Eusebius regarding Christian literature, he largely quoted previous lists and decretals. But he added a sentence of his own on Dionysius: "Dionysius the Areopagite, ordained bishop of the Corinthians, has left many volumes as testimony of his mental ability."[5] Nothing more is said about these writings, and there is no mention of Paris. In *De vanitate mundi*, however, the long narrative about Christian martyrs starts with St. Peter and then: "Dionysius the Areopagite, accepting his mandate, penetrated Gaul," fought for the truth, and showed the power of life by carrying his head in his hands.[6]

These minimal allusions and the relative absence of Dionysius from Hugh's major works raise questions about his *Commentary*, his one work directly on the Dionysian corpus. Long and thorough, his only nonbiblical commentary, the Victorine's exposition of *The Celestial Hierarchy* became a major part of a twelfth-century surge of interest in Dionysius, but why he originally took on the project is never fully explained. On the one hand, it seems to have originated in lectures for novice students, and at their request.

> I said first off and I say again now, lest I lead you on in (false) expectation, that I took up your request regarding the "Hierarchy" of Dionysius not to attempt a full scrutiny of the depths of these subjects but only to uncover the surface of the words and expose them to the light. For this [introduction] is first of all more suited for beginners, especially because we know that what we have undertaken for discussion is too great and beyond our possibilities.[7]

Surely Paris students, whether Victorine novices or external scholars who moved about the area, knew that the Abbey of Saint Denis housed not only the bodily remains but also the literary legacy of its patron saint. It would not be surprising if they as beginners asked Master Hugh to introduce them to the local saint who was the first of the Fathers. On the other hand, Poirel speculates that Hugh knew Dionysius before coming to Paris and may have initiated the project himself.[8]

Hugh's *Prologue*, although separable and in fact often separated from the *Commentary* itself, twice confirms that this project was for beginners, literally "for those who should be introduced" to Dionysius,[9] and he there makes a rudimentary introduction. In his complex *Prologue*, Hugh introduces Dionysius in one place as a "theologian and describer of the hierarchies" and elsewhere as a "theologian and narrator of the hierarchies."[10] By itself, this duplication would not cause much attention, but the *Prologue* also duplicates quite redundantly both its specification that these "hierarchies" are three (the divine Trinity, the triadic angelic hierarchy, and the human counterpart) and the explanation for why Dionysius starts with the angelic (*The Celestial Hierarchy*), proceeds to the human (*The Ecclesiastical Hierarchy*), and culminates with the divine (*The Divine Names*).[11] For this and other reasons, the *Prologue* seems to be a composite of introductory remarks by Hugh, perhaps written after the *Commentary* itself, and surely assembled later, probably after Hugh's death. These and other textual questions must await Poirel's edition and further studies.[12] For now, however, regarding the purpose of Hugh's *Commentary*, the *Prologue* confirms and amplifies the point that this is for beginners. However deep and difficult the Dionysian concepts may be, Hugh's first task is a "moderate, common, and simple explanation unto understanding. Indeed perhaps this will be an explanation more fitting for those who are to be introduced" to such great material.[13] Hugh's patient way of presenting the entire Dionysian text first, passage by passage, before offering his own comments on specific wording and overall meaning, supports this view of his pedagogical plan, although such was also the pattern in Eriugena's commentary.[14]

The Celestial Hierarchy is a substantial treatise in size and complexity. Its fifteen chapters present the nine kinds of biblical angels in three triads, such as the seraphim, cherubim, and thrones at the top of the angelic hierarchy, receiving divine illumination and passing it on down in sequential mediation. However, before any such specific discussion of the celestial orders, the initial trio of chapters provides a foundation not merely for this work but for the Dionysian corpus as a whole. The Areopagite first presents his principles of revelation, apophatic (negative) theology, and hierarchy. Eriugena's *Expositiones* had already explained many of these Dionysian themes, in the Latin vocabulary used in his own translation. This Latin Dionysius was supplemented by some further comments on the original Greek text by Anastasius, the papal librarian.[15] Hugh knew this legacy of the Latin Dionysius, and may even be subtly refuting Eriugena on certain points, but never named him or any other commentator.[16]

A comprehensive analysis of Hugh's commentary, noting his special emphases and relationship to Eriugena's work, is a separate full-length project. Here, only a few general observations can be offered, with limited examples. Hugh's *Commentary* cannot be dated precisely and may have been done in stages over time, but it seems to stem largely from the middle portion of his career, perhaps a little before the midpoint. As a mature author, Hugh's basic emphases were already in place, yet this project could still influence his later writings. The timing allows us to look for Hugh's own imprint in his comments on Dionysius, and also for a Dionysian imprint on Hugh's other works.

Going through Hugh's commentary line by line confirms the judgment of previous scholars such as R. Roques and R. Baron that Hugh is here a diligent and faithful expositor of the Dionysian text who does not force it into his own mold.[17] The whole point is to present the Areopagite's own words (in Eriugena's Latin translation) sentence by sentence, usually phrase by phrase, so that the students can become acquainted with this Father's text on a basic level. Hugh here follows his own *Didascalicon* advice to work with the "letter" of the text first and then move to the "sense." Outside the *Prologue*, Hugh never interjects into the Areopagite's thought, for example, his early and prominent pairing of the works of creation and restoration, even when the Dionysian language of "procession and return" might suggest it, as in the first chapter of *The Celestial Hierarchy*. Similarly, when Dionysius interprets the scriptural presentations of the angelic ranks and their activities, Hugh presents this exegesis on its own terms, never importing his own hermeneutical pattern of the threefold sense. The result of this fidelity to Dionysius is that the Victorine's commentary is minimally "Hugonian": very little salvation history, no eschatology, only faint traces of *conditio/restauratio*, nothing about Noah's ark, no mention of allegory or tropology, and very little on pride and humility outside the (pointed) discussion in the *Prologue*.

There are a few obvious Hugonian touches, such as the brief mention of "the three eyes"[18] and the emphasis on the angels as teachers, as an extension of the Dionysian stress on angelic mediation.[19] Further, Hugh consistently adds to the Areopagite's texts about knowing (or unknowing) God his own pairing of knowledge and love, including service to the neighbor.[20] One prominent excursus, pursued here, puts love above knowledge in a decidedly non-Dionysian way. Finally, the Victorine grants the Areopagite's point about apophatic or negative theology, that God transcends our categories and language,[21] yet without ever applying it as rigorously as the Dionysian corpus does. In general, Hugh defers to Dionysius, patiently presenting the Areopagite's text phrase by phrase for the students' sake. In the end, he even apologizes if his own words have covered up the Dionysian authority, like mud on marble.[22] With all this deference to the apostolic authority, Hugh's *Commentary* is explicitly Hugonian only rarely, as in the excursus on love above knowledge presented later as a case study.

There is another side to the relationship of Hugh to Dionysius, the converse of his commentary not being decisively Hugonian: is the rest of Hugh's corpus in any decisive way Dionysian? That is, how did this deferential encounter with *The Celestial Hierarchy* and the other "apostolic" writings by the Areopagite influence Hugh's thoughts and other works? Briefly, as others have noted, Hugh's overall corpus does not show much of a Dionysian imprint at all, whether from *The Celestial Hierarchy* or in general. As Poirel concludes, there are no sudden signs of Dionysian influence in Hugh's corpus, no new vocabulary or specific themes or overall theological orientation.[23] True, a portion of this commentary, specifically on how the communion elements both symbolize and *are* the body and blood of Christ, was incorporated into the later *De sacramentis*, as noted before.[24] Hugh also offers a compact and influential definition of *symbol* here.[25] Yet this isolated example also involved an excursus within Hugh's *Commentary*, perhaps a critique of Eriugena, not a specifically Dionysian point.

Other than his *Commentary* on *The Celestial Hierarchy,* Hugh shows no particular Dionysian imprint in his presentation of the angels, in *De sacramentis*, for example, choosing to draw on Gregory the Great but not using the specific triple triad of angelic ranks distinctive to the Areopagite. Nor does he even use the language of "hierarchy" except in the *Commentary*,[26] although the possibility that the *Commentary* itself was dedicated to King Louis VII and "friendly to secular power and monarchy" is worth exploring further.[27] Grover Zinn sees the Dionysian triad of "purification, illumination, and perfection" in the Ark treatises,[28] but the texts do not seem Dionysian enough to argue any real influence. Even someone coming to Hugh to find the tracks of the Areopagite will find little hard evidence. Hugh's descriptions of specific sacraments or orders show no trace of *The Ecclesiastical Hierarchy*; his presentation of Moses and the cloud on Mt. Sinai is completely independent of *The Mystical Theology*. *The Divine Names* makes no difference in Hugh's doctrine of God, the divine names, or attributes. Further, the occasional nod to apophatic theology is more generic than Dionysian, as seen before this Areopagite in Augustine himself. Overall, Hugh reflects an Augustinian, not Dionysian, appropriation of Platonism. Even with Eriugena's thoroughly Dionysian versions of theophany, "procession and return," and the anagogical thrust of the symbolic in his *Expositiones* well known to Hugh, the Victorine remains relatively non-Dionysian. In fact, Eriugena provides the decisive contrast, for his encounter with Dionysius left a deep and broad imprint on his thought and overall corpus. John the Scot became a Dionysian, but Hugh of St. Victor remained an Augustinian or, rather, was his own Victorine. Thus the basic contours of his thought, presented previously, needed no Dionysian material. One specific excursus can illustrate how Hugh could take the Dionysian text, as mediated through Eriugena, and make it his own, leaving an enormous legacy for Victorine spirituality and medieval mysticism generally. Otherwise, Hugh's Dionysian *Commentary* remains largely peripheral to his overall corpus.

A Case Study: "Love above Knowledge"

Commenting on a passage in the Dionysian *Celestial Hierarchy* regarding the angels, Hugh wrote some influential words: "Love [*dilectio*] surpasses knowledge, and is greater than intelligence. [God] is loved more than understood; and love enters and approaches where knowledge stays outside."[29] The context concerns the etymologies of the angelic designations Seraphim and Cherubim. *The Celestial Hierarchy* had carefully noted that the word *seraphim* means "fire-makers or carriers of warmth," and the word *cherubim* means "fullness of knowledge" or "carriers of wisdom." Dionysius discussed the angels, their names, and various angelic ranks frequently, not only in *The Celestial Hierarchy*, and he explicated the symbolism of fire quite fully: mobile, warm, sharp, and so forth. But Dionysius never identified the seraphic fire as the fire *of love*. To Hugh, with his overall interest in fire, as seen elsewhere as well, it was plain that the Seraphim's fire was, indeed, the fire of love: the fire of *love* is mobile, warm, sharp, and so forth.

On this point, Hugh is himself adapting a long tradition in Latin exegesis. The deep background is represented by Jerome, Augustine, and Gregory the Great; the crucial discussion is in the ninth century by Eriugena. In Gregory's gospel homilies, especially on Luke 15 and the lost coin, he discusses the angels, their various ranks and names, and the precedent set by the apostolic Dionysius. Three times he refers to the Seraphim and their fiery love, as part of an exegetical commonplace. Yet he never claims that this is the Dionysian understanding of the name Seraphim or of the angelic ranks.

As with many aspects of the medieval appropriation and adaptation of Dionysius, the key is Eriugena.[30] In his translation of *The Celestial Hierarchy*, chapter 7 (the chapter and the translation used by Hugh), John accurately presents the various attributes of the seraphic fire—warm, superburning, inextinguishable, and the like—and does so without adding any references to charity or love. In his commentary, however, Eriugena poetically explains warmth as the warmth of charity, and fire as the ardor of love.

> Their motion is "warm" because it burns with the inflammation of charity and . . . "super-burning" because the first hierarchy of celestial powers burns above all who come after them in love of the highest good.[31]

Ten times in a single passage, love (*caritas* or *amor*) is associated with fire—warmth, ardor, burning, or flaming. "The fire itself of the celestial Seraphim is . . . 'inextinguishable' because the divine love always burns in it."[32]

Eriugena provided Hugh with the linkage between the seraphic fire and love, but he did not argue that the Seraphim and love were thus higher than the Cherubim and knowledge. On the contrary, he discusses the various and apparently conflicting orders used by Dionysius such as that in *The Celestial Hierarchy*, chapter 6, where the thrones are first and the Seraphim last in the supreme triad. But in general, as Hugh pointed out, the Seraphim are the highest in the Dionysian hierarchy, especially in chapter 7 of *The Celestial Hierarchy*, where they are superior to the Cherubim, the bearers of knowledge. Thus armed with Eriugena's linkage of seraphic fire and love, Hugh came to a specific Dionysian text, wrote his long excursus, and left behind the influential conclusion that love is superior to knowledge, as the Seraphim are higher than the Cherubim.[33]

Hugh's commentary on *The Celestial Hierarchy* has several smaller digressions, some of them sounding homiletical and usually on the same issue of love and knowledge,[34] but nothing like the long excursus at the beginning of chapter 7. A single Dionysian sentence about the name Seraphim received fully nine columns of Hugonian expansion in the familiar Migne edition.[35] Besides the length, this excursus is extraordinary for the way it begins and ends. After quoting the Areopagite's sentence on the Seraphim, Hugh first marvels at these words, so profound and divine, he says, that they must have been revealed to the one who penetrated the "third heaven" into the paradise of God. Thus the authority of St. Paul is first invoked for special insights into the celestial heights which were then passed on to his disciple Dionysius, who wrote down such amazing words for us.[36] The long discussion of love and knowledge that follows is finally concluded nine columns later by breaking off and starting a new book with an explicit admission: "long intervals require a new beginning."[37] Hugh then reorients the reader to the Dionysian passage at hand and finally moves on to the Cherubim and their "fullness of knowledge."

Within this mini-essay on fire and love, on love and knowledge, Hugh employs a complex exegetical strategy, as Grover Zinn has already explored. What is this fire, moving and warm and sharp?

> If we have said that this is love [*dilectio*] perhaps we seem to have said too little, not knowing what love is. Whoever says love never says little, unless perhaps he speaks of a little love. Now this [author] did not wish to speak of a little love, who has said so many things of love. "Mobile," he says, and "unceasing and warm and sharp and superheated.[38]

The fire of love, now applied to human longing, is mobile, warm, and sharp, in that order, as seen in the Gospel of Luke's road to Emmaus. "Walking and loving, igniting and fervoring, what were they saying about Jesus, whom they heard and yet did not know along the way?"[39] When the walking disciples felt their hearts burn within them, they had mobility and warmth but did not yet have the sharpness of knowledge. "Because, however, they loved first, then they knew, so that 'sharp' might be in love as also 'warm.' First 'warm,' then 'sharp.'"[40] The sharpness of love penetrates to comprehension. "This love . . . goes through and penetrates all things until it arrives at the beloved, or rather goes into the beloved. For if you do not go into the beloved, you still love externally, and you do not have the 'sharp' of love."[41] With this conjugal imagery, we are ready for the *Song of Songs*, with the melting and entrance and embrace.

> Therefore he himself will approach you, so that you may go in to him. You approach him then, when he himself goes in to you. When this love penetrates your heart, when his delight/love reaches as far as the innermost [space] of your heart, then he himself enters into you, and you indeed enter yourself so that you may go in to him.[42]

It is in this context of the bridal chamber that Hugh says: "This is not . . . a great love, unless it go through as far as the bridal chamber, and enter the room, and penetrate as far as the interior things, and rest in your innermost [spaces]."[43] Then comes the well-known passage quoted earlier: "Love [*dilectio*] surpasses knowledge, and is greater than intelligence. He [the beloved of the *Song*] is loved more than understood, and love enters and approaches where knowledge stays outside."[44] Hugh was rarely that interested in the apophatic, but the image of a threshold here is the end of knowledge and thus the beginning of *un*knowing. These angels "surround by desire what they do not penetrate by intellect."[45] The bridal chamber of love is beyond the realm of knowing, and thus later authors can associate it with the darkness of unknowing, whether the cloud of Mt. Sinai or the dark night of the lovers' embrace. Bonaventure, of course, became the master of these poetic associations, but it is Hugh of Saint Victor's excursus that opened the way for this influential turn of the Dionysian apophatic toward the Franciscan affective.

Yet there is still more in Hugh's mini-treatise, as he waxes rhapsodic on every Dionysian word about the seraphim: "warm, sharp, intimate, etc."

> Because of this kind of marvelous operations of love, he [Dionysius] has said so many things about it, in which he would perhaps have said everything, if everything could be said. Still, we fear that we may have been negligent or fastidious. It is hard for us regarding something so sweet to leave anything out that we have received, and again it seems reckless to us to add something that we ought not. What is love [*dilectio*], do you think? When will everything be said? Behold we called it itself "mobile and unceasing and warm and sharp and superheated and intent and intimate and unbending and exemplative and re-leading and active and re-heating and reviving." And this seems to be much, and perhaps even enough, except that other marvelous things still follow, I do not

know whether they are even more marvelous. "Fiery," he says "from heaven, and purifying like a holocaust." Two things should be noted, that he calls it "fiery," and at the same time "from heaven." For there is another "fiery" from earth, but it is not similar to that which is "fiery" from heaven.[46]

He goes on to speak of a purifying fire, as a purifying love, and so on.

This tangential exposition by Hugh marks a decisive step in a larger tradition of spiritual theology, not only that love surpasses knowledge in the human approach to union with God but also that this insight stems from a higher celestial realm and from privileged apostolic revelation through St. Paul to Dionysius, for in the "third heaven" seraphic love is higher than cherubic knowledge.

The *Commentary* is here (only) appended because it seems peripheral to Hugh's corpus and concerns, as sketched before. Yet even if the rest of Hugh's works may have been minimally Dionysian, the attention he brought to the Areopagite's corpus, and the way he interpreted it, left a considerable legacy for Richard of St. Victor, Thomas Gallus, Bonaventure, and thus many other medieval spiritual writers such as Ruysbroek and Gerson.[47]

NOTES

CHAPTER I

1. Charles H. Haskins, *The Renaissance of the Twelfth Century* (Cambridge, Mass: Harvard University Press, 1939). For a recent overview of literature, see Leidulf Melve, "'The Revolt of the Medievalists.' Directions in Recent Research on the Twelfth-Century Renaissance." *Journal of Medieval History* 32 (2006): 231–252.

2. *Didascalicon* VI, 3, FC 27: 364.16; Taylor, 137. The *Didascalicon* is cited by book and chapter (in this case, VI, 3), followed by the page and line number of the Latin text reprinted in Thilo Offergeld's *Studienbuch* (Freiburg: Herder, 1997) as *Fontes Christiani* 27 (in this case, FC 27: 364.16) and then by the page number in Jerome Taylor's English translation of *Fontes Christiani* 27, *The Didascalicon of Hugh of St. Victor* (New York: Columbia University Press, 1961 and 1991) (here, Taylor, 137). FC 27 replaces PL 176: 741–812. See also C. H. Buttimer's edition of *Didascalicon de studio legendi* (Washington, D.C.: Catholic University Press, 1939).

3. David Luscombe and Jonathan Riley-Smith, "Introduction" to *The New Cambridge Medieval History*, vol. 4 c. 1024–1198, part 1 (Cambridge: Cambridge University Press, 2004), 2.

4. Haskins, *Renaissance*, 258. For a more balanced introduction to the theology of this century, see M. D. Chenu, *Nature, Man, Society in the Twelfth Century: Essays on New Theological Perspectives in the Latin West* (Chicago: University of Chicago Press, 1968).

5. On William's teaching, before St. Victor, see Jean Jolivet, "*Données* sur Guillaume de Champeaux: dialectician et théologien." In *L'Abbaye Parisienne de Saint-Victor au Moyen Age: communications présentées au XIIIe Colloque d'Humanisme médiéval de Paris (1986–1988) et réunies par Jean Longère*, Bibliotheca Victorina 1 (Paris: Brepols, 1991), 235–251.

6. Abelard, *Historia calamitatum,* tr. Betty Radice, *The Letters of Abelard and Heloise* (New York: Penguin Books, 1974), 58–61. PL 178:115–116, 120.

7. On the early history of Saint Victor, see especially Robert-Henri Bautier, "Les origines et les premiers développements de l'abbaye Saint Victor de Paris," *L'Abbaye Parisienne de Saint-Victor au Moyen Age: communications présentées au XIIIe Colloque d'Humanisme médiéval de Paris (1986–1988) et réunies par Jean Longère*, Bibliotheca Victorina 1 (Paris: Brepols, 1991), 23–52.

8. J. C. Dickinson, *The Origins of the Austin Canons and Their Introduction into England* (London: S.P.C.K., 1950), 191. PL 171: 141–143. For more of this letter, and on William, see C. Stephen Jaeger, *The Envy of Angels: Cathedral Schools and Social Ideals in Medieval Europe, 950–1200* (Philadelphia: University of Pennsylvania Press, 1994), 244–247.

9. Caroline Walker Bynum, *Docere Verbo et Exemplo: An Aspect of Twelfth-Century Spirituality*, Harvard Theological Studies 31 (Missoula, Mont.: Scholars Press, 1979).

10. Beryl Smalley, *The Study of the Bible in the Middle Ages* (Oxford: Blackwell, 1952), 83.

11. Bautier, "Les origines," 43.

12. Dickinson, *Origins*, 86.

13. *Liber Ordinis Sancti Victoris Parisiensis*, L. Jocqué and L. Milis, eds., CCCM 61 (Turnholt: Brepols, 1984) (hereafter, *Liber Ordinis*). For analysis and bibliography, especially on the officers, see Luc Jocqué, "Les structures de la population claustrale dans l'ordre de Saint-Victor au XIIᵉ siècle: un essai d'analyse du 'Liber ordinis,'" *L'Abbeye parisienne de Saint-Victor au Moyen Age*, 53–95.

14. *Liber ordinis*, chapter 63, pp. 244–249.

15. Jaeger, *Envy of Angels*, 247–254.

16. Bautier, "Les origines," 44.

17. This well-known story is told well in Stephen C. Ferruolo, *The Origins of the University: The Schools of Paris and Their Critics, 1100–1215* (Stanford, Calif.: Stanford University Press, 1985), 31. See discussion of Piazzoni's "Sententiae" in chapter 4.

18. *Didascalicon* III, 19; FC 27: 268.11f.; Taylor, 101.

19. The passage, from *On the Vanity of the World* (PL 176: 718B–719C), is discussed in chapter 8.

20. *De arrha anime*, Prologue, lines 1–18, *L'oeuvre de Hugues de Saint-Victor* 1 (Turnhout: Brepols, 1997), p. 226 (to be abbreviated as OHSV 1); PL 176: 951B–952B; *Soliloquy*,13; discussed in chapter 9.

21. *De virtute orandi*, OHSV 1, p. 126, discussed in chapter 7. For the general context of Halberstadt and this community in Hamersleben, see Karlotto Bogumil, *Das Bistum Halberstadt im 12. Jahrhundert* (Cologne: Böhlau, 1972), especially 106–113.

22. E. Croydon, "Notes on the Life of Hugh of St. Victor." *Journal of Theological Studies* 40 (1939): 232–253; Jerome Taylor, *The Origin and Early Life of Hugh of St. Victor: An Evaluation of the Tradition* (Notre Dame, Ind.: Medieval Institute, 1957).

23. Roger Baron, "Notes biographiques sur Hugues de Saint-Victor." *Revue d'histoire ecclésiastique* 51 (1956): 930.

24. Thomas D. McGonigle notes that the family language of "nephew" for the younger Hugh (relative to a Saxon uncle) would argue against a Flemish birthplace, but he also offers a harmonizing if forced solution. If "nepos" meant protégé instead of blood nephew, then the young Flemish exile "from boyhood" could have been befriended and patronized by the archdeacon Hugh. Thomas D. McGonigle, "Hugh of St. Victor's Understanding of the Relationship between the Sacramental and Contemplative Dimensions of Christian Life" (Ph.D. diss., Harvard Divinity School, 1976), 53f. This seems to be the last attempt at harmonizing the Flemish and Saxon claims.

25. Dominique Poirel, *"Hugo Saxo.* Les origines germaniques de la pensée d'Hugues de Saint-Victor." *Francia. Forschungen zur westeuropäischen Geschichte* 33/1 (2006): 163–169. Poirel further speculates that Hugh must have come to Paris, fully developed, and started teaching as early as 1115 and had already fully assimilated Dionysius, yet without specific evidence. On this last point, see the appendix.

26. Poirel, *"Hugo Saxo,"* 164 and 171.

27. PL 175: CLXIII.

28. Damien van den Eynde, *Essai sur la succession et la date des écrits de Hugues de Saint-Victor*, Spicilegium Pontificii Athenaei Antoniani 13 (Rome: Pontificium Athenaeum Antonianum, 1960); see Baron, "Notes biographiques," and Poirel, *Livre de la nature et débat trinitaire au XIIe siècle: le De tribus diebus de Hughes de Saint-Victor*, Bibliotheca Victorina 14 (Turnhout: Brepols, 2002), 131–154.

29. *De Reductione Artium ad Theologiam*, Preface; Quarrachi V, 32; St. Bonaventure's *De Reductione Artium ad Theologiam*, tr. Sister Emma T. Healy (Saint Bonaventure, N.Y.: Saint Bonaventure University, 1955), 27f. (*Works of Saint Bonaventure*, 1).

30. First published from an Oxford manuscript (Merton Coll., 49) by J. de Ghellinck, "La table des materières de la première édition des oeuvres de Hugues de Saint-Victor." *Recherches de sciences religieuses* 1 (1910): 270–289, 385–396. Discussed recently in D. Poirel, *Livre*, chapter 2, "Une édition victorine: les *volumina* de l'abbé Gilduin," 27–86; and Ralf M. Stammberger, "Die Edition der Werke Hugos von Sankt Viktor (d. 1141) durch Abt Gilduin von Sankt Viktor (d. 1155)—Eine Rekonstruktion," in *Schrift, Schreiber, Schenker: Studien zur Abtei Sankt Viktor in Paris und den Viktorinern*, edited by Rainer Berndt, Corpus Victorinum: Instrumenta, vol. 1 (Berlin: Akademie Verlag, 2005), 119–231. Stammberger has also recently identified another manuscript, containing sermons by Hugh that was perhaps originally part of Gilduin's edition. Ralf M. W. Stammberger, "The *Liber Sermonum Hugonis*: The Discovery of a New Work by Hugh of Saint Victor," *Medieval Sermon Studies* 52 (2008): 63–71.

31. For a fuller start to Gilduin's list, see the bibliographical presentation of Hugh's works on pp. 215–217.

CHAPTER 2

1. William Green, "Hugo of St. Victor: *De tribus maximis circumstantiis gestorum.*" *Speculum* 18 (1943): 484.

2. *The Medieval Craft of Memory: An Anthology of Texts and Pictures*, ed. Mary Carruthers and Jan M. Ziolkowski (Philadelphia: University of Pennsylvania Press, 2002), 32–40, a revision of Mary Carruthers, *The Book of Memory* (Cambridge: Cambridge University Press, 1990), 261–266.

3. For the edited portions of this material, see Stammberger, "Die Edition," 194.

4. Green, 484.

5. Carruthers, 33, translated from Green, 488, line 5.

6. Green, 484.

7. Green, 490, line 30f., Carruthers, 38; see also "pueris puerilia" at Green, 490, line 38, "basics to children" in Carruthers, 39.

8. Green, 491, lines 3–8; Carruthers, 39; adjusted, e.g., translating "historiam" as "history" instead of as "literal."

9. Green, 491, lines 11–16; Carruthers, 39.

10. Green, 491, lines 34f.; Carruthers, 40.

11. E.g., Patrice Sicard, *Hugues de Saint-Victor et son école: introduction, choix de texte, traduction et commentaires*, Témoins de Notre Histoire (Tournhout: Brepols, 1991), 24.

12. Grover A. Zinn, "Hugh of St. Victor's 'De scripturis et scriptoribus sacris' as an *Accessus* Treatise for the Study of the Bible." *Traditio* 52 (1997): 115, citing the chronological arguments of van den Eynde, *Succession*. The text itself

is at PL 175: 9–28. An earlier and shorter version has been edited very recently by Ralf M. W. Stammberger, *"Diligens scrutator sacri eloquii:* An Introduction to Scriptural Exegesis by Hugh of St. Victor Preserved at Admont Library (MS 672)," *Manuscripts and Monastic Culture*, ed. Alison I. Beach (Turnhout: Brepols, 2007), 241–283.

13. Zinn, *"Accessus* Treatise," 116.

14. PL 175: 11 A–D, my translation.

15. PL 175: 12AB.

16. PL 175: 12B.

17. PL 175: 12B–D, cited more fully in chapter 3.

18. PL 175: 13CD.

19. PL 175: 14A. This wording is repeated in *Didascalicon* III, 13; FC 27: 254.6; Taylor, 95; and in *Didascalicon* VI, 3; FC: 27: 364.4f.; Taylor, 137.

20. PL 175: 14D.

21. PL 175: 15A.

22. See especially Grover Zinn, " '*Historia fundamentum est*': The role of history in the contemplative life according to Hugh of St Victor," *Contemporary Reflections on the Medieval Christian Tradition; Essays in Honor of Ray C. Petry*, George H. Shriver, ed. (Durham, N.C.: Duke University Press, 1974), 135–158.

23. PL 175: 24 AB.

24. Zinn, *"Accessus* Treatise," 134.

25. See chapter 1, note 2, for the Latin editions and English translation of the *Didascalicon*. Besides the German translation mentioned there (Offergeld), see also the French by Michel Lemoine, *L'Art de lire* (Paris: Editions du Cerf, 1991); Ivan Illich's free-wheeling *In the Vineyard of the Text: A Commentary to Hugh's "Didascalicon"* (Chicago: University of Chicago, 1993); and the edition forthcoming from Ralf Stammberger.

26. *Didascalicon* Preface; FC 27: 106.20 to 108.3; Taylor, 44. Taylor's endnotes also contain further helpful information.

27. *Didascalicon*, Preface; FC 27: 108.15–23; Taylor, 44f.

28. Taylor's notes supply the specifics for these and other names; Taylor, 175–183.

29. *Didascalicon* I, 4; FC 27: 126.6f; Taylor, 51.

30. *Didascalicon* I, 4; FC 27: 126.11f; Taylor, 51. See also *Didascalicon* II, 1; FC 27: 154.2; Taylor, 61.

31. *Didascalicon* I, 5; FC 27: 128.1–4; Taylor, 51f.

32. *Didascalicon* I, 5; FC 27: 128.11f; Taylor, 52.

33. *Didascalicon* I, 7; FC 27: 136.8–11; Taylor, 54.

34. *Didascalicon* I, 8; FC 27: 136.22 to 138.6; Taylor, 55.

35. *Didascalicon* I, 8; FC 27: 138.10–15; Taylor, 55.

36. *Didascalicon* II, 1; "ut divina similitudo in nobis reparetur," FC 27: 154.14f; Taylor, 61.

37. *Didascalicon* II, 1; FC 27: 156.20 to 158.5; Taylor, 62.

38. *Didascalicon* II, 6; FC 27: 172.1–3; Taylor, 67.

39. *Didascalicon* II, 19; FC 27: 188.18; Taylor, 74.

40. *Didascalicon* II, 16; FC 27: 182.14–17; Taylor, 71. Yet perhaps Hugh knew Eriugena's commentary on Martianus Capella, where there was such a category.

41. *Didascalicon* II, 25; FC 27: 202.1f.; Taylor, 78.

42. *Didascalicon* II, 23; FC 27: 198.6–8; Taylor, 77.

43. *Didascalicon* II, 30; FC 27: 214.8–10; Taylor, 82.

44. *Didascalicon* III, 1; FC 27: 216.1–10; Taylor, 83.

45. Again, Taylor's notes supply further information on these and other authors; *Didascalicon* III, 2; FC 27: 216.20 to 228.5; Taylor, 83–86.

46. *Didascalicon* III, 3; FC 27: 228.14–16; Taylor, 87.

47. *Didascalicon* III, 3; FC 27: 230.9; Taylor, 87.

48. *Didascalicon* III, 5; FC 27: 236.8f.; Taylor, 89.

49. *Didascalicon* III, 5; FC 27: 238.3–8; Taylor, 90.

50. *Didascalicon* III, 8; FC 27: 242.20 to 244.1; Taylor, 92.

51. *Didascalicon* III, 10; FC 27: 246.24f.; Taylor, 93.

52. *Didascalicon* III, 11; "arcula memoriae," FC 27: 248.15; Taylor, 94. See the opening of the "Chronicles," discussed earlier in this chapter.

53. *Didascalicon* III, 13; FC 27: 256.1–18; Taylor, 96f. See Offergeld, 256 n. 67, and Taylor, 215 n. 68. On this text and Hugh's relationship to Abelard in general, see David Luscombe, *The School of Peter Abelard: The Influence of Abelard's Thought in the Early Scholastic Period*, Cambridge Studies in Medieval Life and Thought, New Series 14 (Cambridge: Cambridge University Press, 1970), 183–197, where he concludes: "Hugh's mistrust of Abelard has to be pieced together from implicit indications" (196).

54. *Didascalicon* III, 13; FC 27: 254.6f.; Taylor, 95f. Taylor's loose paraphrase obscures the similarities of one sentence (Quidam dum magnum saltum facere volunt, praecipitium incident) to a passage quoted earlier from *De scripturis*: Noli ergo saltum facere, ne in praecipitium incidas, PL 175 14A.

55. *Didascalicon* III, 19; FC 27: 268.8–14; Taylor, 101. See Taylor, 216 nn. 85–88, for the allusions to Vergil, Cicero, and Horace.

56. *De scripturis* 2, PL 175: 11C, discussed previously.

57. *Didascalicon* IV, 2; FC 27: 272.9–13; Taylor, 103.

58. See Rainer Berndt, "Gehören die Kirchenväter zur Heiligen Schrift? Zur Kanontheorie des Hugo von St Viktor," *Zum Problem des biblischen Kanons,* Jahrbuch für biblische Theologie, vol. 3. (Neukirchen-Vluyn: Neukirchener Verlag, 1988), 191–199.

59. *Didascalicon* IV, 14; FC 27: 306.20f.; Taylor, 116.

60. *Didascalicon* V, 2; FC 27: 318.11–13; Taylor, 120.

61. *Didascalicon* V, 2; FC 27: 320.24 to 322.2; Taylor, 121.

62. *Didascalicon* V, 3; FC 27: 332.3f.; Taylor, 121.

63. *Didascalicon* V, 4; FC 27: 324.13 to 332.13f.; Taylor, 122–125.

64. *Didascalicon* V, 6; FC 27: 336.23 to 338.4; Taylor, 127. This passage duplicates Hugh's *De scripturis* 13, PL 175: 20C.

65. *Didascalicon* V, 9; FC 27: 348.17f.; Taylor, 132. See the expansion of these steps in Dominique Poirel, *Hugues de Saint-Victor,* Initiations au Moyen-Age (Paris: Cerf, 1998), 123ff.

66. *Didascalicon* V, 10; FC 27: 354.21 to 356.4; Taylor, 134.

67. *Didascalicon* VI, 1; FC 27: 358.1; Taylor, 135.

68. *Didascalicon* VI, 2; FC 27: 358.15 to 360.2; Taylor, 135.

69. *Didascalicon* VI, 3; "neque ut quidem, dum magnum saltum facere volunt, praecipitium incidunt," FC 27: 364.4ff.; Taylor, 137. See *De scripturis* 5, PL 175: 14A, and *Didascalicon* III, 13; FC 27: 254.6; Taylor, 95, cited previously.

70. *Didascalicon* VI, 3; "Omnia disce." FC 27: 364.14–16; Taylor, 137.

71. *Didascalicon* VI, 3; "fundamentum autem et principium doctrinae sacrae historia est." FC 27: 366.25f., Taylor, 138.

72. *Didascalicon* VI, 3; FC 27: 368.6–8; Taylor, 138.

73. *Didascalicon* VI, 4; FC 27: 374.9–23; Taylor, 141.

74. *Didascalicon* VI, 6; FC 27: 384.12f.; Taylor, 145.

75. *Didascalicon* VI, 11; FC 27: 396.25; Taylor, 150.

76. *Didascalicon* VI, 13, FC 27: 400.8–10; Taylor, 151; *Didascalicon*, Preface; FC 27: 106.13f.; Taylor, 44.

77. *Didascalicon* III, 10; FC 27: 246.5–7; Taylor, 93. On meditation, see also *In Ecclesiastes* 1, *Selected Spiritual Writings*, 183–187.

78. *Didascalicon* VI, 13; FC 27: 400.7f.; Taylor, 151.

79. "Finis libri: Ydromancia primum a persis venit." Stammberger, "Die Edition," 196.

80. *Didascalicon* VI, 14 (Appendix A); FC 27: 402.4–7; Taylor, 152.

81. *Didascalicon* I, 5; FC 27: 128.2–5; Taylor, 51f.

82. *Didascalicon* I, 5; FC 27: 128.11f.; Taylor, 52.

83. *Didascalicon* VI, 14 (Appendix A): FC 27: 402.1–406.14; Taylor, 152–154.

84. Baron, *Opera*, 200, lines 330–344, and p. 206.

85. Baron, *Opera*, 194, lines 176–183.

86. Baron, *Opera*, 190, lines 98–99. "Finis enim omnis philosophie agnitio est summi boni quod in solo rerum omnium factore situm est."

87. Zinn, "*Accessus* Treatise," 114.

88. B. McGinn, *The Presence of God*, The Growth of Mysticism, vol. 2 (New York: Crossroads, 1994), 372: "more organized and pedagogically coherent presentation of Christian teaching."

89. McGinn, 374. "For Hugh, *tropologia* was a broad term that embraced moral purification, meditative illumination, and contemplative ascent to God." 90. *De scripturis* 14A. *Didascalicon* III, 13; FC 27: 254.6f.; Taylor, 95. *Didascalicon* VI, 3; FC 27: 364.4; Taylor, 137.

CHAPTER 3

1. *De sacramentis*, PL 176: 204B, p. 27; One, one, xxviii.
2. *Didascalicon* VI. 14 (Appendix A); FC 27: 402.4–7; Taylor, 152.
3. *Didascalicon* II. 21–27; FC 27: 194.6–206.2; Taylor, 75–79.
4. See chapter 4.
5. *De archa Noe* II, iii, p. 37f. 5–16 [638AB]; my own translation; see also *Noah's Ark*, in *Hugh of Saint-Victor; Selected Spiritual Writings*, A. Squire, ed. (London: Faber and Faber, 1962), 77f.
6. Roger Baron, *Hugonis de Sancto Victore Opera Propaedeutica*, University of Notre Dame Publications in Mediaeval Studies 20 (Notre Dame, Ind.: University of Notre Dame Press, 1966), 165.
7. *De grammatica* will be cited according to the page number and lines of the edition in Baron, *Opera Propaedeutica*; here, *De grammatica* 76, lines 1–11.
8. *De grammatica* 153, lines 2237–2244.
9. Baron, *Opera Propaedeutica*, 70.
10. *Didascalicon* II, 9 and 13; FC 27: 172.9–5 and 178.15–180.3; Taylor, 68 and 70.
11. To be cited as *Practica geometriae*, by page and lines in Baron, *Opera Propaedeutica*; followed by corresponding citation for the English translation of Frederick A. Homann, *Practical Geometry* (Milwaukee, Wisc.: Marquette University Press, 1991).
12. *Practica geometriae*, 15, lines 1–2; Homann, 33.
13. *Practica geometriae*, 17f., lines 53–55; Homann's paraphrase, 34.
14. Homann, 23–24.
15. Poirel, "*Hugo Saxo*," 171.
16. Baron, "Introduction," in *Opera Propaedeutica*, 5.
17. *De archa Noe* I, iv, p. 21f. 81–138; PL 176: 628C–629C; Homann, Appendix F, 85f.
18. See Dominique Poirel, "*Symbolice et anagogice*: l'école de Saint-Victor et la naissance du style gothique," in *L'abbé Suger, le manifeste gothique de Saint-Denis et la pensée victorine*, Rencontres médiévales européennes, vol. 1 (Turnhout: Brepols, 2001), 141–170, and the "Discussions" of Poirel's essay, pp. 171–175 in the same volume.

19. "mare altum et celum profundum," *Practica geometriae*, 17, line 42; Homann, 34.

20. *Practica geometriae*, 38, lines 396–398; Homann, 50.

21. Baron, "Introduction," in *Opera Propaedeutica*, 5.

22. Homann, 17.

23. PL 176: 925–952B; to be cited by lines in OHSV 1, with page number added.

24. See especially C. Stephen Jaeger, "Humanism and Ethics at the School of St. Victor in the Early Twelfth Century." *Mediaeval Studies* 55 (1993): 51–79; revised as chapter 9 in Jaeger's *Envy of Angels*, 244–268.

25. *De institutione*, lines 55–58, OHSV 1, p. 20.

26. *De institutione*, lines 1229–1230, OHSV 1, p. 98.

27. See Poirel's "Introduction," OHSV 1, pp. 7–10.

28. See Poirel's note 34 on p. 103 of OHSV 1 for the implied critique of Abelard and company.

29. *De institutione*, lines 389–393, 402, OHSV 1, p. 44.

30. *De institutione*, lines 451–455, OHSV 1, p. 48; translation from Jaeger, "Humanism and Ethics," 58, with echoes of earlier tradition such as Cassian.

31. Jean-Claude Schmitt, chapter 5 in *La raison des gestes dans l'Occident médiéval*, Bibliothèque des histoires (Paris: Éditions Gallimard, 1990), 173–205. See also Poirel's notes 80–92 on p. 110f. of OHSV 1.

32. Jaeger, "Humanism and Ethics," 69; *Envy of Angels*, 254–268.

33. On humility, see Poirel's note 32 on p. 103 of OHSV 1.

34. Poirel, "Introduction," 15.

35. Bynum, *Docere Verbo et Exemplo*, esp. 45–48 on this treatise. See also her excellent essay on "The Spirituality of Regular Canons in the Twelfth Century," in *Jesus as Mother: Studies in the Spirituality of the High Middle Ages*, Publications of the Center for Medieval and Renaissance Studies, UCLA, 16 (Berkeley: University of California Press, 1982), 22–58.

36. Jaeger, "Humanism and Ethics," 73; see also his *Envy of Angels*, 246.

37. *Didascalicon* VI, 3; FC 27: 368.1–5; Taylor, 138. Gregory the Great, *Moralia in Iob,* Epistola ad Leandrum 3; CC 143.110–114, p. 4; SC 32, p. 118; PL 75: 513.

38. *De scripturis* III, PL 175: 12BC.

39. *De scripturis* III, PL 175: 12C.

40. *Didascalicon*, V.9; FC 27: 350.1–9; Taylor, 132.

41. Smalley, 83–106; Dale Coulter, *Per Visibilia ad Invisibilia: Theological Method in Richard of St. Victor (d. 1173)*, Bibliotheca Victorina 18 (Turnhout: Brepols, 2006), esp. 61–92.

42. Zinn, "*Historia*," 136.

43. PL 176: 184BC, *De sacramentis,* Prologue III; p. 4.

44. PL 176: 183; p. 3.

45. "The Preparation to Allegory: Hugh of St. Victor's *De Sacramentis* and His Notes on the Octateuch." *Nederlands archief voor kerkgeschiedenis* 68 (1988): 17–22.

46. H. J. Pollitt, "Some Considerations on the Structure and Sources of Hugh of St. Victor's Notes on the Octateuch," *Recherches de théologie ancienne et médiévale* 33 (1966): 5–38.

47. Pollitt, 8.

48. PL 175: 33A.

49. PL 175: 35C; PL 17: 1191A "Magnae Deus potentiae."

50. PL 176: 203D, *De sacramentis*, One, one, xxvii, p. 26.

51. van Zwieten, 21.

52. PL 175: 35AB; PL 176: 202B, *De sacramentis,* One, one, xxiii, 24f.

53. PL 176: 187C-189B, *De sacramentis*, One, one, ii–iii, pp. 8–9.

54. *De scripturis*, PL 175: 33C.

55. "pulchrum esse atque beatum esse," PL 176: 189A, *De sacramentis*, One, one, iii; p. 9. For much more on this phrasing, indeed a judicious overview of Hugh's theology as a whole, see Boyd T. Coolman, "*Pulcrum esse*: The Beauty of Scripture, the Beauty of the Soul, and the Art of Exegesis in Hugh of St. Victor," *Traditio* 58 (2003): 175–200.

56. PL 175: 33D.

57. Poirel, *Hugues*, 72.

CHAPTER 4

1. "Praefatiuncula," PL 176: 173–174; Deferrari, 1. As an additional textual challenge, the Deferrari translation needs to be corrected at many points, and the PL Latin text will be replaced soon by a critical edition (see note 6). Meanwhile, the Deferrari version is the only access for many readers.

2. "Praefatiuncula," PL 176: 173–174; Deferrari, 1.

3. Heinrich Weisweiler first summarized prior work on this pattern, especially by L. Ott, and then extended it considerably: "Die Arbeitsmethode Hugos von St. Viktor: Ein Beitrag zum Entstehen seines Hauptwerkes *De sacramentis*." *Scholastik* 20–24 (1949): 59–87, 232–267.

4. Van den Eynde, *Essai sur la succession*, 100.

5. In general, book 1 shows a complete integration of source material, but book 2 quotes prior material without fully digesting it.

6. According to the Web site of the Hugo von Sankt-Viktor-Institut (http://www.sankt-georgen.de/hugo/), this task falls to the director Rainer Berndt.

7. PL 176: 17C.

8. PL 176: 23A and 284C; *De sacramentis* One, six, xxxv; Deferrari, 117.

9. H. Weisweiler, "Hugos von St. Viktor Dialogus de sacramentis legis naturalis et scriptae als frühscholastisches Quellenwerk," in *Miscellanea Giovanni Mercati* II, Studi e Testi 122 (Vatican City: Biblioteca Apostolica Vaticana, 1946), 179–219, esp. 196–198. See also Weisweiler, "Arbeitsmethode," 256–266.

10. On the category of "reportatio," including this example, see Smalley, 200–207.

11. Epistola Laurentii, 19–30; in A. M. Piazzoni, "Ugo di San Vittore 'auctor' delle 'Sententiae de divinitate." *Studi medievali* 23.2 (1982): 912.

12. Piazzoni, 928–936, 936–948, 948–953; Piazzoni discusses Hugh's interesting understanding of three "primordial causes" (God's will, wisdom, and power) on pp. 886–894.

13. Piazzoni, *Prologue*, 918, lines 169–171; 920, lines 232–241; and 927, lines 490–511. See Piazzoni's discussion of the parallel passages on 876f., 888f., and 896f. See also Poirel's layout of the overlap between the *Dialogus*, the *Sententiae*, and *De sacramentis* in *Hugues*, 89.

14. *De tribus diebus*, ed. D. Poirel (Turnholt: Brepols, 2002), *Corpus Christianorum* 177; idem, *Livre*. J. Van Zwieten, ed. and trans., *Hugh van St. Victor, De drie dagen* (Kampen: Kok Agora, 1996). For a discussion in English, see Wanda Cizewski, "Reading the World as Scripture: Hugh of St. Victor's *De Tribus Diebus*." *Florilegium* 9 (1987): 65–88. In 1577, Wylliam Brome apparently printed "A Treatise of the Workes of three days," by "an old wryter Hugo," under the title "An Exposition of certayne words of S. Paule to the Romaynes." I owe this reference to David Sytsma.

15. For the polemics with Abelard, see Poirel, *Livre*, 267–420; for the legacy to later authors such as Richard and Bonaventure, see Poirel, *Livre*, 169–198. For an earlier and more general discussion of Hugh and Abelard, their similarities and differences, see David Luscombe, *The School of Peter Abelard: The Influence of Abelard's Thought in the Early Scholastic Period*. Cambridge Studies in Medieval Life and Thought, New Series 14 (Cambridge: Cambridge University Press, 1970), 183–197.

16. *De tribus diebus*, lines 6–15, pp. 3f. (811CD). Hugh's various treatments of the trio of *potentia, sapientia*, and *benignitas* are fully documented in Poirel, *Livre*.

17. *De tribus diebus* 15–32, pp. 4f. (812C–813A).

18. *De tribus diebus* 94–98, p. 9 (814B). On the prior history of the (Augustinian) idea of a "book of nature," see Poirel, *Livre*.

19. *De tribus diebus* 336–353, 22f. (819B–D); 373–382, p. 24 (820B).

20. *De tribus diebus* 407–462, pp. 26–29 (820D–821D).

21. *De tribus diebus* 464–505, pp. 29–31 (822A–D).

22. *De tribus diebus* 529–543, p. 33 (823B–C).

23. *De tribus diebus* 1072–1078, p. 60 (835A). See the diagram in Poirel, *Livre*, 252.

24. *De tribus diebus* 1079–1106, pp. 61f. (835A–D).

25. *De tribus diebus* 1110–1112, p. 62 (835D).

26. *De tribus diebus* 1118–1123, p. 63 (836A).

27. *De tribus diebus* 1131f., p. 64 (836B).

28. "assignavit potestatem Patri, sapientiam Filio, bonitatem Spiritui sancto," *De sacramentis,* One, two, vi and x–xiii, PL 176: 208D and 210C–211C. See also *De sacramentis,* One, three, 26–28.

29. *De tribus diebus* 1242–1245, p. 69 (838C–D).

30. Poirel, *Livre*, 261.

31. Poirel, *Livre*, Appendix V, 461–464.

32. Poirel, *Livre*, 114–128.

33. *Libellus* IV, p. 143.109–116 [693D].

34. PL 176: 183–184; p. 3, quoted in chapter 3, p. 51.

35. "*brevem quamdam summam,*" PL 176: 183–184, p. 3.

36. PL 176: 183A–B, p. 3.

37. PL 176: 183C, p. 4.

38. PL 176: 184C, p. 4.

39. PL 176: 185D, p. 6.

40. PL 176: 185D–186D, pp. 6–7.

41. PL 176: 371C, p. 206; Two, one, i.

42. Marcia Colish has even labeled it "redundant and disorganized"; she claims that Hugh is "flailing about" and that "the logic of Hugh's scheme is more apparent than real" ("Systematic Theology" 88, in *Studies in Scholasticism* I, Variorum Collected Studies Series, CS838 [Aldershot, U.K.; Burlington, Vt.: Ashgate Variorum, 2006], 144–145).

CHAPTER 5

1. The titles of the parts are taken from Deferrari's translation, sometimes abbreviated.

2. PL 176: 187A, p. 7.

3. PL 176: 173–174, p. 1.

4. PL 176: 205B, p. 28; One, two, i.

5. PL 176: 325A, p. 162; One, nine, v; and PL 176: 403A, p. 240; Two, one, xi.

6. PL 176: 519D, p. 369; Two, twelve, i.

7. PL 176: 187A, p. 7. Grover Zinn (in private correspondence, September 2007) notes the parallels with Gregory the Great's comments upon taking up the book of Job.

8. Chapter 3.

9. PL 176: 195C, p. 16; One, one, xii; the "mysteries of the light" at PL 176: 198D, p. 20; One, one, xiv.

10. E.g., One, one, xii, xix, xxvii.

11. PL 176: 203D–204A, p. 26; One, one, xxviii.

12. PL 176: 204B, p. 27; One, one, xxviii.

13. PL 176: 204C, 27; One, one, xxix.

14. PL 176: 205A–206A, 27; One, one, xxx; reiterated later: PL 176: 263B, p. 93; One, six, i.

15. *Didascalicon* VI.3; FC 27: 374.9–23; Taylor, 141.

16. PL 176: 263B, p. 93.

17. Discussed in chapter 4.

18. PL 176: 208D, p. 32; One, two, vi.

19. PL 176: 211D–214A, pp. 35–38; One, two, xiv–xxi.

20. PL 176: 214B–216C, pp. 38–41; One, two, xxii. The argument about omnipotence, apparently against Abelard, is taken directly from Hugh's own exposition of the *Magnificat* ("he who is mighty") discussed in chapter 7. *Super Canticum Mariae*, lines 564–663, OHSV 2, pp. 64–72; PL 175: 425A–427A. See Weisweiler, "Arbeitsmethode," 61–63. On Abelard in this connection, see also Luscombe, *The School of Peter Abelard*, 189–191.

21. PL 176: 234BC, p. 60; One, three, xxxi.

22. PL 176: 233D, p. 61.

23. PL 176: 236A and B/C, pp. 62 and 63; One, four, v and vi.

24. PL 176: 246BC, p. 74; the "primordial causes," those ideas of things to be created, well known from Eriugena, were mentioned earlier at PL 176: 206D, p. 29; One, three, ii, especially in the headings.

25. PL 176: 245D, p. 74.

26. PL 176: 250AB, p. 78; One, five, viii.

27. PL 176: 258C, "ordinator," p. 88.

28. PL 176: 263C–264C, p. 94; *De Vanitate Mundi* III, PL 176: 721B–723B; Weisweiler, "Arbeitsmethode," 67–71.

29. PL 176: 264C, p. 95.

30. PL 176: 264C, p. 95; One, six, ii.

31. PL 176: 265A, p. 95.

32. PL 176: 266D, p. 97.

33. PL 176: 267A, pp. 97f.; One, six, v.

34. PL 176: 277A–280B, pp. 109–111; One, six, xxii–xxv.

35. PL 176: 284BC, p. 117; One, six, xxxv. Deferrari follows PL with "damnation," whereas Hugh's earlier version (*Dialogus*; PL 176: 23A) supplies the more natural "domination."

36. PL 176: 287B, p. 121; One, seven, i.

37. PL 176: 288CD, p. 122; One, seven, iv.

38. PL 176: 289B, p. 123.
39. PL 176: 291A, p. 125.
40. PL 176: 299A, p. 134; One, seven, xxviii.
41. PL 176: 301C, p. 136; One, seven, xxxi.
42. PL 176: 305C, p. 141; One, eight, i.
43. PL 176: 305D–306C, p. 142.
44. PL 176: 306C–307B, pp. 142f.
45. PL 176: 312D, p. 149; One, eight, xi.
46. PL 176: 309B, p. 145.
47. PL 176: 310BC, p. 146; One, eight, vi.
48. PL 176: 310C–311D, pp. 146–148; One, eight, vii–x.
49. PL 176: 311D–312A, p. 148; One, eight, x.
50. PL 176: 312A, p. 148; One, eight, xi.
51. PL 176: 313CD, p. 150; One, eight, xii. On sacraments from the beginning, see also Hugh's use of his near-contemporary Ivo of Chartres (PL 162: 506C), discussed later.
52. PL 176: 314A–318A, pp. 150–154; One, eight, xii–xiii. When Hugh comes back to marriage more fully in book 2, part 11, he there quotes Augustine at length on this issue.
53. PL 176: 317B, p. 154; One, nine, i.
54. "sacramentum est sacrae rei signum," PL 176: 317C, p. 154; One, nine, ii.
55. PL 176: 317D, p. 155; One, nine, ii.
56. PL 176: 318B, p. 155; One, nine, ii.
57. PL 176: 318D, p. 155; One, nine, ii.
58. "accedit verbum sanctificationis ad elementum et fit sacramentum," PL 176: 319A, p. 155; One, nine, ii. Augustine: "accedit verbum ad elementum, et fit sacramentum," CCSL 36: 529.
59. PL 176: 319A, p. 155; One, nine, ii.
60. PL 176: 319A, p. 156; One nine, iii.
61. PL 176: 320A, p. 157; One, nine, iii.
62. PL 176: 320AB, p. 157; One, nine, iii.
63. PL 176: 320B–322A, pp. 157–159; One, nine, iii.
64. PL 176: 323B, p. 160; One, nine, iv.
65. PL 176: 324C, p. 162; One, nine, v. The polemic may involve Abelard. Hugh had written to Bernard of Clairvaux to ask about four sacramental questions, especially on baptism, raised by an unnamed opponent. Bernard's reply (Letter 77), including material Hugh incorporated into *De Sacramentis*, is discussed by Hugh Feiss, "*Bernardus Scholasticus:* The Correspondence of Bernard of Clairvaux and Hugh of Saint Victor on Baptism," *Bernardus Magister: Papers Presented at the Nonacentenary Celebration of the Birth of Saint Bernard of Clairvaux, Kalamazoo, Michigan, sponsored by the Institute of Cistercian Studies,*

Western Michigan University, 10–13 May 1990, edited by John Sommerfeldt, Cistercian Studies 135 (Spencer, MA: Cistercian Publications, 1992), 349–378; and by Emero Stiegman, "Three Theologians in Debate: Saint Bernard's Tract on Baptism," in *Bernard of Clairvaux: On Baptism and the Office of Bishops, on the Conduct and Office of Bishops, on Baptism and Other Questions: Two Letter-Treatises*, trans. Pauline Matarasso, Cistercian Fathers Series 67 (Kalamazoo, Mich.: Cistercian Publications, 2004), 85–147.

66. PL 176: 326CD, p. 164; One, nine, vi.

67. PL 176: 327AB, p. 164; One, nine, viii.

68. PL 176: 328AB, pp. 164f.; One, nine, viii.

69. PL 176: 327C, p. 165; One, ten, ii.

70. PL 176: 329A–330A, pp. 166f.; One, ten, ii. The "three eyes" are discussed more fully in PL 175: 975D–976A.

71. PL 176: 330C, p. 168; One, ten, ii; when this definition is repeated later in the paragraph, the Deferrari translation wrongly reads "certainly" for "certainty" (168).

72. PL 176: 331B–332B, pp. 169f.; One, ten, iii.

73. PL 176: 332B, p. 170; One, ten, iv.

74. PL 176: 332C, p. 170; One, ten, iv.

75. PL 176: 334AB, p. 172; One, ten, v.

76. PL 176: 334B, p. 172; One, ten, v. *Opera conditionis, opera restaurationis*.

77. PL 176: 334B, p. 172; One, ten, v.

78. PL 176: 334D, p. 173; One, ten, v.

79. See Feiss, "Bernardus Scholasticus," and Stiegman, "Three Theologians in Debate," 112–114, with the translation on 165–169.

80. Augustine at PL 176: 336B, p. 174; One, ten, vi. Gregory at PL 176: 337D, p. 176; One, ten, vi. Augustine again and Bede at PL 176: 340A and D, pp. 178f.; One, ten, vii. See the discussion in Weisweiler, "Arbeitsmethode," 63–64.

81. PL 176: 339 BC, p. 178; One, ten, vi. "Hugh must be complimented on what he decided to borrow" from Bernard (Stiegman, "Three Theologians in Debate," 114).

82. PL 176: 339D, p. 178; One, ten, vii.

83. PL 176: 341A and BC, p. 179 and 180; One, ten, viii.

84. PL 176: 342C, p. 181; One, ten, ix.

85. PL 176: 342D, p. 181; One, ten, ix.

86. PL 176: 343B, p. 182; One, eleven, i.

87. PL 176: 343B–345C, pp. 182–184; One, eleven, i–v.

88. "sive decimas videlicet, sive sacrificia, sive oblationes," PL 176: 344B, p. 183; One, eleven, iii.

89. PL 176: 351D, p. 191; One, twelve, iv.

90. PL 176: 346A, p. 185; One, eleven, vi (viii in Deferrari).

91. PL 176: 346CD, p. 186; One, eleven, vi (end of viii in Deferrari).

92. PL 176: 350A, p. 189; One, twelve, ii.

93. PL 176: 351B, p. 190; One, twelve, iii.

94. PL 176: 351CD, p. 191; One, twelve, iv.

95. PL 176: 352BC, p. 192; One, twelve, v.

96. The earlier work's first two chapters (PL 176: 9A–13C) are reused in *De sacramentis* One, twelve, vi–vii, PL 176: 352C–356B (vi–x in Deferarri, pp. 192–196); the third chapter (14BC) is reused in viii, 359CD (xxii in Deferarri, p. 200). See Weisweiler, "Arbeitsmethode," 64–67, for further documentation.

97. PL 176: 352CD, p. 192; One, twelve, vi.

98. PL 176: 354AB, p. 194; One, twelve, vi (vii in Deferarri).

99. PL 176: 354CD–355A, pp. 194f.; One, twelve, vi (viii in Deferrari). The Deferrari translation here dropped the "third Sabbath," the one commanded to serve the people of God, in oblique reference to Jesus' comment on the Sabbath "made for man," (354D).

100. PL 176: 355A, p. 195; One, twelve, vi (viii in Deferrari).

101. PL 176: 355AB, p. 195; One, twelve, vii (ix–x in Deferrari).

102. PL 176: 356D–358D, pp. 197–199; One, twelve, vii (xiv–xix in Deferrari). See Weisweiler, "Arbeitsmethode," 65.

103. PL 176:359B–360C, pp. 200f.; One, twelve, viii (xxii in Deferrari); cf. PL 176: 14BC.

104. PL 176: 360C–362B, pp. 201–203; One, twelve, ix (xxiii in Deferrari).

105. PL 176: 362B–364A, pp. 203f.; One, twelve, x (xxiv in Deferrari).

CHAPTER 6

1. PL 176: 363–364, p. 205. "Nam ipse Deus humiliari dignatus est, ad humana descendens, ut hominem postmodum, ad divina sublevaret."

2. Poirel, "'Alter Augustinus—Der Zweite Augustinus': Hugo von Sankt Viktor und die Väter der Kirche," in *Väter der Kirche: Ekklesiales Denken von den Anfängen bis in die Neuzeit: Festgabe für Hermann Josef Sieben SJ zum 70. Geburtstag*, edited by Johannes Arnold, Rainer Berndt, and Ralf Stammberger (Munich: Ferdinand Schöningh, 2004), 643–668.

3. PL 176: 371C, pp. 205f.; Two, one, i.

4. Prologue to the First Book, PL 176: 183B, p. 3. Hugh also discusses Christology in other works, such as "On the Four Wills of Christ" and *De scientia Christi*; see Poirel, *Hugues*, 42 and 94f.

5. PL 176: 376A–381B, pp. 210–216; Two, one, iv.

6. Weisweiler, "Arbeitsmethode," 71f.

7. Besides Weisweiler ("Arbeitsmethode") and his predecessors such as L. Ott, see especially Poirel, "'Alter Augustinus,'" 655: "*De sacramentis* ist unvollendet."

8. PL 176: 381C–383A, pp. 217f; Two, one, v.

9. PL 176: 383D, p. 219; Two, one, vi; see also Two, eight, viii, quoted later.

10. "Deus humanitatem suscepit; homo divinitatem accepit." PL 176: 394C, p. 231; Two, one, ix.

11. PL 176: 391D–393D, pp. 228–230; Two, one, viii duplicates PL 176: 870D–872D; OHSV 2, lines 686–781, pp. 232–238.

12. PL 176: 413A–416A, pp. 250–253; Two, one, xiii; Aug. Ep. 187, PL 33:833–848. For example, PL 176: 413BC equals PL 33: 835 no. 10, and PL 176: 413CD equals PL 33: 837 no. 14. For further details, see Weisweiler, "Arbeitsmethode," 73.

13. "Quod per hominem Verbo unitum Deo uniuntur omnes qui membra sunt illius." PL 176: 412A, p. 249; Two, one, xii.

14. PL 176: 4121B, p. 249; Two, one, xii.

15. PL 176: 412C, p. 250; Two, one, xii.

16. *De quatuor voluntatibus in Christo.* PL 176: 841B–846C. See the full discussion in Boyd Coolman, "Hugh of St. Victor on 'Jesus Wept': Making Christological Sense of Jesus' Tears and Conceiving Ideal *Humanitas* in the Twelfth Century," *Theological Studies* 69 (2008): 528–556. PL 176: 383C, p. 219; Two, one, vi.

17. PL 176: 415D, p. 254; Two, two, i.

18. PL 176: 416BC, p. 254; Two, two, ii.

19. PL 176: 417B, p. 255; Two, two, iii. Deferrari unaccountably has "clerics" here for "*laici.*"

20. PL 176: 417C, p. 255; Two, two, iii.

21. PL 176: 418C, p. 256; Two, two, iv.

22. PL 176: 418D, p. 256; Two, two, iv.

23. PL 176: 418D–419B, p. 257; Two, two, v.

24. PL 176: 419B–422A, pp. 257–259; Two, two, v–viii.

25. PL 176: 422AB, p. 259; Two, two, viii–ix.

26. PL 176: 421B, p. 259; Two, three, i.

27. PL 176: 421C, p. 260; Two, three, i.

28. PL 176: 423A, p. 261; Two, three, iv.

29. PL 176: 423C, p. 261; Two, three, iv.

30. For the full story on the many generations of literature on what Roger Reynolds calls the "ordinals of Christ," see his *The Ordinals of Christ from Their Origins to the Twelfth Century* (Berlin: de Gruyter, 1978), supplemented by his "Christ as Cleric: The Ordinals of Christ," in *Clerics in the Early Middle Ages* (Aldershot, U.K.: Ashgate, 1999), II.1–50, and many related essays.

31. PL 176: 423D–424A, p. 262; Two, three, v (vi in PL). Weisweiler ("Arbeitsmethode," 77f.) documents this example of Hugh's free use of Isidore and Ivo.

32. PL 176: 428BC, p. 267; Two, three, xi. See also PL 176: 430B, p. 269; Two, three, xii.

33. PL 176: 430D–431A, p. 270; Two, three, xiv.

34. PL 176: 432C–434A, p. 272; Two, three, xxii and xxiii.

35. Weisweiler, "Arbeitsmethode," 75–82; "fast ganz, und zwar wörtlich," 76.

36. *De significationibus indumentorum sacerdotalium*, PL 162: 519–527; Weisweiler, "Arbeitsmethode," 82–83, especially n. 55.

37. PL 176: 433D, p. 273; Two, four, ii.

38. PL 176: 435C, p. 275; Two, four, v.

39. PL 176: 435CD, p. 275; Two, four, vi.

40. PL 176: 435D, p. 275; Two, four, vi. Ivo's version was not quite so sharp about it, referring to truth but not to superstition (PL 162: 523A).

41. PL 176: 436A, p. 275; Two, four, vii.

42. PL 176: 436C, p. 276; Two, four, viii.

43. PL 176: 437A, p. 277; Two, four, ix.

44. PL 162: 524C: Ivo's slightly earlier use of Jerome's letter *ad Fabiolam* (524A) is presented in Weisweiler, "Arbeitsmethode," 83.

45. PL 176: 437D, p. 277; Two, four, xiii.

46. PL 176: 438D, p. 278; Two, four, xvii. On Amalar, see Christopher A. Jones, *A Lost Work by Amalarius of Metz* (London: Henry Bradshaw Society, 2001).

47. PL 176: 439A, p. 279; Two, five, i.

48. PL 162: 527–535. Weisweiler, "Arbeitsmethode," 84–86.

49. PL 176: 439C, p. 279; Two, five, i.

50. PL 176: 441A, p. 281; Two, five, iii.

51. PL 176: 442BC, p. 282; Two, five, iii.

52. PL 176: 441D, p. 282; Two, six, i.

53. PL 176: 461D, p. 304; Two, eight, i.

54. PL 176: 443AB, p. 283; Two, six, iii. "accedat verbum ad elementum, et sic sacramentum" echoes Hugh's earlier wording (One, nine, ii) and Augustine's dictum (*CCSL* 36, 529).

55. PL 176: 443B–447D, pp. 283–288; Two, six, ii.

56. PL 176: 447D–449B, pp. 288–290; Two, six, iii.

57. PL 176: 449C–451C, pp. 290–292; Two, six, iv–v.

58. PL 176: 451CD, p. 292; Two, six, vi.

59. PL 176: 452A–453B, pp. 293f.; Two, six, vii.

60. PL 176: 453CD, pp. 294f.; Two, six, vii.

61. PL 176: 454B, p. 295; Two, six, vii. See Feiss, "*Bernardus Scholasticus*," and Stiegman, "Three Theologians in Debate," regarding the material by Bernard that was used in *De sacramentis*.

62. PL 162: 505C–512D; see Weisweiler, "Arbeitsmethode," 233–235.

63. PL 176: 454C–455C, pp. 295f.; Two, six, viii.

64. PL 176: 455C, p. 296; Two, six, viii. Ivo's text is in PL 162: 507D–508A.

65. PL 176: 455D, p. 297; Two, six, viii. "Haec sunt sacramenta fidei Christianae ab initio condita in fide credenda, sine fine profutura."

66. PL 176: 456AB, p. 297; Two, six, ix.

67. PL 176: 456BC, pp. 297f.; Two, six, ix. Here again, echoing Ivo, PL 162: 508BC, as well as other sources noted by Weisweiler, "Arbeitsmethode," 235f.

68. PL 176: 456C–457B, p. 298; Two, six, x.

69. PL 176: 457CD, p. 299; Two, six, xi.

70. PL 176: 457D–458A, p. 299; Two, six, xi.

71. PL 176: 458BC, pp. 299f.; Two, six, xii. Ivo, *Panormia* I, 77–82; PL 161: 1063B–1064A.

72. PL 176: 458D–459A, p. 300; Two, six, xiii. Ivo, *Panormia* I, 88; PL 161: 1064D–1065A.

73. PL 176: 459A–460A, pp. 300f.; Two, six, xiii.

74. PL 176: 460AB, p. 301; Two, six, xiii.

75. PL 176: 459CD, p. 302; Two, seven, i; Isidore, PL 83: 823A; Weisweiler, "Arbeitsmethode," 238.

76. PL 176: 460D–461A, pp. 302f.; Two, seven, iii.

77. PL 176: 461C–462C, pp. 303f.; Two, seven, v–vi. For Amalar and other sources, see Weisweiler, "Arbeitsmethode," 240–242.

78. "salus constat;" PL 176: 461D, p. 304; Two, eight, i.

79. PL 176: 461D, p. 304; Two, eight, i. For the earlier linkage of salvation to these two sacraments, see PL 176: 327A, p. 164; One, nine, vii. For the parallel language regarding baptism, see PL 176: 441D, p. 282; Two, six, i.

80. PL 176: 461D, p. 304; Two, eight, ii.

81. PL 176: 462D–464C, pp. 304–306; Two, eight, iii.

82. PL 176: 464CD, pp. 306f.; Two, eight, iv.

83. PL 176: 465C, p. 307; Two, eight, v.

84. PL 176: 466A, p. 308; Two, eight, vi.

85. PL 176: 466B, p. 308; Two, eight, vi.

86. Two, eight, vi–viii (461D–472C), duplicates PL 176: 951C–953D.

87. PL 176: 466C, p. 308; Two, eight, vii.

88. PL 176: 467AB, p. 309; Two, eight, viii.

89. PL 176: 467D–468A, p. 310; Two, eight, viii. "quoniam divinos facit, et participes divinitatis."

90. PL 176: 468A, 310; Two, eight, ix.

91. PL 176: 468C–469A, pp. 311f.; Two, eight, x.

92. Amalar, *Lib. Off.* 3.35 ST 139; PL 105: 1154D–1155A; perhaps via Ivo's fifth sermon, PL 162: 560BC.

93. PL 176: 469B–470B, pp. 312f.; Two, eight, xi–xii.

94. PL 176: 470C, p. 313; Two, eight, xiii.

95. PL 176: 470D, p. 314; Two, eight, xiii.
96. PL 176: 471A, p. 314; Two, eight, xiii.
97. *Confessions* VII, x (16).
98. PL 176: 472A–C, pp. 314f.; Two, eight, xiv. (Pseudo-) Alcuin, perhaps Remigius of Auxerre, PL 101: 1246CD. See Weisweiler, "Arbeitsmethode," 242f.
99. PL 176: 472D–473A, pp. 315f.; Two, nine, i.
100. PL 176: 473AB, p. 316; Two, nine, ii.
101. PL 176: 473C, pp. 316f.; Two, nine, iii.
102. PL 176: 473D, p. 317; Two, nine, iv.
103. PL 176: 474A, p. 317; Two, nine, v. Amalar, *Lib. Off.* I. 17–18 (ST 139; PL 105: 1033B–D).
104. PL 176: 474B–475A, pp. 317f.; Two, nine, v–vi. Amalar, *Lib. Off.* 3.1 (ST 139; PL 105: 1101D). Weisweiler ("Arbeitsmethode," 243–249) here also considers Rupert of Deutz.
105. PL 176: 475A, p. 318; Two, nine, viii.
106. PL 176: 475B, p. 319; Two, nine ix.
107. Weisweiler, "Arbeitsmethode," 245.
108. PL 176: 475C–476C, pp. 319f.; Two, nine, ix.
109. PL 176: 476 CD, p. 320; Two, nine, ix.
110. PL 176: 476D, p. 320; Two, nine, x.
111. PL 176: 477A–478B, p. 321; Two, nine, x.
112. PL 176: 477CD, p. 322; Two, ten, i–ii.
113. PL 176: 477D–479B, pp. 322f.; Two, ten, iii.
114. PL 176: 479B–480D, pp. 323f.; Two, ten, iv–v.
115. On this whole section, see Weisweiler, "Arbeitsmethode," 245–252, and his earlier studies.
116. See also the specific case of the marriage of the Virgin Mary in chapter 7.
117. PL 176: 314A–318A, pp. 150–54; One, eight, xii–xiii.
118. PL 176: 481B, p. 325; Two, eleven, iii.
119. PL 176: 485C, p. 330; Two, eleven, iv; the "some" at the start of this chapter (483A, p. 327) includes Isidore of Seville by way of the tracts of the school of Anselm and William of Champeaux, in Weisweiler, "Arbeitsmethode," 249.
120. PL 176: 485D–488C, pp. 330–333; Two, eleven, v.
121. PL 176: 488C–494A, pp. 333–339; Two, eleven, vi.
122. PL 176: 494B, p. 339; Two, eleven, vii.
123. PL 176: 494B, p. 339; Two, eleven, vii; and PL 176: 495A, p. 340; Two, eleven, viii.
124. PL 176: 495B–496B, pp. 340f., Two, eleven, viii; citing *De Bono Conjugali*, "On the Good of Marriage," by Augustine, through Hugh's proximate sources discussed in Weisweiler, "Arbeitsmethode," 249.

125. PL 176: 496C–497C, pp. 342f.; Two, eleven, ix–x.

126. PL 176: 497D–499B, pp. 343–345; Two, eleven, xi.

127. PL 176: 499B–504D, pp. 345–351; Two, eleven, xii.

128. PL 176: 504D, p. 351; end of Two, eleven, xii.

129. PL 176: 501D–510C, pp. 351–357; Two, eleven, xiii.

130. PL 176: 510C–516B, pp. 357–365; Two, eleven, xiv.

131. PL 176: 516B–520A, pp. 365–369; Two, eleven, xv–xvii.

132. PL 176: 520 BC, p. 369; Two, eleven, xviii–xix, including the fraud of concealing a partner's enslavement.

133. PL 176: 519D–524D, pp. 369–374; Two, twelve. The earlier discussion of vows was under "bearing false witness"; PL 176: 358BC, p. 199; One, twelve, viii (xix in Deferrari). Hugh's earlier inclusion of sacramental words, such as the invocation, was restricted to texts of the Mass and never mentioned vows. PL 176: 475C–476D, pp. 319f.; Two, nine, ix.

134. PL 176: 519D, pp. 369f.; Two, twelve, i, discussed at the beginning of chapter 5 regarding the *De sacramentis*, book 1. Speaking directly to the reader-hearers gives this whole chapter the appearance of a prior letter.

135. PL 176: 520D–521C, pp. 370f.; Two, twelve, ii–iii.

136. PL 176: 521CD, p. 371; Two, twelve, iv.

137. PL 176: 522A–523B, pp. 371–373; Two, twelve, v.

138. PL 176: 523C–524D, pp. 373f.; Two, twelve, vi.

139. PL 176: 525A, pp. 374f.; Two, thirteen, i.

140. PL 176: 525CD, p. 375; Two, thirteen, i. See *De quinque septenis* 2 (PL 175: 406B; Baron SC 155, lines 50–56, p. 104), also mentioned in chapter 7.

141. PL 176: 526C–527B, pp. 376f.; Two, thirteen, ii.

142. PL 176: 527B, p. 377; Two, thirteen, iii.

143. PL 176: 527C–528D, pp. 377f.; Two, thirteen, iv–v. The section on the four fears is taken from Hugh's *Super Canticum Mariae*, as documented in chapter 7.

144. PL 176: 528D–531C, pp. 378–381; Two, thirteen, vi.

145. PL 176: 531C–534A, pp. 381–384; Two, thirteen, vii. See also "when you love your God, you love your good . . . and when you love your good, you love yourself." PL 176: 535AB, p. 385; Two, thirteen, viii at end.

146. PL 176: 534C, p. 384; Two, thirteen, viii.

147. PL 176: 535B–536A, pp. 385f.; Two, thirteen, ix.

148. PL 176: 536 BC, pp. 386f.; Two, thirteen, x.

149. PL 176: 539B, pp. 389f.; Two, thirteen, x.

150. PL 176: 539B–542C, pp. 390–393; Two, thirteen, xi.

151. PL 176: 542C–545C, pp. 393–396; Two, thirteen, xi.

152. PL 176: 545D–546B, pp. 396f.; Two, thirteen, xii.

153. PL 176: 546B–550C, pp. 397–401; Two, thirteen, xii.

154. PL 176: 549D, 401; Two, fourteen, i.

155. PL 176: 552A, p. 403; Two, fourteen, i.

156. James 5.16; PL 176: 552B, p. 403; Two, fourteen, i.

157. PL 176: 553D, pp. 404f; 554D, p. 406; Two, fourteen, i.

158. PL 176: 555B, p. 406; Two, fourteen, ii.

159. PL 176: 556B, p. 407; Two, fourteen, iii.

160. PL 176; 556C, p. 408; Two, fourteen, iii.

161. PL 176: 557B, pp. 408f.; Two, fourteen, iv. Also considered in Hugh's letter 2, question 4 (PL 176: 1013CD). See Weisweiler, "Arbeitsmethode," 252–254.

162. "tamen melior est sera quam nulla." PL 176: 560B, p. 412; Two, fourteen, v.

163. "Totum ergo meritum in voluntate est. Quantum vis, tantum mereris." PL 176: 561AB, p. 413; Two, fourteen, vi.

164. PL 176: 564B, p. 416; Two, fourteen, vii.

165. PL 176: 564C–570C, pp. 416–422; Two, fourteen, viii.

166. PL 176: 578A, p. 430; Two, fourteen, ix. The example of a second homicide is at PL 176: 573AB, pp. 425f.; Two, fourteen, ix.

167. PL 176: 577BC, pp. 430f.; Two, fifteen, i.

168. PL 176: 577D, p. 431; Two, fifteen, ii.

169. PL 176: 580B, p. 432; Two, fifteen, iii.

170. *Summa sententiarum*, PL 176: 41–174; Poirel, "'Alter Augustinus,'" p. 657.

171. PL 176: 579C–580D, p. 433; Two, sixteen, i.

172. PL 176: 582C, pp. 435f.; Two, sixteen, ii.

173. PL 176: 582C–584C, pp. 436–438; Two, sixteen, ii.

174. PL 176: 585A, p. 438; Two, sixteen, iii.

175. PL 176: 586A, p. 440; Two, sixteen, iv.

176. PL 176: 586C–587C, pp. 440f.; Two, sixteen, iv.

177. PL 176: 589B, p. 443; Two, sixteen, v.

178. PL 176: 593C–594A, p. 448; Two, sixteen, vi. *Enchiridion* 110, chapter xxix, pp. 405f. in Outler, LCC VII.

179. PL 176: 594AB, p. 449; Two, sixteen, vii. *City of God* XXI, 27; O'Meara (Penguin), 1019f.

180. PL 176: 595BC, p. 450; Two, sixteen, ix–x. Gregory the Great, *Dialogues* 4.57–58.

181. PL 176: 596B, p. 451; Two, sixteen, xi.

182. PL 176: 601CD, p. 457; Two, seventeen, xiii. Gregory, *Moralia* 14. 50.70 (PL 75: 1076BC).

183. PL 176: 602A–603B, pp. 458f.; Two, seventeen, xiv. *Enchiridion,* 84–87 ch. 23 pp. 390f.; *City of God* XXII. 13.

184. PL 176: 603B–605C, pp. 459–461; Two, seventeen, xv–xix. *Enchiridion*, 88–91; *City of God* XXII, 15.

185. PL 176: 605C–606A, p. 462; Two, seventeen, xx.

186. PL 176: 607CD, p. 464; Two, seventeen, xxii–xxiii.

187. PL 176: 607D–608D, pp. 464f.; Two, seventeen, xxiv–xxvii. *The City of God* XX. 1–2.

188. PL 176: 609B–612A, pp. 466–469; Two, eighteen, i–xii. Gregory at x.

189. PL 176: 612A, p. 469; Two, eighteen, xiii.

190. PL 176: 613A, p. 470; Two, eighteen, xvi.

191. PL 176: 613A–614B, pp. 470–472; Two, eighteen, xvi.

192. PL 176: 614C–615D, pp. 472f.; Two, eighteen, xvii. See Augustine's *Usefulness of Belief*.

193. PL 176: 616A, pp. 473f.; Two, eighteen, xviii; *The City of God* XXII.29, 1082f.

194. PL 176: 616BC, p. 474; Two, eighteen, xix.

195. PL 176: 616D, p. 474; Two, eighteen, xx, quoting from *The City of God* XXII, 30, p. 1087.

196. "Idem in eodem." PL 176: 616D–617B, pp. 474f.; Two, eighteen, xx, quoting at length from *The City of God* XXII, 30, p. 1088.

197. PL 176: 617B, p. 475; Two, eighteen, xxi.

198. PL 176: 618AB, p. 475; Two, eighteen, xxii; *The City of God* XXII, 30, pp. 1089f.

199. PL 176: 618B, p. 476; Two, eighteen, xxii; *The City of God* XXII, 30, p. 1091. Where this PL text reads "vocabimus" ("we shall call"), Augustine's read "vacabimus" ("we shall be still," as in Psalm 46).

CHAPTER 7

1. *Didascalicon* V, 6; FC 27: 336.23f., 338, 3; Taylor, p. 137. The Taylor translation of "moribus ornat" reads "*equips* it with morals," but the familiar image of a building constructed and then "adorned" is also suggested.

2. *Didascalicon* V. 9; FC 27: 348.17f.; Taylor, 132.

3. PL 175: 12BC; quoted in chapter 3.

4. In OHSV 1, *De virtute orandi* and *De laude caritatis* follow *De institutione novitiorum*, already discussed, and precede *De arrha animae*.

5. *De virtute orandi* will be cited according to the lines and page of the edition mentioned (OHSV 1) and in PL 176, in this case, *De virtute orandi* lines 2 and 14, OHSV 1 p. 126; PL 176: 977A. For a glimpse of the wide diffusion (266 manuscripts), see the introduction by D. Poirel, OHSV 1, p. 118.

6. See especially Poirel's notes and his appendices in OHSV 1, pp. 315f.

7. See Poirel's presentation of the plan or outline of the treatise, along with its principal themes, including his expression "progression pédagogique" on p. 123.

8. "Ostendamus foris verbis habere nos intus erga Deum affectum devotionis." *De virtute orandi*, lines 360f., OHSV 1 p. 150; PL 176: 984C.

9. "in affectibus pietatis est omnis virtus orandi." *De virtute orandi*, line 391, OHSV 1 p. 152; PL 176: 985B.

10. For example, *De virtute orandi*, lines 331–338, OHSV 1 p. 148; PL 176: 984A.

11. *De laude caritatis*, lines 164f., OHSV 1 p. 192; PL 176: 974B.

12. *De laude caritatis*, lines 166–180, OHSV 1 pp. 192/194; PL 176: 974BC; my translation.

13. *De laude caritatis*, line 215, OHSV 1 p. 196; PL 176: 975B; citing 1 John 4.16.

14. *Liber Ordinis* 20.75–85; CCCM 61, pp. 90f. On Adam of St. Victor and the development of Victorine liturgical materials, see Margot Fassler, *Gothic Song: Victorine Sequences and Augustinian Reform in Twelfth-Century Paris*, Cambridge Studies in Medieval and Renaissance Music (New York: Cambridge University Press, 1993).

15. OHSV 2, p. 12.

16. *De beatae Mariae virginitate*, lines 2–18, OHSV 2 p. 182; PL 176: 857A.

17. "Matrimonium non facit coitus, sed consensus." *De beatae Mariae virginitate*, lines 49f., OHSV 2 p. 186; PL 176: 858A. Jollès supplies some of the patristic background in note 4, OHSV 2 p. 254.

18. For example *De beatae Mariae virginitate*, lines 312–338, OHSV 2 pp. 204/206; PL 176: 863B–D.

19. Summarized in *De beatae Mariae virginitate*, lines 805–810, OHSV 2 p. 240; PL 176: 873A. Part of this text was incorporated into *De sacramentis*: Two, one, viii; PL 176: 391D–393D.

20. *De beatae Mariae virginitate*, lines 811–972, OHSV 2 pp. 242–252; PL 176: 873B–876C. See Jollès's comments on pp. 176–178 and note 56 on p. 258.

21. See "spiritualis intelligentie mysteria" in the Prologue to *Super Canticum Mariae*, line 13, OHSV 2 p. 24; PL 175: 413B.

22. *Super Canticum Mariae*, lines 149–266, OHSV 2 pp. 34–42; PL 175: 417A–419B.

23. *Super Canticum Mariae*, lines 267–400, OHSV 2 pp. 42–53; PL 175: 419B–421D.

24. *Super Canticum Mariae*, lines 564–664, OHSV 2 pp. 64–72; PL 175: 425A–427A. *De sacramentis* One, two, xxii, pp. 38–41; PL 176: 214B–216C. See Jollès's notes 47–48 on p. 96.

25. *Super Canticum Mariae*, lines 702–744, OHSV 2 pp. 76–78; PL 175: 427D–428D. *De sacramentis* Two, thirteen, v, pp. 377f.; PL 176: 528A–D.

26. *Pro Assumptione Virginis,* lines 21–16, OHSV 2 p. 112, PL 177: 1209–1210; Jollès's "Introduction," 103f.

27. *Pro Assumptione Virginis*, lines 51–55, OHSV 2 p. 116; PL 177: 1211A.

28. *Pro Assumptione Virginis*, lines 168–176, OHSV 2 p. 124; PL 177: 1213C.

29. Emphasis added. *Pro Assumptione Virginis*, lines 28f. OHSV 2, p. 134; PL 177: 1215D.

30. "Taste and see": *Pro Assumptione Virginis*, lines 394–400, OHSV 2, p. 142; PL 177: 1217D–1218A; "tree of life": lines 463–472, OHSV 2, p. 146; PL 177: 1219BC.

31. See Jollès's introduction for the frequencies of certain phrases and especially words for love. OHSV 2, p. 109.

32. Jollès, OHSV 2, p. 104 n. 3; see also p. 9 n. 11.

33. *De amore sponsi ad sponsam*, PL 176: 987B–994A. Much of this (987B–992B) is translated in *The Song of Songs Interpreted by Early Christian and Medieval Commentators*, tr. and ed. by Richard A. Norris Jr. (Grand Rapids, Mich.: Wm. B. Eerdmans, 2003), 167–172.

34. PL 176: 989BC for myrrh, 994A for the climax "de multis ad unum."

35. *Egredietur virga*, OHSV 2 pp. 270–280, is not in the PL edition, being first edited in 1955 by R. Baron. See the Jollès introduction, OHSV 2, pp. 263–269.

36. *Egredietur virga*, lines 1–37; OHSV 2, pp. 270/272.

37. *Egredietur virga* 126–128 and 140f.; OHSV 2, pp. 278 and 280.

38. *Maria porta*, lines 1–13 (complete), OHSV 2, p. 282. Hugh took no overt position, apparently, in the controversy over the immaculate conception.

39. "Contemplation and Its Forms" has been edited by Roger Baron in *Hugues de Saint-Victor. La Contemplation et ses espèces* (Desclée: Tournai, 1955). Partially translated by Bernard McGinn in *The Essential Writings of Christian Mysticism* (New York: Random House, 2006), 336–340, it itemizes many forms and types of contemplation in a more systematic or even more scholastic way than Hugh ever does in his undisputed writings.

40. Hugues de Saint-Victor, *Six Opuscules Spirituels*, Roger Baron, ed. (Paris: Les éditions du Cerf, 1969), *Sources chrétiennes* 155; to be abbreviated as Baron, SC 155. "On the Nature of Love" is translated in Hugh of Saint-Victor, *Selected Spiritual Writings*, Aelred Squire, ed. (London: Faber and Faber, 1962), 187–191.

41. *De meditatione*, Baron SC 155, lines 7–15 for creation (p. 44), lines 16–64 for scripture (pp. 46–48). The rest of the essay (lines 65–200; pp. 46–58) is "Meditatio in moribus." Also in PL 176: 993B–998A. See also *In Ecclesiastes,* in *Selected Spiritual Writings*, 183–187.

42. *De meditatione*, Baron SC 155, lines 64–94, pp. 48–50.

43. See chapter 3; some parallels are indicated in OHSV I, p. 100, n. 13, p. 106 n. 55, and p. 107 n. 62.

44. *De Verbo Dei*, Baron SC 155, pp. 60–81, also in PL 177: 289A–294D. For Baron's summary, including his admiration for Hugh's *virtuosité*, see pp. 17–24.

45. *De Verbo Dei*, Baron SC 155, lines 212–214, p. 74; PL 177: 293A.

46. *De quinque septenis* and *De septem donis Spiritus Sancti*, Baron SC 155, pp. 100–118 and 120–132; PL 175: 405B-410C, 410C-414A.

47. For this example, see *De quinque septenis*, Baron SC 155, lines 151–159, p. 110; PL 175: 408B.

48. *De quinque septenis*, Baron SC 155, lines 33–37, p. 102; PL 175: 405D.

49. *De quinque septenis*, Baron SC 155, lines 50–56, p. 104; PL 175: 406BC. *De sacramentis* Two, 13, i, p. 375; PL 176: 525CD.

50. "Of the Nature of Love" (see note 39) pp. 187–191; *De substantia dilectionis*, Baron SC 155, pp. 82–92; PL 176: 15A–18B, there printed as chapter 4 of the *Institutiones in Decalogum Legis Dominicae*.

51. *Quid vere diligendum sit*, Baron SC 155, lines 56–68, p. 98; PL 177: 564D–565A.

CHAPTER 8

1. *De archa Noe* and *Libellus de formatione arche*, P. Sicard, ed. (Turnhout: Brepols, 2001), *CCCM* 176, to be abbreviated as *De archa Noe* and *Libellus*. An English translation of the first is found in *Selected Spiritual Writings*, Aelred Squire, ed. (London: Faber and Faber, 1962) and will be referred to as "*Noah's Ark*" followed by the page number. These two treatises, in the Migne edition, are called *De arca Noe morali* and *De arca Noe mystica* (PL 176: 617–680 and 681–704), a most unfortunate pair of names given the weak and absent warrant, respectively, in the manuscript evidence, and the misleading results for modern readers. See editor Sicard's comments at *CCCM* 176, 205* and 255*.

2. Quoted more fully later, the question is posed immediately: *De archa Noe* [*CCCM* 176] I i, p. 3, lines 1–12; see also PL 176: 617–618; *Noah's Ark*, 45. The answer is summarized much later: *De archa Noe* IV, viii, p. 110. 143–159 [677AB]; *Noah's Ark*, 146. For "the author of creation and restoration," see *De archa Noe* IV, vi. p. 102. 24f. [672D]; *Noah's Ark*, 138.

3. *De archa Noe* I, i, p. 3. 3–9 [617–618]; *Noah's Ark*, p. 45.

4. *De archa Noe* I, i, p. 5. 46–57 [619], *Noah's Ark*, 47.

5. *De archa Noe* I, ii, p. 7. 23–45 [620AB–621A]; *Noah's Ark*, 48f.

6. *De archa Noe* I, iii, p. 9. 10–13 [621D]; *Noah's Ark*, 51.

7. *De archa Noe* I, iii, p. 9f. 17–29 [622AB]; *Noah's Ark,* 51.

8. *De archa Noe* I, iii, p. 10. 29–34 [622B]; *Noah's Ark*, 51f.

9. *De archa Noe* I, iii, p. 10. 35–44 [622BC]; *Noah's Ark*, 52.

10. *De archa Noe* I, iii, p. 14. 138–142 [624C]; *Noah's Ark*, 56.

11. That the seraphim do not here cover the Lord's face, as in Isaiah 6, is discussed by Grover Zinn in "Hugh of St. Victor, Isaiah's Vision, and *De Arca Noe*," in *The Church and the Arts: Papers Read at the 1990 Summer Meeting and the 1991 Winter Meeting of the Ecclesiastical History Society*, Diana Wood, editor (Oxford: Blackwell, 1992), 99–116.

12. *De archa Noe* I, iii, p. 16. 199–201 [625D]; *Noah's Ark*, 58.

13. *De archa Noe* I, iii, pp. 16f. 210–220. [626A]; *Noah's Ark*, 58f. Such phrases as "in forma visibili depinxi" (10.43) are considered again later when the *Libellus* raises the question of a diagram.

14. *De archa Noe* I, iii, p. 17.229–249 [626BC]; *Noah's Ark*, 59f. Hugh here also mentions a fourth, the "ark of mother grace," but it never receives explicit exposition and seems mostly to round out the symmetry of two visible and two invisible arks.

15. *De archa Noe* I, iv, pp. 18–20. 1–61 [627]; *Noah's Ark*, 60–62. For Hugh's exegetical differences with Origen over the physical shape of the ark, see Grover Zinn, "Hugh of St. Victor and the Ark of Noah: A New Look," *Church History* 40 (1971): 261–272.

16. *De archa Noe* I, iv, pp. 20–22. 62–138 [628–629]; *Noah's Ark*, 62f.; a large section (pp. 21–22) regarding geometry was not translated here but is available in Homann, *Practical Geometry*, 85f.

17. *De archa Noe* I, v, p. 23f. 1–19 [630AB]; *Noah's Ark*, 64.

18. *De archa Noe* I, v, p. 24.19–30 [630B]; *Noah's Ark*, 64.

19. *De archa Noe* I, v, pp. 24–26. 31–70 [630C–631B]; *Noah's Ark*, 65f.

20. *De archa Noe* I, v, pp. 26f. 71–86 [631CD]; *Noah's Ark*, 66f.

21. *De archa Noe* I, v, pp. 27–31. 87–224 [631D–634C]; *Noah's Ark*, 67–72. Along the way, Hugh supplies symbolic meanings to his own suggestion as to differing heights for different stories, from four cubits up to eight.

22. *De archa Noe* I, v, pp. 31f. 225–231 [634CD]; *Noah's Ark*, 72.

23. *De archa Noe* II, i, p. 33. 1–24 [635AB]; *Noah's Ark*, 73.

24. *De archa Noe* II, i, pp. 33f. 25–31 [635C]; *Noah's Ark*, 74.

25. *De archa Noe* II, i, p. 34. 32–42 [636A]; *Noah's Ark*, 74.

26. *De archa Noe* II, ii, p. 35. 1–9 [636C]; *Noah's Ark*, 75.

27. *De archa Noe* II, ii, p. 36. 26–45 [637BC]; *Noah's Ark*, 76f.

28. *De archa Noe* II, ii, pp. 36f. 47–56 [637CD]; *Noah's Ark*, 77; recapitulated in *De archa Noe* II, iv, pp. 39f. 22–24 [639B]; *Noah's Ark*, 80.

29. *De archa Noe* II, ii–iii, pp. 37f. 57–63, 1–30 [638A–C]; *Noah's Ark*, 77f.; see chapter 3, pp. 39–40.

30. *De archa Noe* II, iii, p. 38. 31–39 [638CD] *Noah's Ark*, 78f.

31. *De archa Noe* II, iii–iv, pp. 38f. 39–42, 1–21 [638D–639A]; *Noah's Ark*, 79f.

32. *De archa Noe* II, v, p. 41. 36f. [640C]; *Noah's Ark*, 82.

33. *De archa Noe* II, vi, p. 42. 5–8 [640D]; *Noah's Ark*, 82.

34. *De archa Noe* II, vii, p. 43. 5f. [641A]; *Noah's Ark*, 83.

35. *De archa Noe* II, vii, pp. 43f. 25f., 31f., 38 [641BC]; *Noah's Ark*, 84.

36. *De archa Noe* II, vii, p. 45. 70–73 [642B]; *Noah's Ark*, 86.

37. On the details of the ascents, see Grover Zinn, "Exile, the Abbey of St-Victor at Paris, and Hugh of Saint Victor," in *Medieval Paradigms: Essays in Honor of Jeremy duQuesnay Adams,* vol. 2, edited by Stephanie A. Hayes-Healy, New Middle Ages (New York: Palgrave Macmillan, 2005), 83–111.

38. *De archa Noe* II, vii, p. 45. 87f. [642D]; *Noah's Ark*, 86.

39. *De archa Noe* II, viii, p. 46. 12–14 [643A]; *Noah's Ark,* 87.

40. *De archa Noe* II, viii, p. 47. 24–27 [643B]; badly translated in *Noah's Ark*, 87f., as if to suggest the opposite.

41. *De archa Noe* II, xii, p. 49. 1–13 [644B]; *Noah's Ark*, 89. *De archa Noe* II, xv, p. 53. 1–10 [646A]; *Noah's Ark*, 92.

42. *De archa Noe* II, xvii, p. 54. 1–10 [646C]; *Noah's Ark*, 93. The Latin has the same preposition (*per*) for all fifteen phrases.

43. *De archa Noe* III, i, p. 55. 1–5 [647A], *Noah's Ark*, 94.

44. *De archa Noe* III, ii, pp. 55f. 1–19 [647AB]; *Noah's Ark*, 94f.

45. *De archa Noe* III, v, p. 61. 76f. [650D]; *Noah's Ark*, 100.

46. *De archa Noe* III, vii, p. 67. 92–96 [653C]; *Noah's Ark*, 105.

47. *De archa Noe* III, ix, p. 69. 19–37 [655AB]; *Noah's Ark*, 107.

48. *De archa Noe* III, xi, p. 71. 2–9 [655CD]; *Noah's Ark,* 108.

49. *De archa Noe* III, xi [655D–661B]; *Noah's Ark*, 108–117.

50. *De archa Noe* III, xi, pp. 73f. 75–84 [657AB]; *Noah's Ark*, 111.

51. *De archa Noe* III, xvii, pp. 83f. 1–42 [662B–664A].

52. *De archa Noe* III, xvii, p. 85. 43–49 [664A]; *Noah's Ark*, 121, with "construction" for *fabricatione*.

53. Emphasis added; "de fabricatione arche sapientie prosequamur," *De archa Noe* III, xvii, p. 85. 48f. [664A]; *Noah's Ark*, 121 (adjusted translation). "De edificatione domus Domini loqui volumus," *De archa Noe* IV, i. p. 86. 2 [663B]; *Noah's Ark*, 122. The emphasis on the process of building the ark rather than on the ark as object continues later in book 4: what God is doing is "producing in our hearts the form of an invisible ark," *De archa Noe* IV, v, p. 100. 63f. [672A]; *Noah's Ark*, 137; "so that a spiritual house of wisdom could be built in us," *De archa Noe* IV, viii, p. 110. 153f. [677B]; *Noah's Ark*, 146 (adjusted translation).

54. *De archa Noe* IV, i, p. 86. 7–9 [663B]; *Noah's Ark*, 122.

55. *De archa Noe* IV, i, p. 86, 16f. [663C]; *Noah's Ark*, 122; "Dilata ergo cor tunum" ("Enlarge your heart therefore") is repeated several times in the next few lines.

56. *De archa Noe* IV, i, pp. 87f. 50–52 [664C]; *Noah's Ark*, 123f.

57. *De archa Noe*, IV, i–ii, pp. 89–91. 82–90, 1–49 [665C-666C]; *Noah's Ark*, 125–127.

58. "modum reparationis," *De archa Noe* IV, ii, p. 91. 48f. [666C]; *Noah's Ark*, 127, "manner of reintegration."

59. *De archa Noe* IV, iii, p. 93. 21–23 [667C]; *Noah's Ark*, 129. The general (re)statement of the works of creation and reparation/restoration is at *De archa Noe* IV, iii, p. 92. 1–10 [667B]; *Noah's Ark*, p. 128, a parallel to *De sacramentis*, PL 176: 183AB, p. 3, Prologue, and elsewhere.

60. *De archa Noe* IV, iii, p. 94. 58–60 [668B]; *Noah's Ark*, 130.

61. *De archa Noe* IV, iii, p. 94. 70f. [668C]; *Noah's Ark*, 131.

62. *De archa Noe* IV, iv, pp. 95–97 [668D–670B]; *Noah's Ark*, 132–134.

63. *De archa Noe* IV, iv, p. 98. 86–88 [670C]; *Noah's Ark*, 134.

64. *De archa Noe* IV, v, pp. 98–100. 1–60 [670D–671D]; *Noah's Ark*, 134–137. The passage also contains an interesting correlation of creation with power and redemption with love.

65. *De archa Noe* IV, v, p. 100. 60–64 [671D]; *Noah's Ark*, 137, with "minds" for *mentes*.

66. *De archa Noe* IV, vi, pp. 101f. 1–20 [672BC]; *Noah's Ark*, 137f.

67. *De archa Noe* IV, vi, p. 102. 20–27 [672CD]; *Noah's Ark*, 138. "Per visibilia ad invisibilia" (102.21) is also Dale Coulter's title for a recent book on Richard of St. Victor (Turnhout: Brepols, 2006), including some discussion of Hugh, although not (unfortunately) this passage.

68. *De archa Noe* IV, vii, pp. 102f. 1–19 [673A]; *Noah's Ark*, 138f.

69. *De archa Noe* IV, vii, p. 104. 51–53, [673D]; *Noah's Ark*, 140.

70. *De archa Noe* IV, viii, pp. 105f. 1–42 [674A–D]; *Noah's Ark*, 141f.

71. *De archa Noe* IV, viii, p. 107. 55f. [675A]; *Noah's Ark*, 143.

72. *De archa Noe* IV, viii, p. 107. 61–65 [675B]; *Noah's Ark*, 143.

73. *De archa Noe* IV, viii, p. 108. 91–94 [676A]; *Noah's Ark*, 144.

74. *De archa Noe* IV, viii, p. 110. 143–154 [677A]; *Noah's Ark*, 146.

75. *De archa Noe* IV, viii, p. 110. 154–160 [677B]; *Noah's Ark*, 146f.

76. *De archa Noe* IV, ix, p. 111. 2–4 [677B]; *Noah's Ark*, 147.

77. *De archa Noe* IV, ix, pp. 111f. 6–35 [677C–678A]; *Noah's Ark*, 147f.

78. *De archa Noe* IV, ix, pp. 112f. 35–55 [678AB]; *Noah's Ark*, 148.

79. *De archa Noe* IV, ix, p. 113. 67–73 [678D]; *Noah's Ark*, 149.

80. *De archa Noe* IV, ix, p. 114. 81–102 [679AB]; *Noah's Ark*, 150, although this translation left out "body."

81. *De archa Noe* IV, ix, p. 115. 103–119 [679C]; *Noah's Ark*, 151.

82. "Non laberintus, sed requies intus." *De archa Noe* IV, ix, p. 115. 120–122 [679D]; *Noah's Ark*, 151.

83. *De archa Noe* IV, ix, pp. 115f. 130–141 [680AB]; *Noah's Ark*, 151f.

84. *De archa Noe* IV, ix, p. 116. 141–162 [680BC]; *Noah's Ark*, 152.

85. *De archa Noe* IV, ix, pp. 116f. 162–165 [680D]; *Noah's Ark*, 152.

86. "arche nostre exemplar . . . quod exterius depingimus." *De archa Noe* IV, ix, p. 117. 166–172, *Noah's Ark*, 153. This passage is not included in the PL edition.

87. *De archa Noe* I, iii, p. 10. 35–44 [622BC]; *Noah's Ark*, 52.

88. To be cited as *Libellus* from CCCM 176 by chapter, page, and lines with added reference to the PL 176 location. The translation (of the PL text) by Jessica Weiss in *The Medieval Craft of Memory: An Anthology of Texts and Pictures*, ed. Mary Carruthers and Jan W. Ziolkowski (Philadelphia: University of Pennsylvania Press, 2002), 45–70, will be cited as *Little Book*.

89. Zinn, "Hugh of St. Victor, Isaiah's Vision," 100, and "Exile," 94–95; Patrice Sicard, *Diagrammes médiévaux et exégèse visuelle: Le Libellus de formatione arche de Hugues de Saint-Victor* (Paris/Turnhout: Brepols, 1993), to be abbreviated as Sicard, *Diagrammes;* CCCM 176A is a set of eleven diagrams accompanying the *Libellus;* Conrad Rudolph, *"First, I Find the Center Point": Reading the Text of Hugh of Saint Victor's The Mystic Ark*, Transactions of the American Philosophical Society, v. 94, pt. 4 (Philadelphia: American Philosophical Society, 2004).

90. "il n'est guère possible de se tromper plus lourdement," CCCM 176: 255*.

91. E.g.: *de pictura, de pictura arche, depinctio arche*, CCCM 176: 256*.

92. "in forma visibili depinxi," *De archa Noe* I, iii, p. 10. 43 [622C]; *Noah's Ark*, 52. "quod exterius depingimus," *De archa Noe* IV, ix, p. 117. 169; *Noah's Ark*, 153.

93. *Libellus* I, p. 121. 1–3 [681A]; *Little Book*, p. 45. Translating from PL 176:681A, Weiss includes Migne's editorial addition "ad mysticam arcae Noe descriptionum."

94. *Libellus* I, p. 122. 26–28 and 34f. [681C and 682A]; *Little Book*, 45f.

95. *Libellus* I, pp. 123f. 48–57 [682C–683C]; *Little Book*, 46f.

96. *Libellus* I, pp. 124f. 87–107 [683CD]; *Little Book*, 47.

97. *Libellus* I, p. 126. 133–139 [684C]; *Little Book*, 48.

98. *Libellus* I, p. 126. 151–157 [685A]; *Little Book*, 48f.

99. *Libellus* II, pp. 127f. 1–32 [685B–D]; *Little Book*, 49.

100. *Libellus* II, pp. 128f. 32–72 [686A–C]; *Little Book*, 50.

101. *Libellus* II, p. 129. 72–81 [686D]; *Little Book*, 50f.

102. *Libellus* II, p. 130. 86–96 [687A]; *Little Book*, 51.

103. *Libellus* II, pp. 130f. 96–125 [687CD]; *Little Book*, 51f.

104. *Libellus* II–III, pp. 131f. 126–138, 1–6 [688AB]; *Little Book*, 52.

105. *Libellus* III, p. 133. 28f. [688D]; *Little Book*, p. 53. The overall passage about this complicated color scheme is *Libellus* III as a whole, pp. 132–138 [688B–691B]; *Little Book*, 52–56.

106. *Libellus* IV, p. 139. 7–35 [671D–692A]; *Little Book*, 56f. *Noah's Ark* explained that fifty cubits "denotes the breadth of all believers everywhere," seven times seven, plus the One who is the Head. *De archa Noe* I, v, p. 24. 10–16 [630A]; *Noah's Ark*, 64.

107. *Libellus* IV, p. 140. 36–46 [692B]; *Little Book*, 57, putting "discipline" for "doctrine" and "teaching."

108. *Libellus* IV, p. 140. 47–52 [692C]; *Little Book*, 57.

109. *Libellus* IV, pp. 140f. 53–61 [692C]; *Little Book*, 57.

110. *Libellus* IV, p. 141. 62–146.186 [692D–695B]; *Little Book*, 57–60.

111. *Libellus* IV, p. 147. 206–217 [695D–696A]; *Little Book*, 61.

112. *Libellus* IV–V, pp. 147f. 224–242, 1–22 [696A–D]; *Little Book*, 61f.

113. *Libellus* V, pp. 149f. 23–40 [697AB]; *Little Book*, 62f.

114. *Libellus* VI, p. 151. 12–27 [697CD]; *Little Book*, 63.

115. *Libellus* VII–VIII, pp. 151f. [698A–D]; *Little Book*, 63f. At this point, the Weiss translation dropped a line (bottom of p. 63); see 151f. 6–8. The door and window, complete with raven and dove, were thoroughly discussed in *De archa Noe* II, ii, pp. 35–37 [637]; *Noah's Ark*, 75f., as noted earlier (pp. 133–134).

116. *Libellus* IX, pp. 153f. 1–12 [698D–699A]; *Little Book*, 64f. See *De archa Noe* I, iv, p. 20. 55–60 [627D–628A]; *Noah's Ark*, 62.

117. *Libellus* IX, p. 154. 12–21 [699A]; *Little Book*, 65, citing Numbers 35.

118. *Libellus* IX, p. 155. 31–37 [699C]; *Little Book*, 65.

119. "in descriptione mappe mundi," *Libellus* IX, p. 155. 48 [699D]; *Little Book*, 66. See the discussion later as to whether this refers to another work as well.

120. *Libellus* IX–X, pp. 155f. 50–55, 1–28 [699D–700C]; *Little Book*, 66f. Here Hugh seems to promise still more detail about these rooms/stations in yet another work on the ark (156. 24–28) as mentioned later.

121. "Hec ad constructionem arche . . . sufficere possunt." *Libellus* XI, p. 157. 1–2 [700C]; *Little Book*, 67.

122. *Libellus* XI, pp. 157–159. 1–69 [700C–701D]; *Little Book*, 67f.

123. *Libellus* XI, p. 157. 8–10 [700D]; unfortunately missing from *Little Book*, 67. See Rudolph's comments, *Center Point*, 28.

124. *Libellus* XI, p. 160. 70–73 [702A]; *Little Book* 68. *De archa Noe* I, iii, 10f. 35–51; *Noah's Ark*, 52.

125. *Libellus* XI, p. 160. 73–85 [702AB]; *Little Book*, 68f.

126. *Libellus* XI, p. 160. 86–101 [702BC]; *Little Book*, 69.

127. *Libellus* XI, p. 161. 102–118 [702CD]; *Little Book*, 69f. These references to the angelic numbers stem from Gregory the Great, not the Dionysian *Celestial Hierarchy*.

128. *Libellus* XI, p. 162. 119–123 [703A–704A]; *Little Book*, 70.

129. *De archa Noe* I, iii, p. 10. 35–37 [622B]; *Noah's Ark*, 52.

130. For a yet wider view, see Grover Zinn, "Mandala Symbolism and Use in the Mysticism of Hugh of St. Victor," *History of Religions* 4 (1973): 317–341.

131. Mary Carruthers and Jessica Weiss, for example, in their introduction to *Little Book*, 41f.: "there is no reason to suppose that it was ever materially realized or that it described an actual painting."

132. Sicard, 1993, 40–45, p. 55–59; Zinn, "Exile," 107 n. 46.

133. Conrad Rudolph, *Center Point*, vii and p. 87 n. 7.

134. "in eo libro quam de archa dictavi," *Libellus* VIII, p. 153. 12 [698D]; *Little Book*, 64. "tractatum quem fecimus, qui intitulatur *De tribus diebus*," *Libellus* IV, p. 143. 115f. [693D]; *Little Book*, 59.

135. *Libellus* X, p. 156. 24–28 [700C]; *Little Book*, 67.

136. "in descriptione mappe mundi postea clarebit," *Libellus* X, p. 155. 48f. [699D]; *Little Book*, 66.

137. Patrick Gautier Dalché, *La "Descriptio mappe mundi" de Hugues de Saint-Victor. Texte inédit avec introduction et commentaire* (Paris: Études Augustiniennes, 1988), followed by "La 'Descriptio mappe mundi' de Hugues de Saint-Victor: retractatio et additamenta," in *L'abbaye parisienne de Saint-Victor au Moyen Age*, ed. Jean Longère (Paris/Turnhout: Brepols, 1991), 143–179, which was revised and reprinted as "Nouvelles lumières sur la *Descriptio mappe mundi* de Hugues de Saint-Victor," in Patrick Gautier Dalché, *Géographie et culture, La représentation de l'espace du VIe au XIIe siècle*, Variorum collected studies series, CS592 (Aldershot, U.K.; Brookfield, Vt.: Ashgate, 1997), XII. 1–27.

138. Gautier Dalché, *La "Descriptio*," 48–50, 100–107, 111–113.

139. *De vanitate mundi*, PL 176: 703ff.; to be abbreviated as *De vanitate*; there is a partial translation in *Selected Spiritual Writings*, to be abbreviated as *Vanity*.

140. *De vanitate*, PL 176: 705C–706B; *Vanity*, 160f.

141. *De vanitate*, PL 176: 706B–709C; *Vanity*, 162–167.

142. *De vanitate*, PL 176: 709CD; *Vanity*, 167f.

143. *De vanitate*, PL 176: 710B; *Vanity*, 168f.

144. *De vanitate*, PL 176: 711A–713C; *Vanity*, 171–174; "certiorem mansionem" at 713B; *Vanity*, 174.

145. *De vanitate*, PL 176: 713D–714A; this very passage is dropped from the English translation, oddly called "five lines of repetition," *Vanity*, 175 n. 1.

146. *De vanitate*, PL 176: 714AB; *Vanity*, 175f.

147. *De vanitate*, PL 176: 714C–715A; here, too, the English translation has omitted thirty-five lines, including the *viam salutis* and *salutaris legni* evoking the cross at 714D.

148. *In intimis etiam seipsum transire*. *De vanitate*, PL 176: 715B; *Vanity*, 176.

149. *De vanitate*, PL 176: 715BC and 716B; omitted in *Vanity*, 176 and 177.

150. *De vanitate*, PL 176: 716D; also omitted from *Vanity*, 177.

151. *De vanitate*, PL 176: 717B–D; *Vanity*, 177. Parallels with *De archa Noe* are indexed in CCCM 176: 195f.

152. *De vanitate*, PL 176: 717D; *Vanity*, 177.

153. *De vanitate*, PL 176: 718B–719B; *Vanity*, 178–180.

154. *De vanitate*, PL 176: 719B–D; *Vanity*, 180f.

155. *De vanitate*, PL 176: 719D–720D; *Vanity*, 181f.

156. Weisweiler, "Arbeitsmethode," 67–71.

157. *De vanitate*, PL 176: 724D–725A, 726B.

CHAPTER 9

1. *De arrha anime*, line 3, OHSV 1, p. 226; PL 176: 951B; *Soliloquy*, p. 13. The English translation is by Kevin Herbert, *Soliloquy on the Earnest Money of the Soul* (Milwaukee: Marquette University Press, 1956), adjusted as needed. This essay was the first of Hugh's works to be printed, in 1473 (Poirel, *Hugues*, 10). On the manuscript diffusion and translations, see Poirel's introduction in OHSV 1, pp. 212f. A newly discovered manuscript confirms that the recipient is Brother Gunther; Julie Hotchin, "*Dilecto fratri Gunthero*: Provost Gunther of Lippoldsberg and the Reception of Hugh of St. Victor in Northern Germany" in *Texte in Kontexten. Gesammelte Studien zur Abtei Sankt-Viktor und den Viktorinen*, 2, ed. by Matthias Tischler. Corpus Victorinum, Instrumenta 3 (Berlin: Akademie, forthcoming).

2. *De arrha anime*, lines 6–9, OHSV 1, p. 226; PL 176: 951B; *Soliloquy*, 13.

3. Poirel (OHSV 1, pp. 212f.) notes Bede's and Hugh's other uses of this format, such as the *Epitoma Dindimi* and the *Vanity of the World* sampled previously, as well as the diffusion of more than three hundred manuscripts and specific successors.

4. Augustine, Sermon 156, 15 (PL 38: 858) and other texts cited by Poirel, OHSV 1 p. 211, nn. 1 and 4.

5. *De arrha anime*, lines 11f.; OHSV 1, p. 226; PL 176: 951B; *Soliloquy*, 13. See Poirel, OHSV 1, p. 284, n. 10.

6. *De arrha anime*, lines 24f., OHSV 1, p. 226; PL 176: 951C; *Soliloquy*, 13.

7. *De arrha anime*, lines 76f., OHSV 1, p. 230; PL 176: 953D; *Soliloquy*, 15.

8. "Sponsum habes, sed nescis." *De arrha anime*, line 121, OHSV 1, p. 234; PL 176: 954C; *Soliloquy*, 16.

9. . . . sed munera misit, arram dedit pignus amoris, signum dilectionis. *De arrha anime*, lines 123f., OHSV 1, p. 234; PL 176: 954D, *Soliloquy*, 16.

10. *De arrha anime*, lines 144–146, OHSV 1, p. 234; PL 176: 955A; *Soliloquy*, 17.

11. *De arrha anime*, lines 146–171, OHSV 1, p. 236; PL 176: 955D; *Soliloquy*, 17.

12. *De arrha anime*, lines 179–185, OHSV 1, p. 238; PL 176: 955D–956A; *Soliloquy*, 17f.

13. *De arrha anime*, lines 207–220, OHSV 1, p. 240; PL 176: 956A–C; *Soliloquy*, 18.

14. *De arrha anime*, lines 233f., OHSV 1, p. 240; PL 176: 956D–957A; *Soliloquy*, 19.

15. *De arrha anime*, lines 270–274, OHSV 1, p. 244, PL 176: 957D; *Soliloquy*, 20.

16. *De arrha anime*, lines 274–299, OHSV 1, pp. 244f.; PL 176: 957D–958B; *Soliloquy*, 20.

17. *De arrha anime*, lines 317–319, OHSV 1, p. 246; PL 176: 958D; *Soliloquy*, 21.

18. *De arrha anime*, lines 329–343, OHSV 1, p. 248; PL 176: 959AB; *Soliloquy*, 21, translation adjusted.

19. "affectu et effectu," *De arrha anime*, lines 349–352, OHSV 1, p. 248; PL 176: 959C; *Soliloquy*, 22.

20. *De arrha anime*, lines 353–366, OHSV 1, pp. 248/250; PL 176: 959CD; *Soliloquy*, 22.

21. *De arrha anime*, lines 391–406, OHSV 1, p. 252; PL 176: 960BC; *Soliloquy*, 23.

22. *De arrha anime*, lines 413–423, OHSV 1, pp. 252/254; PL 176: 960D; *Soliloquy*, 23f.

23. *De arrha anime*, lines 437–455, OHSV 1, pp. 254/256; PL 176: 960BC; *Soliloquy*, 24.

24. *De arrha anime*, lines 456–469, OHSV 1, p. 256; PL 176: 961CD; *Soliloquy*, 24f.

25. *De arrha anime*, lines 469–480, OHSV 1, p. 256; PL 176: 962A; *Soliloquy*, 25.

26. *De arrha anime*, lines 481–487, OHSV 1, p. 258; PL 176: 962B; *Soliloquy*, 25f.

27. *De arrha anime*, lines 487–495, OHSV 1, p. 258; PL 176: 962BC; *Soliloquy*, 26.

28. *Eulogium*, PL 176: 987CD; see Poirel, OHSV 2, p. 294, n. 78.

29. *De arrha anime*, lines 496–509, OHSV 1, p. 258; PL 176: 962CD; *Soliloquy*, 26.

30. *De arrha anime*, lines 519–522, OHSV 1, p. 260; PL 176: 962D–963A; *Soliloquy*, 26.

31. *De arrha anime*, lines 551–554, OHSV 1, p. 262; PL 176: 963CD; *Soliloquy*, 27.

32. *De arrha anime*, lines 560–579, OHSV 1, pp. 262/264; PL176: 963D–964B; *Soliloquy*, 28.

33. *"exemplum utile," De arrha anime*, lines 580–600, OHSV 1, p. 264; PL 176: 964BC; *Soliloquy*, 28f.

34. *De arrha anime*, lines 601f., OHSV 1, p. 266; PL 176: 964D; *Soliloquy*, 29.

35. *De arrha anime*, lines 602–619, OHSV 1, p. 266; PL 176: 964D–965A; *Soliloquy*, 29.

36. *De arrha anime*, lines 619f., OHSV 1, p. 266; PL 176: 956A; *Soliloquy*, 29.

37. *De arrha anime*, lines 628f., OHSV 1, p. 266; PL 176: 965B; *Soliloquy*, 30.

38. *De arrha anime*, lines 630–650, OHSV 1, p. 268; PL 176: 965CD; *Soliloquy*, 30.

39. *De arrha anime*, lines 651–699, with the quotation from 696–699, OHSV 1, pp. 268/270; PL 176: 965D–966D; *Soliloquy*, 30f.

40. *De arrha anime*, lines 715–717, OHSV 1, p. 272; PL 176: 967A; *Soliloquy*, 32.

41. *De arrha anime*, lines 731–733, OHSV 1, p. 274; PL 176: 967C; *Soliloquy*, 32.

42. *De arrha anime*, lines 735–743, OHSV 1, p. 224; PL 176: 967CD; *Soliloquy*, 32f.

43. *De virtute orandi*, lines 147–157, OHSV 1, p. 136; PL 176: 980BC.

44. *De arrha anime*, lines 743–747, OHSV 1, p. 274; PL 176: 967D; *Soliloquy*, p. 33.

45. *De arrha anime*, lines 748–766, OHSV 1, pp. 274/276; PL 176: 967D–968B; *Soliloquy*, 33, adding translation for "quando iui, deduxisti me; quando ueni, suscepisti me."

46. *De arrha anime*, lines 767–774, OHSV 1, p. 276; PL 176: 968B; *Soliloquy*, 33.

47. *De arrha anime*, lines 775–780, OHSV 1, p. 276; PL 176: 968C; *Soliloquy*, 33.

48. *De arrha anime*, lines 795f., OHSV 1, p. 278; PL 176: 968D; *Soliloquy*, 34.

49. *De arrha anime*, lines 819–823, OHSV 1, p. 280; PL 176: 969B; *Soliloquy*, 34.

50. *De arrha anime*, lines 824–826, OHSV 1, p. 280; PL 176: 969C; *Soliloquy*, 34.

51. *De arrha anime*, lines 826–830, OHSV 1, p. 280; PL 176: 969C: *Soliloquy*, 35.

52. *De arrha anime*, lines 831–843, quoting from 834–837, OHSV 1, p. 280; PL 176: 969C–979A; *Soliloquy*, 35.

53. *De arrha anime*, lines 844–861, OHSV 1, pp. 280/282; PL 176: 970 AB; *Soliloquy*, 35.

54. Genesis 32; Bernard on the Song of Songs, Sermon 74, J. Leclercq vol. 2, p. 242.

55. *De arrha anime*, lines 862–877, OHSV 1, p. 282; PL 176: 970CD; *Soliloquy*, 35f.

APPENDIX

1. PL 175: 923–1154. A modern edition is being prepared by D. Poirel, who kindly supplied a copy of his basic text, to appear as *Hugonis de Sancto Victore Opera III: Super Ierarchiam Dionysii* (Turnhout: Brepols), CCCM 178. Besides the prefatory material in that forthcoming volume, the major study on this entire topic of Dionysius and Hugh is Poirel's companion volume, *Hugues de Saint-Victor et le réveil dionysien du XIIe siecle: Le 'Super Ierarchiam beati Dionisii,'* Bibliotheca Victorina (Paris/Turnhout: Brepols, forthcoming). All other studies are provisional, awaiting Poirel's two books, although some of his conclusions have been previewed in briefer essays: "L'ange gothique," in *L'architecture gothique au service de la liturgie*, ed. A. Bos and X. Dectot (Turnhout: Brepols, 2003), 115–142; "*Hugo Saxo:* Les origines germaniques de la pensée d'Hugues de Saint Victor," *Francia: Forschungen zur westeuropäischen Geschichte* 33/1 (2006): 163–174. See also his "Le 'chant dionysien'" and "*Symbolice et anagogice:* l'école de Saint-Victor et la naissance du style gothique," cited in chapter 3 regarding geometry and Gothic.

2. I have summarized this general material in *Pseudo-Dionysius: A Commentary on the Texts and an Introduction to Their Influence* (New York: Oxford University Press, 1993), 14–18. For the Dionysian works, see *Pseudo-Dionysius: The Complete Works,* translated by Colm Luibheid (New York: Paulist Press, 1987).

3. For details, see my study of Eriugena and Dionysius, *Eriugena's Commentary on the Dionysian "Celestial Hierarchy"* (Toronto: Pontifical Institute of Mediaeval Studies, 2005). To be abbreviated as *Eriugena's Commentary.*

4. David Luscombe, "The Commentary of Hugh of Saint-Victor on the Celestial Hierarchy," in *Die Dionysius Rezeption im Mittelalter*, ed. T. Boiadjiev, G. Kapriev, and A. Speer (Turnhout: Brepols, 2000), 160–164; to be abbreviated as Luscombe, "Commentary." D. Poirel, "Le 'chant dionysien.'"

5. *Didascalicon* IV, 3; FC 27: 306.20f.; Taylor, 116.

6. PL 176: 737A.

7. PL 175: 960CD.

8. Poirel, "*Hugo Saxo,*" 173f. This speculation could be confirmed if the peculiarities in Hugh's text of *The Celestial Hierarchy*, including traces of marginalia, match the German group of Dionysian manuscripts rather than the Parisian.

9. "Introducendis," PL 175: 928B, 931BC.

10. "theologus et hierarchiarum descriptor," ch. 2 PL 175: 927C; "theologus et narrator hierarchiarum," ch. 3 PL 175: 929C.

11. PL 175: 929C/930C and 931C/932B.

12. See n. 1.

13. PL 175: 931B.

14. See editor J. Barbet's introductory comments in *Expositiones in Ierarchiam Coelestem* (Turnholt: Brepols, 1975), x. Eriugena's Commentary will be abbreviated as *Expositiones*.

15. My thanks to Ralf M. W. Stammberger for a prepublication copy of his essay "*Theologus nostri temporis Ioannes Scotus*: Hugh of St. Victor's Assessment of John Scotus Eriugena's Reception of Pseudo-Dionysius," a paper given at the 2000 Maynouth meeting of the Society for the Promotion of Eriugenian Studies, forthcoming in *Irish Theological Quarterly*.

16. Heinrich Weisweiler, "Die Pseudo-Dionysiuskommentare 'In Coelestem Hierarchiam' des Skotus Eriugena und Hugos von St. Viktor," *Recherches de théologie ancienne et médiévale* 19 (1952): 26–47; Jean Châtillon, "Hugues de Saint-Victor critique de Jean Scot," *Jean Scot Érigène et l'histoire de la philosophie*, ed. E. Jeauneau, G. Madec, and R. Roques (Paris: CNRS, 1977), 415–431.

17. René Roques, "Connaissance de Dieu et théologie symbolique d'après l' '*In hierarchiam coelestem sancti Dionysii*' de Hugues de Saint-Victor," *Structures théologiques de la gnose à Richard de Saint-Victor* (Paris: Press Universitaires de France, 1962), 294–364; R. Baron, "Le Commentaire de la 'Hiérarchie céleste' par Hugues de Saint-Victor," *Études sur Hugues de Saint-Victor* (Paris: Desclée de Brouwer, 1963), 133–218.

18. PL 175: 975D/976AB, also in *De sacramentis*, One, ten, ii (PL 176: 329C). See Van der Eynde, 59f.

19. See D. Poirel's contrast of Gregorian and Dionysian angelology in "L'ange gothique," n. 1.

20. Jong Won Seouh, "Knowledge and Action in Hugh of St. Victor's Commentary on the Dionysian *Celestial Hierarchy*," Ph.D. dissertation, Princeton Theological Seminary, 2007.

21. PL 175: 972C–978AD, esp. 974AB–975A.

22. PL 175: 1154C. On this text, and the other few where Hugh comments on his own commentary, see D. Poirel, "La boue et le marbre: le paradoxe de l'exégèse du Pscudo-Denys par Hugues de Saint-Victor," forthcoming.

23. Poirel, "Le 'chant dionysien,'" 172f. See also Luscombe, "Commentary," 173. Curiously, Poirel later speculates from this absence of discernible Dionysian influence that Hugh must have been a subtle Dionysian all along, already incorporating the Areopagite's thought into his own, even before coming to Paris

("*Hugo Saxo*," 173f.). The alternative argument, suggested here, is that Hugh was never that deeply affected by the encounter with Dionysius.

24. PL 175: 951B–953D in PL 176: 465D–468A; *De sacramentis*, Two, three, vi–viii.

25. PL 175: 960D.

26. Poirel, "Chant," 173.

27. Luscombe, "Commentary," 171.

28. Zinn, "*De gradibus ascensionum*: The Stages of Contemplative Ascent in Two Treatises on Noah's Ark by Hugh of St. Victor," *Studies in Medieval Culture* V, ed. J. R. Sommerfeldt (Kalamazoo, Mich.: Medieval Institute, 1975), 61–79.

29. PL 175, 1038D. Also discussed in Poirel, *Hugues*, 120–123.

30. In general, see Rorem, *Eriugena's Commentary*.

31. *Expositiones* 7, lines 139–143, p. 95.

32. *Expositiones* 7, lines 170–174, p. 95.

33. Hugh also links love and knowledge, without nuance, in his homilies on Ecclesiastes (PL175: 175D and 195C).

34. PL 175: 1043D, 1062–1066C, 1118B–1119C, 1130B.

35. PL 175: 1038–1044.

36. PL175: 1036A; see also 1029C.

37. PL 175: 1045A. This comment may also suggest a long hiatus in the composition of the work; see Poirel, *Livre*, p. 110; Baron, "Le Commentaire," 134f.

38. PL 175: 1037A.

39. PL 175: 1037B; Luke 24, as discussed by Grover Zinn, "Texts within Texts: The Song of Songs in the Exegesis of Gregory the Great and Hugh of St. Victor," in *Studia Patristica* 25 (Leuven: Peeters, 1993), 209–215.

40. PL 175: 1037C.

41. PL 175: 1037D.

42. PL 175: 1038BC. The Poirel text will delete "*intrat, et*" between "*cor tuum*" and "*penetrat.*"

43. PL 175: 1038C.

44. PL 175: 1038D.

45. PL 175: 1041A.

46. PL 175: 1044AB.

47. For the Dionysian presence in the scholasticism of the thirteenth century, see H. F. Dondaine, *Le corpus dionysien de l'Université de Paris au XIIIe Siècle* (Rome: Edizioni di Storia e Letteratura, 1953).

BIBLIOGRAPHY OF EDITIONS OF HUGH'S WORKS IN THE ORDER DISCUSSED IN THIS TEXT

OHSV   *L'oeuvre de Hugues de Saint-Victor* (Turnhout: Brepols, 1997ff.)

CHAPTER 2

De Tribus Maximis (The Chronicles)

Latin

Green, William. "Hugo of St. Victor: *De tribus maximis circumstantiis gestorum.*" *Speculum* 18 (1943): 488–492.

English

"The Three Best Memory Aids." In *The Medieval Craft of Memory: An Anthology of Texts and Pictures,* 32–40. Mary Carruthers and Jan M. Ziolkowski, eds. Philadelphia: University of Pennsylvania Press, 2002; a revision of Mary Carruthers, *The Book of Memory,* 261–266. Cambridge: Cambridge University Press, 1990.

De Scripturis et scriptoribus sacris (On the Scriptures)

Latin

PL 175: 9–28.

Stammberger, Ralf. *"Diligens scutator sacri eloquii:* An Introduction to Scriptural Exegesis by Hugh of St. Victor Preserved at Admont Library (MS 672)." In *Manuscripts and Monastic Culture,* 241–283. Alison I. Beach, ed. Turnhout: Brepols, 2007.

Didascalicon (de studio legendi)

Latin

PL 176: 741–812.
Buttimer, C. H. *Didascalicon.* Washington, D.C.: Catholic University Press, 1939.
Offergeld, Thilo, ed. *Didascalicon de studio legendi (Studienbuch).* Latin text with German translation on facing pages and notes. Fontes Christiani 27. Freiburg: Herder, 1997.

English

Didascalicon of Hugh of St. Victor: A Medieval Guide to the Arts. Jerome Taylor, tr. and ed. Records of Civilization, Sources and Studies 64. New York: Columbia University Press, 1961 and 1991.

French

Lemoine, Michel. *L'Art de lire.* Paris: Editions du Cerf, 1991.

German

Studienbuch (Didascalicon de studio legendi). Latin text with German translation on facing pages and notes by Thilo Offergeld. Fontes Christiani 27. Freiburg: Herder, 1997.

Epitoma Dindimi in Philosophiam

Baron, Roger. In *Hugonis de Sancto Victore Opera Propaedeutica,* 187–208. University of Notre Dame Publications in Mediaeval Studies 20. Notre Dame, Ind.: University of Notre Dame Press, 1966.

CHAPTER 3

On Grammar (De grammatica)

Latin

Baron, Roger. In *Hugonis de Sancto Victore Opera Propaedeutica,* 75–156. University of Notre Dame Publications in Mediaeval Studies 20. Notre Dame, Ind.: University of Notre Dame Press, 1966.

Practica Geometriae (Practical Geometry)

Latin

Baron, Roger. In *Hugonis de Sancto Victore Opera Propaedeutica,* 15–64. University of Notre Dame Publications in Mediaeval Studies 20. Notre Dame, Ind.: University of Notre Dame Press, 1966.

English

Homann, Frederick A. *Practical Geometry.* Milwaukee, Wisc.: Marquette University Press, 1991.

Notulae/adnotationes

Latin

PL 175: 29–114.

De Institutione Novitiorum (On the Formation of Novices)

Latin

PL 176: 925–952B.
OHSV 1: 18–98.

French

OHSV 1: 19–99.

CHAPTERS 4–6

De Sacramentis Christianae Fidei (On the Sacraments)

Latin

PL 176: 173–618.
Berndt, Rainer. *De sacramentis Christianae fidei.* Munster: Aschendorff, 2008.

English

Deferrari, Roy J., tr. *On the Sacraments of the Christian Faith (De sacramentis).* Mediaeval Academy of America 58. Cambridge, Mass.: Mediaeval Academy of America, 1951.

Dialogus de sacramentis legis naturalis et scriptae

Latin

PL 176: 17–40.

Sententiae de divinitate

Piazzoni, A. M., ed. *"Sententiae de divinitate." Studi Medievali* 23.2 (1982): 912–955.

De tribus diebus (On the Three Days)

Latin

PL 176: 811–838.
Poirel, Dominique, ed. *De tribus diebus*. Corpus Christianorum Continuatio Mediaevalis 177. Turnhout: Brepols, 2002, 3–70.

Dutch

Van Zwieten, J., ed. and tr. *Hugh van St. Victor, De drie dagen*. Kampen: Kok Agora, 1996.

Institutiones in decalogum legis dominicae

PL 176: 9–18.

De quatuor voluntatibus in Christo

Latin

PL 176: 841B–846C.

CHAPTER 7

De Virtute Orandi (On the Power of Prayer)

Latin

PL 176: 977A–984C.
OHSV 1: 126–160.

French

OHSV 1: 127–161.

De Laude Charitatis (On Praise of Charity)

Latin

PL 176: 970D–976D.
OHSV 1: 180–200.

French

OHSV 1: 181–201.

De beatae Mariae virginitate (On the Virginity of the Blessed Mary)

Latin

PL 176: 857–876.
OHSV 2: 182–252.

French

OHSV 2: 183–253.

Super Canticum Mariae

Latin

PL 175: 413D–432B.
OHSV 2: 24–90.

French

OHSV 2: 25–91.

Pro Assumptione Virginis

Latin

PL 177: 1209–1222.
OHSV 2: 112–160.

French

OHSV 2: 113–161.

De amore sponsi ad sponsam/Eulogium sponsi ad sponsam
("On the Love of the Bridegroom toward the Bride")

Latin

PL 176: 987B–994A.

English

Norris, Richard A., Jr., tr. and ed. Excerpt from PL 176: 987B–992B. In *The Song of Songs Interpreted by Early Christian and Medieval Commentators,* 167–172. Grand Rapids, Mich.: Eerdmans, 2003.

Egredietur virga

Latin

OHSV 2: 270–280.

French

OHSV 2: 271–281.

Maria porta

Latin

OHSV 2: 282.

French

OHSV 2: 283.

De contemplatione et ejus speciebus

Latin

Baron, Roger. In *Hughes de Saint-Victor. La Contemplation et ses especes,* Paris: Desclée, 1963.

English (partial translation)

McGinn, Bernard, tr. In *The Essential Writings of Christian Mysticism,* 336–340. New York: Random House, 2006.

De Meditatione (On Meditation)

Latin

Baron, Roger, ed. In *Six Opuscules Spirituels,* 44–58. Sources Chrétiennes 155. Paris: Les éditions du Cerf, 1969.

French

Baron, Roger, ed. In *Six Opuscules Spirituels,* 45–59. Sources Chrétiennes 155. Paris: Les éditions du Cerf, 1969.

De Verbo Dei (On the Word of God)

Latin

PL 177: 289A–294.
Baron, Roger, ed. In *Six Opuscules Spirituels,* 60–80. Sources Chrétiennes 155. Paris: Les éditions du Cerf, 1969.

French

Baron, Roger, ed. In *Six Opuscules Spirituels,* 61–81. Sources Chrétiennes 155. Paris: Les éditions du Cerf, 1969.

De quinque septenis

Latin

PL 175: 405B–410C.
Baron, Roger, ed. In *Six Opuscules Spirituels,* 100–118. Sources Chrétiennes 155. Paris: Les éditions du Cerf, 1969.

French

Baron, Roger, ed. In *Six Opuscules Spirituels,* 101–119. Sources Chrétiennes 155. Paris: Les éditions du Cerf, 1969.

De Septem Donis Spiritus Sancti (Seven Gifts of the Holy Spirit)

Latin

PL 175: 410C–414A.

Baron, Roger, ed. In *Six Opuscules Spirituels,* 120–132. Sources Chrétiennes 155. Paris: Les éditions du Cerf, 1969.

French

Baron, Roger, ed. In *Six Opuscules Spirituels,* 121–133. Sources Chrétiennes 155. Paris: Les éditions du Cerf, 1969.

De Substantia Delictionis (Of the Nature of Love)

Latin

PL 176: 15A–18B.
Baron, Roger, ed. In *Six Opuscules Spirituels,* 82–92. Sources Chrétiennes 155. Paris: Les éditions du Cerf, 1969.

English

Squire, Aelred, ed. In *Hugh of Saint-Victor: Selected Spiritual Writings,* 187–191. London: Faber and Faber, 1962.

French

Baron, Roger, ed. In *Six Opuscules Spirituels,* 83–93. Sources Chrétiennes 155. Paris: Les éditions du Cerf, 1969.

Quid Vere Diligendum Sit (What Should Be Truly Loved)

Latin

PL 177: 564D–565A.
Baron, Roger, ed. In *Six Opuscules Spirituels,* 94–98. Sources Chrétiennes 155. Paris: Les éditions du Cerf, 1969.

French

Baron, Roger, ed. In *Six Opuscules Spirituels,* 95–99. Sources Chrétiennes 155. Paris: Les éditions du Cerf, 1969.

In salomonis Ecclesiastes

Latin

PL 176: 113–256.

English

Squire, Aelred, ed. In *Hugh of Saint-Victor: Selected Spiritual Writings,* 183–187. London: Faber and Faber, 1962.

CHAPTER 8

De Archa Noe (Noah's Ark)

Latin

PL 176: 617–680 (*De Arca Noe Morali*).
Sicard, Patrice, ed. *De archa Noe* and *Libellus de formatione arche.* Corpus Christianorum; Continuatio Mediaevalis 176. Turnhout: Brepols, 2001.

English

Squire, Aelred, ed. "*Noah's Ark:* 1." In *Hugh of Saint-Victor: Selected Spiritual Writings,* 45–153. London: Faber and Faber, 1962.

Libellus de Formatione Arche (The Making of the Ark)

Latin

PL 176: 681–704 (*De Arca Noe Mystica*).
Sicard, Patrice, ed. *De archa Noe* and *Libellus de formatione arche.* Corpus Christianorum; Continuatio Mediaevalis 176. Turnhout: Brepols, 2001.

English

Weiss, Jessica, tr. "Little Book." In *The Medieval Craft of Memory: An Anthology of Texts and Pictures,* 45–70. Mary Carruthers and Jan W. Ziolkowski, eds. Philadelphia: University of Pennsylvania Press, 2002.

Descriptio Mappe Mundi

Latin

Dalché, Patrick Gautier. *La "Descriptio mappe mundi" de Hugues de Saint-Victor. Texte inédit avec introduction et commentaire.* Paris: Études Augustiniennes, 1988.

De Vanitate Mundi (On the Vanity of the World)

Latin

PL 176: 703–740.

English (partial text)

Squire, Aelred, ed. In *Hugh of Saint-Victor: Selected Spiritual Writings,* 157–182. London: Faber and Faber, 1962.

CHAPTER 9

Soliloquy (De arrha anime)

Latin

PL 176: 951B–970D.
OHSV 1: 226–282.

English

Herbert, Kevin. *Soliloquy on the Earnest Money of the Soul.* Milwaukee, Wisc.: Marquette University Press, 1956.

French

OHSV 1: 227–283.

APPENDIX

Commentaria in hierarchiam coelestem s. dionysii areopagitae (Commentary on the Celestial Hierarchy)

Latin

PL 175: 923–1154.
Poirel, Dominique. *Hugonis de Sancto Victore Opera III: Super Ierarchiam Dionysii.* CCCM 178. Turnhout: Brepols, forthcoming.

BIBLIOGRAPHY OF SECONDARY
STUDIES CITED

Barbet, Jeanne. "Introduction." In *Expositiones in Ierarchiam Coelestem*, ix–liv. Corpus Christianorum. Continuatio Mediaevalis 31. Turnholt: Brepols, 1975.

Baron, Roger. "Le Commentaire de la 'Hiérarchie céleste' par Hugues de Saint-Victor." In *Études sur Hugues de Saint-Victor*. Paris: Desclée de Brouwer, 1963.

————. "Introduction." In *Hugonis de Sancto Victore Opera Propaedeutica*, 3–31. University of Notre Dame Publications in Mediaeval Studies 20. Notre Dame, Ind.: University of Notre Dame Press, 1966.

————. "Notes biographiques sur Hugues de Saint-Victor." *Revue d'histoire ecclésiastique* 51 (1956): 920–934.

Bautier, Robert-Henri. "Les origines et les premiers développements de l'abbaye Saint Victor de Paris." In *L'Abbaye Parisienne de Saint-Victor au Moyen Age: Communications présentées au XIIIe Colloque d'Humanisme médiéval de Paris (1986–1988) et réunies par Jean Longère*, 23–52. Bibliotheca Victorina 1. Paris: Brepols, 1991.

Berndt, Rainer. "Gehören die Kirchenväter zur Heiligen Schrift? Zur Kanontheorie des Hugo von St Viktor." In *Zum Problem des biblischen Kanons*, 191–199. Jahrbuch für biblische Theologie, vol. 3. Neukirchen-Vluyn: Neukirchener Verlag, 1988.

————, ed. *Schrift, Schreiber, Schenker: Studien zur Abtei Sankt Viktor in Paris und den Viktorinern*. Corpus Victorinum: Instrumenta, vol. 1. Berlin: Akademie Verlag, 2005.

Bogumil, Karlotto. *Das Bistum Halberstadt im 12. Jahrhundert; Studien zur Reichs und Reformpolitik des Bischofs Reinhard und zum Wirken der Augustiner-Chorherren.* Cologne: Böhlau, 1972.

Bynum, Caroline Walker. *Docere Verbo et Exemplo: An Aspect of Twelfth-Century Spirituality.* Harvard Theological Studies 31. Missoula, Mont.: Scholars Press, 1979.

———. "The Spirituality of Regular Canons in the Twefth Century." In *Jesus as Mother: Studies in the Spirituality of the High Middle Ages,* 22–58. Publications of the Center for Medieval and Renaissance Studies, UCLA, 16. Berkeley: University of California Press, 1982.

Carruthers, Mary, and Jan M. Ziolkowski, eds. *The Medieval Craft of Memory: An Anthology of Texts and Pictures.* Philadelphia: University of Pennsylvania Press, 2002.

Châtillon, Jean. "Hugues de Saint-Victor critique de Jean Scot." In *Jean Scot Érigène et l'histoire de la philosophie,* 415–431. E. Jeauneau, G. Madec, R. Roques, eds. Paris: CNRS, 1977.

Chenu, M. D. *Nature, Man, Society in the Twelfth Century: Essays on New Theological Perspectives in the Latin West.* Chicago: University of Chicago Press, 1968.

Cizewski, Wanda. "Reading the World as Scripture: Hugh of St. Victor's *De Tribus Diebus.*" *Florilegium* 9 (1987): 65–88.

Colish, Marcia. *Studies in Scholasticism.* Variorum Collected Studies Series CS838. Aldershot, U.K.: Ashgate Variorum, 2006.

Coolman, Boyd T. "Hugh of St. Victor on 'Jesus Wept': Making Christological Sense of Jesus' Tears and Conceiving Ideal *Humanitas* in the Twelfth Century." *Theological Studies* 69 (2008): 528–556.

———. "Hugh of St. Victor" (on the Sermon on the Mount). In *The Sermon on the Mount through the Centuries,* 59–80. J. Greenman, T. Larsen, and S. Spencer, eds. Grand Rapids, Mich.: Brazos, 2007.

———. "Pulcrum esse: The Beauty of Scripture, the Beauty of the Soul, and the Art of Exegesis in Hugh of St. Victor." *Traditio* 58 (2003): 175–200.

Coulter, Dale. *Per Visibilia ad Invisibilia: Theological Method in Richard of St. Victor (d. 1173).* Bibliotheca Victorina 18. Turnholt: Brepols, 2006.

Croydon, E. "Notes on the Life of Hugh of St. Victor." *Journal of Theological Studies* 40 (1939): 232–253.

Dickinson, J. C. *The Origins of the Austin Canons and Their Introduction into England.* London: S.P.C.K., 1950.

Dondaine, H. F. *Le corpus dionysien de l'Université de Paris au XIIIe Siècle.* Rome: Edizioni di Storia e Letteratura, 1953.

Eynde, Damien van den. *Essai sur la succession et la date des écrits de Hugues de Saint-Victor.* Spicilegium Pontificii Athenaei Antoniani 13. Rome: Pontificium Athenaeum Antonianum, 1960.

Fassler, Margot. *Gothic Song: Victorine Sequences and Augustinian Reform in Twelfth-Century Paris*. Cambridge Studies in Medieval and Renaissance Music. New York: Cambridge University Press, 1993.

Feiss, Hugh. *"Bernardus Scholasticus:* The Correspondence of Bernard of Clairvaux and Hugh of St. Victor on Baptism." In *Bernardus Magister: Papers Presented at the Nonacentenary Celebration of the Birth of Saint Bernard of Clairvaux, Kalamazoo, Michigan, sponsored by the Institute of Cistercian Studies, Western Michigan University, 10–13 May 1990,* 349–378. John R. Sommerfeldt, ed. Cistercian Studies 135. Spencer, Mass.: Cistercian, 1992.

Ferruolo, Stephen C. *The Origins of the University: The School of Paris and Their Critics, 1100–1215*. Stanford, Calif.: Stanford University Press, 1985.

Gautier Dalché, Patrick. *La "Descriptio mappe mundi" de Hugues de Saint-Victor. Texte inédit avec introduction et commentaire*. Paris: Études Augustiniennes, 1988.

———. "La 'Descriptio mappe mundi' de Hugues de Saint-Victor: retractatio et additamenta." In *L'Abbaye Parisienne de Saint-Victor au Moyen Age: Communications Présentées au XIIIe Colloque d'Humanisme Médiéval de Paris (1986–1988) et réunies par Jean Longère,* 143–179. Jean Longère, ed. Bibliotheca Victorina 1. Paris: Brepols, 1991. Revised and reprinted as "Nouvelles lumières sur la *Descriptio mappe mundi* de Hugues de Saint-Victor." In *Géographie et culture, La représentation de l'espace du VIe au XIIe siècle,* 1–27. Variorum Collected Studies Series CS592. Aldershot, U.K.: Ashgate, 1997.

de Ghellinck, J. "La table des materières de la première édition des oeuvres de Hugues de Saint-Victor." *Recherches de Sciences Religieuses* 1 (1910): 270–289, 385–396.

Green, William. "Hugo of St. Victor: *De tribus maximis circumstantiis gestorum.*" *Speculum* 18 (1943): 484–493.

Haskins, Charles H. *The Renaissance of the Twelfth Century*. Cambridge, Mass.: Harvard University Press, 1939.

Hotchin, Julie. *"Dilecto fratri Gunthero:* Provost Gunther of Lippoldsberg and the Reception of Hugh of St Victor in Northern Germany." In *Texte in Kontexten: Gesammelte Studien zur Abtei Sankt-Viktor und den Viktorinen, 2*. Matthias Tischler, ed. Corpus Victorinum. Instrumenta 3. Berlin: Akademie, forthcoming.

Illich, Ivan. *In the Vineyard of the Text: A Commentary to Hugh's 'Didascalicon.'* Chicago: University of Chicago, 1993.

Jaeger, C. Stephen. *The Envy of Angels: Cathedral Schools and Social Ideals in Medieval Europe, 950–1200*. Philadelphia: University of Pennsylvania Press, 1994.

———. "Humanism and Ethics at the School of St. Victor in the Early Twelfth Century." *Mediaeval Studies* 55 (1993): 51–79.

Jocqué, Luc, ed. with L. Milis. *Liber Ordinis Sancti Victoris Parisiensis: Instrumenta Lexicologica Latina.* Corpus Christianorum, Continuatio Mediaevalis 61. Turnholt: Brepols, 1984.

————. "Le Structures de la population claustrale dans l'ordre de Saint-Victor au XIIe siècle: un Essi d'Analyse du 'Liber Ordinis.' " In *L'Abbaye Parisienne de Saint-Victor au Moyen Age: communications présentées au XIIIe Colloque d'Humanisme médiéval de Paris (1986–1988) et réunies par Jean Longère,* 53–95. Bibliotheca Victorina 1. Paris: Brepols, 1991.

Jolivet, Jean. "*Données* sur Guillaume de Champeaux: dialectician et théologien." In *L'Abbaye Parisienne de Saint-Victor au Moyen Age: Communications Présentées au XIIIe Colloque d'Humanisme Médiéval de Paris (1986–1988) et réunies par Jean Longère,* 235–251. Bibliotheca Victorina 1. Paris: Brepols, 1991.

Jones, Christopher A. *A Lost Work by Amalarius of Metz.* London: Henry Bradshaw Society, 2001.

Luscombe, David. "The Commentary of Hugh of Saint-Victor on the Celestial Hierarchy." In *Die Dionysius Rezeption im Mittelalter: Internationales Kolloquium in Sofia vom 8. bis 11. April 1999 unter der Schirmherrschaft der Société internationale pour l'étude de la philosophie médiévale,* 159–175. T. Boiadjiev, G. Kapriev, and A. Speer, eds. Rencontres de Philosophie Medievale 9. Turnhout: Brepols, 2000.

————. *The School of Peter Abelard: The Influence of Abelard's Thought in the Early Scholastic Period.* Cambridge Studies in Medieval Life and Thought, New Series 14. Cambridge: Cambridge University Press, 1970.

———— and Jonathan Riley-Smith, "Introduction" to *The New Cambridge Medieval History,* vol. 4 c. 1024–1198, part 1 (Cambridge: Cambridge University Press, 2004), 2.

McGinn, B. *The Presence of God.* The Growth of Mysticism, vol. 2. New York: Crossroads, 1994.

McGonigle, Thomas D. "Hugh of St. Victor's Understanding of the Relationship between the Sacramental and Contemplative Dimensions of Christian Life." Ph.D. dissertation, Harvard Divinity School, 1976.

Melve, Leidulf. "The Revolt of the Medievalists: Directions in Recent Research on the Twelfth-Century Renaissance." *Journal of Medieval History* 32 (2006): 231–252.

Milis, L., ed., with Luc Jocqué. *Liber Ordinis Sancti Victoris Parisiensis.* Corpus Christianorum. Continuatio Mediaevalis 61. Turnholt: Brepols, 1984.

Piazzoni, A. M. "Ugo di San Vittore 'auctor' delle 'Sententiae de divinitate.' " *Studi Medievali* 23.2 (1982): 861–955.

Poirel, Dominique. " 'Alter Augustinus—Der Zweite Augustinus': Hugo von Sankt Viktor und die Väter der Kirche." In *Väter der Kirche: Ekklesiales*

Denken von den Anfängen bis in die Neuzeit: Festgabe für Hermann Josef Sieben SJ zum 70. Geburtstag, 643–668. Johannes Arnold, Rainer Berndt, and Ralf Stammberger, eds. Munich: Ferdinand Schöningh, 2004.

————. "L'ange gothique." In *L'architecture gothique au service de la liturgie*, 115–142. A. Bos and X. Dectot, eds. Turnhout: Brepols, 2003.

————. "La boue et le marbre: le paradoxe de l'exégèse du Pseudo-Denys par Hugues de Saint-Victor," forthcoming.

————. "Le 'chant dionysien' du IXe au XIIe siècle." In *Les historiens et le latin médiéval*, 151–176. M. Goullet and M. Parisse, eds. (Paris: Publications de la Sorbonne, 2001).

————. *Hugonis de Sancto Victore Opera III: Super Ierarchiam Dionysii*. CCCM 178 (Turnhout: Brepols, forthcoming).

————. "*Hugo Saxo:* Les origines germaniques de la pensée d'Hugues de Saint-Victor." *Francia. Forschungen zur westeuropäischen Geschichte* 33/1 (2006): 163–169.

————. *Hugues de Saint-Victor*. Initiations au Moyen-Age. Paris: Cerf, 1998.

————. *Hugues de Saint-Victor et le réveil dionysien du XIIe siecle: Le "Super Ierarchiam beati Dionisii."* Bibliotheca Victorina. Paris: Brepols, forthcoming.

————. "Introduction." In *L'œuvre de Hugues de Saint-Victor*, 7–17. H. B. Feiss and P. Sicard, eds. Sous la règle de Saint Augustin 31. Turnholt: Brepols, 1997.

————. *Livre de la nature et débat trinitaire au XIIe siècle: le De tribus diebus de Hughes de Saint-Victor*. Bibliotheca Victorina 14. Turnhout: Brepols, 2002.

————. "*Symbolice et anagogice:* l'école de Saint-Victor et la naissance du style gothique." In *L'abbé Suger, le manifeste gothique de Saint-Denis et la pensée victorine: colloque organisé à la Fondation Singer-Polignac le mardi 21 novembre 2000 par Rencontres médiévales européennes*, 141–170. Rencontres médiévales européennes, vol. 1. Turnhout: Brepols, 2001.

Pollitt, H. J. "Some Consideration on the Structure and Sources of Hugh of St. Victor's Notes on the Octateuch." *Recherches de théologie ancienne et médiévale* 33 (1966): 5–38.

Reynolds, Roger. "Christ as Cleric: The Ordinals of Christ." In *Clerics in the Early Middle Ages*, vol. 2, 1–50. Aldershot, U.K.: Ashgate, 1999.

————. *The Ordinals of Christ from Their Origins to the Twelfth Century*. Berlin: de Gruyter, 1978.

Roques, René. "Connaissance de Dieu et théologie symbolique d'après l' '*In hierarchiam coelestem sancti Dionysii*' de Hugues de Saint-Victor." In *Structures théologiques de la gnose à Richard de Saint-Victor*, 294–364. Paris: Press Universitaires de France, 1962.

Rorem, Paul. *Eriugena's Commentary on the Dionysian "Celestial Hierarchy."* Toronto: Pontifical Institute of Mediaeval Studies, 2005.

————. *Pseudo-Dionysius: A Commentary on the Texts and an Introduction to Their Influence.* New York: Oxford University Press, 1993.

Rudolph, Conrad. *"First, I Find the Center Point": Reading the Text of Hugh of Saint Victor's* The Mystic Ark. Transactions of the American Philosophical Society, vol. 94, pt. 4. Philadelphia: American Philosophical Society, 2004.

Schmitt, Jean-Claude. *La raison des gestes dans l'Occident médiéval.* Bibliothèque des histoires. Paris: Éditions Gallimard, 1990.

Seouh, Jong Won. "Knowledge and Action in Hugh of St. Victor's Commentary on the Dionysian *Celestial Hierarchy.*" Ph.D. dissertation, Princeton Theological Seminary, 2007.

Sicard, Patrice. *Diagrammes médiévaux et exégèse visuelle: Le Libellus de formatione arche de Hugues de Saint-Victor* (Paris: Brepols, 1993).

————. *Hugues de Saint-Victor et son école: introduction, choix de texte, traduction et commentaires.* Témoins de Notre Histoire. Turnhout: Brepols, 1991.

Smalley, Beryl. *The Study of the Bible in the Middle Ages.* Oxford: Blackwell, 1952.

Stammberger, Ralf M. "Diligens scrutator sacri eloquii: An Introduction to Scriptural Exegesis by Hugh of St. Victor Preserved at Admont Library (MS 672)." In *Manuscripts and Monastic Culture,* 241–283. Alison I. Beach, ed. Turnhout: Brepols, 2007.

————. "Die Edition der Werke Hugos von Sankt Viktor (d. 1141) durch Abt Gilduin von Sankt Viktor (d. 1155)—Eine Rekonstruction." In *Schrift, Schreiber, Schenker: Studien zur Abtei Sankt Viktor in Paris und den Viktorinern,* 119–231. Rainer Berndt, ed. Corpus Victorinum: Instrumenta, vol. 1. Berlin: Akademie Verlag, 2005.

————. "The *Liber Sermonum Hugonis*: The Discovery of a New Work by Hugh of Saint Victor," *Medieval Sermon Studies* 52 (2008): 63–71.

————. "*Theologus nostri temporis Ioannes Scotus*: Hugh of St. Victor's Assessment of John Scotus Eriugena's Reception of Pseudo-Dionysius." Forthcoming.

Stiegman, Emero. "Three Theologians in Debate: Saint Bernard's Tract on Baptism." In *Bernard of Clairvaux: On Baptism and the Office of Bishops,* 85–147. Pauline Matarasso, tr. Cistercian Fathers Series 67. Kalamazoo, Mich.: Cistercian, 2004.

Taylor, Jerome. *The Origin and Early Life of Hugh of Victor: An Evaluation of the Tradition.* Notre Dame, Ind.: Medieval Institute, 1957.

van Zwieten, Jan W. M. "The Preparation to Allegory: Hugh of St. Victor's *De Sacramentis* and His Notes on the Octateuch." *Nederlands archief voor kerkgeschiedenis* 68 (1988): 17–22.

Weisweiler, Heinrich. "Die Arbeitsmethode Hugos von St. Viktor: Ein Beitrag zum Entstehen seines Hauptwerkes *De sacramentis*. *Scholastik* 20–24 (1949): 59–87, 232–267.

————. "Hugos von St. Victor Dialogus de sacramentis legis naturalis et scriptae als frühscholastisches Quellenwerk." In *Miscellanea Giovanni Mercati II*, 179–219. Anselmo Maria Albareda, ed. Studi e Testi 122. Vatican City: Biblioteca Apostolica Vaticana, 1946.

————. "Die Pseudo-Dionysiuskommentare 'In Coelestem Hierarchiam' des Skotus Eriugena und Hugos von St. Viktor." *Recherches de théologie ancienne et médiévale* 19 (1952): 26–47.

Zinn, Grover. "Exile, the Abbey of St-Victor at Paris, and Hugh of Saint Victor." In *Medieval Paradigms: Essays in Honor of Jeremy duQuesnay Adams*, vol. 2, 83–111. Stephanie A. Hayes-Healy, ed. New Middle Ages. New York: Palgrave Macmillan, 2005.

————. "*De gradibus ascensionum*: The Stages of Contemplative Ascent in Two Treatises on Noah's Ark by Hugh of St. Victor." In *Studies in Medieval Culture V*, 61–79. J. R. Sommerfeldt, ed. Kalamazoo, Mich.: Medieval Institute, 1975.

————. "'*Historia fundamentum est*': The Role of History in the Contemplative Life according to Hugh of St Victor." In *Contemporary Reflections on the Medieval Christian Tradition; Essays in Honor of Ray C. Petry*, 135–158. George H. Shriver, ed. Durham, N.C.: Duke University Press, 1974.

————. "Hugh of St. Victor and the Ark of Noah: A New Look." *Church History* 40 (1971): 261–272.

————. "Hugh of St. Victor, Isaiah's Vision, and *De Arca Noe*." In *The Church and the Arts: Papers Read at the 1990 Summer Meeting and the 1991 Winter Meeting of the Ecclesiastical History Society*, 99–116. Diana Wood, ed. Oxford: Blackwell, 1992.

————. "Hugh of St. Victor's 'De scripturis et scriptoribus sacris' as an *Accessus* Treatise for the Study of the Bible." *Traditio* 52 (1997): 111–134.

————. "Mandala Symbolism and Use in the Mysticism of Hugh of St. Victor." *History of Religions* 4 (1973): 317–341.

————. "Texts within Texts: The Song of Songs in the Exegesis of Gregory the Great and Hugh of St. Victor." In *Studia Patristica* 25, 209–215. E.A. Livingstone, ed. Leuven: Peeters, 1993.

INDEX